Royal
Horticultural
Society

THE
wildlife
TRUSTS

WILDLIFE GARDENING
FOR EVERYONE

EDITED BY MALCOLM TAIT

YOUR QUESTIONS ANSWERED BY
THE RHS AND THE WILDLIFE TRUSTS

SUPPORTED BY

JACOBI
JAYNE &
COMPANY

THINK
BOOKS

A Think Book

First published in Great Britain in 2006 by
Think Publishing
The Pall Mall Deposit
124-128 Barlby Road, London W10 6BL
www.think-books.com

Published in association with
The Royal Horticultural Society
80 Vincent Square, London SW1P 2PE
www.rhs.org.uk
and
The Wildlife Trusts
The Kiln, Waterside, Mather Road, Newark
Nottinghamshire NG24 1WT
www.wildlifetrusts.org

Copyright © The Royal Horticultural Society and The Royal Society of Wildlife Trusts 2006
Design and layout © Think Publishing 2006
Distributed in the United States and Canada by:
Sterling Publishing Co., Inc. 387 Park Avenue South, New York, NY 10016-8810
The moral rights of the author have been asserted

Editor: Malcolm Tait
Editorial team: Rica Dearman, Simon Maughan, Morag Shuaib
Photographs credited on page 21
Designer: Lou Millward

ISBN-13: 978-1-84525-016-4
ISBN-10: 1-84525-016-8

Printed and bound in Italy by Printer Trento
The publishers and authors have made every effort to ensure the accuracy and currency of the information in
Wildlife Gardening for Everyone. Similarly, every effort has been made to contact copyright holders. We apologise
for any unintentional errors or omissions. The publisher and authors disclaim any liability, loss, injury or damage
incurred as a consequence, directly or indirectly, of the use and application of the contents of this book.
Main cover image: Celia Mannings

Those who contemplate the beauty of the earth find reserves
of strength that will endure as long as life lasts.

RACHEL CARSON

Wherever Swarovski is,
nature becomes
more fascinating.
Swarovski Pocket 8x20 B

www.swarovskioptik.com

Pocket 8x20

**Perfect for all outdoor activities,
ideal for the theatre,
or as a second binocular:**
Swarovski Pocket Binoculars fit into
any pocket and provide a truly great
viewing experience. They have the
world's most complex optical system
for compact binoculars, as well as the
patented SWAROBRIGHT® prism
coating for optimum colour fidelity
across the entire light spectrum.
Individually adjustable, removable,
twist-up eyecups enable
an extremely large visual field – even
for spectacle wearers.

SWAROVSKI
O P T I K

Swarovski UK LTD • Perrywood Business Park • Salfords, Surrey RH1 5JQ • Tel 01737 856812 • Fax 01737 856885

WILDLIFE GARDENING
FOR EVERYONE

CONTENTS

fig. 1

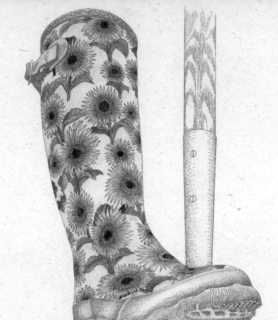

Royal Horticultural Society

Introducing the range of gardener's boots the RHS *does* give a fig about...

A playfully chic exterior, but seriously hard wearing underneath – these boots were made for digging. A metal shank makes light work of even the toughest earth-turning, while the soft cushioned insoles and silky cotton linings ensure a comfort and fit hitherto unheard of on the gardener's grapevine. Constructed of strong natural rubber, they'll provide many seasons of horticultural happiness. Soon everything in your garden will be coming up roses – and sunflowers, and holly...

rhswellies.com

The RHS Digger boot by

HUNTER

The Hunter Rubber Company Limited, Edinburgh Road, Dumfries, DG1 1QA, Scotland, UK. Telephone: +44 (0) 1387 269 591 www.rhs.org.uk

WILDLIFE GARDENING
FOR EVERYONE

CONTENTS

Wildlife Gardening: an introduction

MATTHEW WILSON
Curator and Head of
RHS Garden Harlow Carr

In 2002, the RHS, The Wildlife Trusts and the RSPB organised a joint conference on the theme of Gardens: Heaven or Hell for Wildlife? A range of speakers and delegates were assembled, many of them experts in their respective fields, to consider whether or not the British domestic garden had anything to offer our native wildlife and if so, what? The conclusions drawn were surprising and inspiring; our gardens aren't just good for wildlife, they are vital, and not just the wild and woolly plots that are traditionally associated with wildlife-friendly attitudes.

And what of the legacy of the 2002 conference? Not only has it led to the RHS being even more proactive in encouraging sustainable gardening practices that conserve biodiversity, it has resulted in a hugely beneficial relationship with other organisations, most notably The Wildlife Trusts, with whom the RHS launched the joint Wild About Gardens initiative. The Wild About Gardens website provides plenty of practical information for anyone wanting to improve the diversity in their own garden, and a forum for wildlife gardeners to increase their knowledge. Another of the outcomes of the relationship is this book, designed to be practical yet at the same time inspirational and borne out of the realisation that many gardeners would like to be more active in gardening with wildlife in mind. At the heart of this book is the advice of experts and enthusiasts, keen to pass on the knowledge they have accrued in the best possible circumstances – by doing it themselves.

Gardens form important corridors linking

urban, suburban and rural landscapes, allowing wildlife to move from one environment to another. They can also provide tremendous diversity in comparatively small areas, and offer almost limitless habitat opportunities for everything from the smallest bug upwards. In any street in the UK it is possible to find gardens that range from densely planted plantsman's gardens to those bereft of plants altogether, and all stages in between. And it is this diversity which is all important as it provides different opportunities for different species. Gardens can also help to fill in the gaps by providing environments that are otherwise missing locally. So if there are no natural bodies of fresh water in your area, a well-designed and planted garden pond can make a huge difference to native pond fauna. Best of all, for plant-lovers, is the value that ornamental plants provide for wildlife. Pollen-and nectar-feeding animals get pretty short shrift in winter from our own native flora, but there are plenty of exotic plants that flower during this period and provide sustenance. Plants that produce berries, nuts and fruit will feed everything from mammals to insects, and of course not only will these exotic plants help our wildlife, they will also fill our days with colour, form and fragrance.

However important the content of our gardens, the way in which we garden is the key to wildlife friendliness. Encouraging natural cycles to develop takes time and patience and can often test the nerves of those who seek perfection in their garden. For many gardeners this can be the area of greatest compromise and, consequently, the hardest to embrace. But consider this: a wildflower meadow is beautiful because we deem it so, not because it is neat, tidy and weed-free. It has an inherent perfection, without being 'perfect'. So we have it within us to redefine what is aesthetically acceptable and to measure any compromise against its value to

wildlife. Moreover, the encouragement of natural cycles will help the garden to maintain itself by creating conditions in which natural predators can thrive. And we can further help the balance in our gardens by avoiding monocultures, using modern disease-resistant cultivated varietiess and adopting tried and tested techniques like companion planting.

Now more than ever we need to consider the effect our actions have, and look over the garden fence as well as inside it. Gardens have the capacity to be hugely beneficial to the environment and many gardeners are already enjoying the thrill of seeing their own patch becoming ever more attractive to wildlife. The plants that we use, the habitats we create and the way in which our gardens are maintained have the capacity to preserve and enhance, and surely that must be worth embracing. What could be more satisfying than gardening in a way that not only enhances our own lives, but also that of the biodiversity around us?

FANTASTIC VALUE BREAKS

ONLY £23.95 Bed and Breakfast, per person per night

Wildlife Gardening for Everyone has teamed up with Old English Inns to offer you the chance to escape to our beautiful countryside with super savings. Each of the inns have their own special charm and delightful surroundings – historic buildings, cosy bedrooms, oak-beamed bars and restaurants, comfy armchairs, freshly cooked food, fine wines and real cask ales – perfect for quick get-away!

With the emphasis on relaxation, the traditional inns and hotels offer a warm and friendly welcome and above all, excellent value for money! Perfect for walking, cycling, sightseeing, visiting historic houses and gardens, and golf breaks.

**To take advantage of this fantastic offer and for a list of participating hotels,
Call FREE 0800 917 3085
quoting 'Wildlife Gardening'
or email:central.reservations@oldenglish.co.uk**

Terms & Conditions
- Prices are per person per night, based on two people sharing a twin or double room, for a minimum of two nights. Offer subject to availability
- Must be booked through central reservations on 0800 9173085, not with hotel direct
- Excludes Bank Holidays, Xmas/New Year and St Valentine's Day 2007
- Offer valid until April 2007
- Cannot be used in conjunction with any other offer. Applies to new bookings only
- Calls will be recorded for training purposes
- OEI reserve the right to remove/change the properties during the promotion

Your very own nature reserve

Your garden is a nature reserve waiting to happen. Peter Schofield of the North Wales Wildlife Trust reveals some of the decisions you will need to make as you become 'warden' of your new 'reserve'.

To create your own garden nature reserve you will need to balance the requirements of your gardening interests with the those of plants and animals using the reserve.

First, assess the wildlife which already uses the garden, and occurs in the neighbourhood; it's no good trying to attract species which live miles away. Even if you create the right habitat and introduce species, climate or other factors may make it impossible for them to survive.

Determine your objectives. What do you want or not want? Once decided you can design and manage the garden for specific species. Do plants need damp or dry, acid or alkaline soils, sun or shade? Are introduced plants aggressive and would they take over? Do you want minimal maintenance? Do you want plants to attract specific invertebrates or vertebrates? Remember, each group of animals or species will have specific needs for food, nest sites, shelter, nectar or cover from predators.

The vertical and horizontal structure within the garden is important. Create open spaces, bare ground, low and tall herb areas, and areas for shrubs and trees. Horizontally the structure should grade from bare ground through zones of increasing height of vegetation. Scalloped edges and glades give shelter and act as sun traps for insects. Aspect is also important for some species. Don't forget the value of dead wood, both on trees and on the ground. Your house, too, can provide shelter and nest sites for many species.

Water is especially important. Even the smallest ponds can be good for invertebrates and amphibians. Shallow water is needed for drinking and bathing.

The greater the diversity of structure and of plant life, the greater will be the range of animal species which use the garden.

Remember, even grass can have structure: short or long, and with a diversity of grass and grassland plant species.

But how far do you go in your planning? Nature reserves, even garden nature reserves, need to be managed or, in other words, interfered with. If they are not, they will change; successful species will take over. Such changes are known as succession. The question is when to arrest succession; when to interfere? Before a decision is made you will need to consider if the changes are compatible with your objectives; or if unwanted species are host to more desirable species. Does a new species enhance or detract from the reserve?

It's not only when, but how much to interfere. Identify the problem, and the extent to which it conflicts with your plans or objectives, then make the decision. Occasionally, you may, on reflection, wish to change your objectives.

It's not only plants, but some invertebrates, reptiles, amphibians, birds or mammals may need controlling. Do you always, occasionally or never wish to rid your garden reserve of magpies, jays, squirrels or moles, for example? Some species such as bats, badgers and many birds are protected by law, so before you take action, check with your local Wildlife Trust.

If you have a pond in your garden reserve, you may attract a heron or kingfisher, or a bird-feeder could well interest a sparrowhawk. Such exciting species may soon become unwanted or unwelcomed visitors. When and how do you interfere? Seek advice first.

There are no hard and fast rules about how to manage your garden, but it is certain that at some time every nature reserve will require some interference if it is to remain a diverse and exciting place.

About the Royal Horticultural Society

As the UK's leading gardening charity, the Royal Horticultural Society encourages all gardeners to consider the relationship of their garden to habitats, wildlife and biodiversity.

The RHS put biodiversity firmly on the gardener's agenda in 2002, with a conference entitled Gardens: Heaven or Hell for Wildlife? held in association with The Wildlife Trusts and the RSPB. The conference started to mobilise the gardening public to think of horticulture as an environmentally positive activity and the momentum has been maintained since then with a range of initiatives by the RHS.

These activities have helped to explode some of the myths about wildlife gardening. More people are aware now that you don't have to let your garden go wild to have a garden that's good for wildlife; gardening for wildlife represents an approach to gardening, not a style of garden. It enables a garden to be designed that will be enjoyed by both people and wildlife and does not compromise aesthetics or practicalities.

Recently, the RHS has not just been highlighting how good gardening practice can bring about biodiversity gain in gardens, but also showing how the garden is a particularly special place for contact with wildlife. The Wild About Garden project with The Wildlife Trusts has achieved that by celebrating what gardeners are already doing to encourage wildlife. It also promotes dialogue at a local level between gardeners and wildlife enthusiasts on the Wild About Gardens website at www.wildaboutgardens.org.

The project emphasises that wherever you live and whatever size or type of garden you have, you can take action to make it more wildlife friendly and to create a space to observe, enjoy and support the creatures in your garden.

In 2006, the Britain in Bloom campaign, which is organised by the RHS, has a biodiversity theme. It is hoped that this will help to motivate council staff, businesses and local residents to think about their contribution towards biodiversity when undertaking Bloom projects in gardens, street scenes and other green spaces.

It is possible to have traditional and formal planting schemes in parks and gardens that still support thriving habitats. By incorporating a range of native and non-native planting schemes, people can provide food sources and a range of habitats for wildlife, as well as creating beautiful environments beneficial to people. The RHS has a wealth of information about how to create a biodiverse garden, see www.rhs.org.uk/learning/research/biodiversity/index.asp

REjuvenate

Discover a land rich in history, laced with quiet lanes linking quaint villages surrounded by beautiful countryside. With historic woodlands, rolling wheatfields dotted with poppies and windmills, estuaries and coastal villages, it's the ideal location for rejuvenation.

Why not visit one of the many gardens and historic houses for a relaxing day out?

Please call 0845 600 73 73 or visit our website www.realessex.co.uk and request your complete pack on Essex including our garden guide.

DELIVERED BY

ESSEX DEVELOPMEN
REGENERATION AGEN

About The Wildlife Trusts

The Wildlife Trusts is a partnership of 47 local Wildlife Trusts across the UK plus the Isle of Man and Alderney. The Wildlife Trusts' vision is 'an environment rich in wildlife for everyone' and we are the largest UK charity exclusively dedicated to conserving all our habitats and species. We have a membership of more than 600,000 people, including 100,000 junior members.

Throughout the UK, there are a variety of wildlife gardening schemes and groups run by local Wildlife Trusts. Through these, people can actively join in with gardening for wildlife, whether working in their own gardens using advice provided by their Trust, setting up community gardens or helping to establish and maintain Trust wildlife gardens.

Wildlife gardening is just one element of a wider picture of wildlife conservation that The Wildlife Trusts are involved in throughout the UK.

Habitats and species

The UK has many diverse habitats, including water and wetlands, ancient woodlands, grasslands, uplands, marine and coastline. We work to protect UK species ranging from sharks to spiders, puffins to porpoises, dolphins to dormice, otters to ospreys and of course, many plants and trees.

Our habitats and species conservation work involves managing land, restoring and creating new habitats, surveying and monitoring species, collecting and managing biological data and giving advice to landowners on wildlife-friendly land management. Under the UK Biodiversity Action Plan (BAP) we have responsibility for a number of BAP species and habitats.

Collectively, we also manage more than 2,200 nature reserves covering more than 80,000ha, spanning right across the UK, from the Cornish coasts to the Scottish Islands and incorporating both rural and urban landscapes.

ramble & climb & explore

Our area has several Nature Reserves where visitors can witness all kinds of wildlife in its original habitat. Visit Sussex's finest 'saline lagoons' containing some of the world's rarest plant and invertebrate species. It is the word 'rarest' that should make every visitor realise just how precious and essential these places are and why care and caution should always be exercised. Put simply, the reserves exist to try and keep whole species of plant, animal and insect on the planet.

Experience more at
www.visithastings.com/rambleclimbexplore

Hastings & 1066 Country

Visit the South East's historic coast and countryside where high emotions, extraordinary sensations and unforgettable experiences await you.

Battle ▢ Bexhill ▢ Hastings ▢ Pevensey ▢ Rye
www.1066country.com

Wildlife and people

We're working to highlight the value of wildlife to people of all ages and sectors of society, through our contact with individuals and families, community groups, schools and youth groups (including Wildlife Watch, the Trusts' junior branch), farmers and landowners. We campaign for the protection of wildlife and invest in the future by helping people of all ages to gain a greater appreciation and understanding of wildlife.

Every year, almost 25,000 volunteers give their support to The Wildlife Trusts and over one million people visit our visitor centres and reserves.

Apart from the advice and education we provide to people on wildlife topics, we also advise on environmental issues such as recycling and using natural resources (like water and energy) wisely.

Advocacy – guardians of wildlife

The Wildlife Trusts lobby for better protection of the UK's natural heritage and are dedicated to protecting wildlife for the future. The Trusts' policy work involves campaigning in the UK and Europe, working with local authorities and government agencies, for better legislation and policies to protect these habitats and species.

Join your local Wildlife Trust

The Wildlife Trusts are able to protect wildlife for the future because of the collective support of people like you. Without our members, none of this would be possible. Join us and support one of the 47 local Wildlife Trusts.

There are four possible membership options:
1. Individual adult membership
2. Joint membership (two adults at the same address and sharing publications)
3. Family membership (includes Wildlife Watch* membership for up to four children at the same address sharing publications)
4. Wildlife Watch* junior membership (under-16s only) up to four children at the same address and sharing publication (this option does not include adult membership)

*Please note that individual Wildlife Watch membership is not available for all local Wildlife Trusts. These Trusts offer family membership including Wildlife Watch instead.

Adult membership includes:
- A newsletter or magazine from your local Wildlife Trust, keeping you informed about the wildlife on your doorstep.
- The majority of local Wildlife Trusts send *Natural World* magazine to their members.
- Details of the Wildlife Trust nature reserves in your area
- Opportunities to lend a hand and play a direct role in helping local wildlife
- The knowledge that you have helped keep the UK's precious wildlife safe for the future

Wildlife Watch is The Wildlife Trusts' members club for all young wildlife fans, nature sleuths and young environmentalists. Wildlife Watch is open to any age, but is most suitable for ages 8-15. Most Trusts support a network of Wildlife Watch groups. To find out if your local Trust has a Watch group near you, please visit the Wildlife Watch website at www.wildlifewatch.org.uk.

- If you would like more information about The Wildlife Trusts and how to join, go to our website at www.wildlifetrusts.org or telephone 0870 0367711.

40 foods. 70 feeders. 100 nest boxes. One garden. Yours.

It's your garden, and making it a haven for birds and other wild visitors is a highly personal pleasure we can all enjoy.

If you're a relative newcomer to caring for the wildlife in your garden, the options can seem a little daunting when it comes to picking the right foods, feeders and nest boxes. How can I attract the right species while deterring unwanted predators? What are the most effective ways to ensure that wildlife gets a little extra help during the winter months and other times when it's appreciated most?

Don't feel intimidated: help is at hand. At Jacobi Jayne we've been gathering the very best wildlife care products from all over the world for almost 20 years. As the UK's leading specialist we offer an exceptional range of quality foods and feeders. And that's not all: there's a range of more than 100 nest boxes for birds and other garden visitors... from bees to bats.

Call 0800 072 0130 for your FREE copy of Living with Birds, our 64 page full colour catalogue.

www.livingwithbirds.com

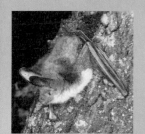

Jacobi Jayne & Company
Canterbury Kent

What a picture!

Enter the RHS Photographic Competition, and your images could appear in books like this

You don't have to be a professional to get your photographs published. Many of the images in this book were taken by amateur naturalists and enthusiastic gardeners who simply love to record the wild world around them. And some of them, like those on this page, are real winners. Each of the images you see here won a prize in the RHS Photographic Competition... and so could you.

The aim of the RHS Photographic Competition is to convey the diversity of plants and the enjoyment of gardening through the medium of photography. The competition is open to amateur and professional photographers and the growing popularity of the competition has seen entries rise to over 4,000 images. The competition 'Photograph of the Year' categories enable photographers to explore opportunities with Plant Portraits, Close-Up, Trees or Shrubs, Wildlife in the Garden and People in the Garden.

For more details please contact RHS Garden Rosemoor on 01805 624067 or write to RHS Garden Rosemoor, Great Torrington, Devon, EX38 8PH.

Some of the photographs in this book were provided by entrants to RHS photo competitions, and are copyright the owners. Our thanks to Barbara Boyce (63), Mike Calvert (cover/167), Torrie Chugg (21), Trevor Davenport (142), James Guilliam (249), Philip Hack (283), Tony Keene (cover/147/201), Celia Mannings (cover/21/142), Stephen Record (cover/71/162-3), Dr Stan Venitt (cover/166).

The other photographs in this book are copyright RHS, The Wildlife Trusts, or the people and organisations listed. We would like to them for helping make this book possible:
Rosemary Atkins, John Black, Peter Cairns, Alison Clarke, Tony Coultiss, Steve Covey, English Nature, Enviromat.co.uk, John Feltwell/Garden Matters, Gloucestershire Wildlife Trust, Graham Game, Gerald Green, GreenSpace, Beth Harker, Gail Harland, Harlequin Survey, Beverley Heath, Neil Hepworth, J Howard, Jerry Kavanagh, Roger Key – Buglife, London Wildlife Trust, Chris Mahon, Gary Mason, Cath Mowat, Northumberland Wildlife Trust, Martin Page, David Plummer, Howard Rice, Royal Horticultural Society, Maddalena Saccon, Tim Sandall, Dragisa Savic – Buglife, M C Sleigh, Darin Smith, Phil Sutton, Sue Tatman, Olive Tayler, Scott Tilley, Tim Webb, Val Welsh, Mick Weston, www.alamy.com, www.harrodhorticultural.com, www.wigglywigglers.co.uk.

How to use this book

Although there are some definite dos and don'ts when it comes to gardening for wildlife, the subject is not always a simple matter of right and wrong. Just as every garden is different, so is every gardener, and each needs to find their own way of sharing their garden with the creatures that also want to live in it. Available time, space, location, soil types and even simple personal taste are all factors in how each garden will be managed. Everyone will have their own opinions, their own favourite wild visitors, and their own tried and tested approaches to the task.

So wouldn't it be wonderful if there was a way to pool these many methods, so that the gardeners of the nation could dip into the collected knowledge and experiences of their peers, and find new and exciting ways to develop their own patches of land for the benefit of wildlife and themselves? The Royal Horticultural Society and The Wildlife Trusts thought so, and in 2005 joined forces to launch a unique new venture. Titled Wild About Gardens, it is an online forum for gardeners, naturalists, and anyone with a love of nature to swap ideas, advice, experiences and opinions on how best to encourage wildlife into their gardens. The forum can be found at www.wildaboutgardens.org.

This book picks up on the 100 commonest themes that were discussed on the website. Each topic – from maybugs to foxes to pond maintenance – starts with a selection of comments from the general public that appeared on the website. Between them, they contribute a wealth of information, some of it from their own direct experience, some from hearsay, some handed down through the generations.

Yet sometimes even the best-informed gardeners need a helping hand, and that's where the RHS and The Wildlife Trusts come in. In this book, experts from across the two charities provide their own experienced advice on each topic, offering the benefits of their professional judgments, pointing out the legalities of dealing with the creatures or plants in question, listing the ideal plants to develop a particular habitat, guiding step by step through more complex gardening processes, charting the requirements of the animals that may visit your garden, and explaining where to go for further information or equipment.

The result is a democratic mixture of public debate and expert comment. Whether you're an experienced gardener, or just starting out with a patch of land at the back of your first new home, this book offers plenty of ideas to draw upon.

And once you've read it, and put those ideas into practice, why not record your experiences? The website forum is growing all the time, adding to the sum of collective knowledge of wildlife gardening.

Come and join us.

Comments from
the public

Expert
advice

OWLS

You said...

Where have all the owls gone in London? They used to hoot every early summer 15 years ago. How can we bring them back? Is it the trees being endlessly lopped at the request of insurance companies?
Cawky, London

Because they're night birds, they're difficult to count, but organisations like the British Trust for Ornithology believe that tawny owls may have dropped in numbers by about a third since 1994. It could well be the reduction of mature trees in many urban places has contributed to this decline, although there's another theory that the constant night-light in towns has made them less effective, too.

Mike Russell, Sussex Wildlife Trust, advises:

To attract owls to your garden you really do have to have one of a reasonable size, preferably with a number of mature deciduous trees and backing on to woodland for tawny owls, or open farmland for barn and little owls.

Tawny owls, although seldom seen, are the most likely to visit your garden, and can be recorded in quite built-up areas, providing there are enough trees around from where it can roost safely during the day. You are more likely to hear the tawny owl, as it is the one that makes the familiar 'hooo' calls, especially in the autumn. They eat rodents, particularly mice and voles, so can be welcome visitors to your garden. If you have a large garden with a number of mature trees, you could try installing an owl nest box, a long funnel-shaped construction to encourage them to breed.

To attract little owls or barn owls you really need to be in a more rural situation, overlooking open ... by hedgerows and, particularly

KEEPING A BALANCE

You said...

I do find gardening for wildlife a difficult balance; I want to see rabbits, but do not want all my shrubs eaten! I like foxes, but not if they eat my chickens! I like moles, but not if they dig up my lawn! Seriously though, it is super to see the garden shared with so many birds, insects and animals. Currently watching a blue tit feeding young in a box outside the kitchen window – pest control in the garden at its best!
Clare Williams, Hertford

I would like to see garden design giving more prominence to bird-life. There should not be designs that are directly harmful – ie those with mirrors which kill birds that fly into them. Steep-sided, deep water features should ensure that hedgehogs which tumble into them can get out and not drown. The products on sale in garden centres should be controlled – poisons for mice and rats become part of the food chain and cause secondary poisoning in birds of prey and badgers. Slug killer kills hedgehogs and birds. I see rows and rows of masses of products designed to kill almost anything. Caterpillars become butterflies, slugs are food, weeds produce seed for food, etc. Rockery stones are taken from wild places destroying habitats. Too many plants are so-called 'architectural' but do nothing to support insects. My garden teems with birdsong. It was silent five years ago when I came here. Think before you buy – you will be rewarded. Jane Parkins, Marlow

A good mixture of habitats – including trees, shrubs and water – should greatly enhance your chance of encouraging wildlife into your garden.

Quick tips for a balanced garden ecosystem

● Always consider creating a pond if you have the space, but ensure the wildlife can get access in and out by not raising it or building hard, steep sides.

● In terms of planting, consider a proportion of native species that provide year-round interest for wildlife. Berry-bearing plants, too, make an excellent food source.

● Do not be tempted to tidy up all of the dead wood in the garden; leave some logs in a small pile to decay and provide vital food and shelter for a wide variety of insects which will in turn provide a meal for some of the birds.

● We all love to see and hear birds in our gardens, so give them another helping hand, especially over the winter, by providing a bird table and squirrel-proof feeders.

Graham Game, Essex Wildlife Trust, advises:

Nature is all about balance. Ecosystems – even in our gardens – need to be balanced to sustain their rich diversity through successive seasons.

If we are to help maintain this balance we need to learn to work with nature and not against it. Our gardens are now becoming vital nature reserves for many species of wildlife struggling to survive in the face of habitat loss due to farming and development. Gardens can even become richer habitats than anything that nature can provide!

But that does not mean we should create wildernesses and turn our gardens over to wildlife completely – gardens are for people, too, and for many of us these days our gardens are our main point of contact with the natural world. We are slowly beginning to realise how beneficial our gardens can be for us as a retreat from the stresses and pressures of our hectic lifestyles. Even scientists are now finding that this contact with nature is actually good for us, and it is well known, for example, that hospital patients can heal more quickly if the view from their beds overlooks a garden.

The trick in our own gardens is to integrate the 'wildlife areas' and the 'people areas' carefully; while decking, sleepers and gravel certainly have a part to play in garden design, hard landscaping – however convenient, should be used with care.

FOCUS ON... INSECTS

Insects are sometimes not the most welcome creatures in a garden. Some sting or suck blood, while others damage plants by sucking sap or eating the foliage, roots, flowers or fruits. However, only about 1% of the 22,000-plus insects in Britain are significant garden pests. Andrew Halstead of the RHS shows that the vast majority of our insects do no harm and some are of real benefit in gardens.

Many insects visit flowers to feed on pollen and/or nectar. In doing so, they frequently pick up pollen on their bodies. When they visit another flower of the same sort, that pollen may get transferred to the stigma of the flower, allowing pollination to occur. Bees are particularly good as pollinators as their hairy bodies readily pick up pollen grains. Most fruits grown in gardens, as well as many vegetables and ornamental plants, are dependent on insects for pollination. Honeybees, of course, also provide us with the additional benefits of honey and beeswax.

Some insects feed on other insects and invertebrate animals, some of which are plant pests. Examples of insects that prey on aphids include ladybirds, some hoverfly larvae and lacewing larvae, while ground beetles or carabids, and rove beetles or staphylinids feed on a wide range of soil-dwelling pests.

Insects, such as ichneumon, chalcid and braconid wasps, and tachinid flies, lay their eggs in the eggs, larvae or pupae of various insects, especially moth and butterfly caterpillars. The parasitoid larvae develop inside the bodies of their host insects, often feeding for several weeks before the host insect is killed. One wasp, *Encarsia formosa*, is used as a biological control of glasshouse whitefly, while *Aphidius colemani* is used against aphids in glasshouses.

Insects are also a significant part of the diet of many other types of animals. Spiders, many birds, amphibians, bats and some other mammals rely on insects for all or most of their food requirements. The pivotal role of insects in many food chains makes them a vital component of garden biodiversity.

Insects, especially some flies and beetles, feed on dead plant material, helping to break it down and making it available to growing plants as humus and nutrients. Insects also play an important role in disposing of animal dung and the corpses of birds and mammals.

Making your garden insect-friendly

Gardens can be regarded as a collection of habitat types, each of which will appeal to certain types of insects. More details can be found in the following pages, but here is an overview of some of the more important habitats for insects.

FLOWERS: Flowers provide a service to insects that is similar to that of petrol stations to cars. They provide a high-energy fuel in the form of nectar, with the added bonus of protein and oil-rich pollen grains. Day and night, flowers will be visited by a steady stream of butterflies, moths, flies, beetles, bees and other insects. Plant your garden so that there is something in flower from early spring to late autumn. Mixing flowers with vegetables and fruit trees may encourage hoverflies to visit and lay their eggs on the fruits and vegetables where aphids can be a problem.

WILDFLOWERS: Some native wildflowers are sufficiently attractive to earn a place in gardens (see page 64 and onwards). Exotic plants can attract a wide range of insects but these are mostly non-specialist insects that can use a wide range of plants. By growing native plants in a garden you can encourage those specialist insects that are entirely dependent on those plants. It is best to select wildflowers that already occur in your area. This links your garden to the wildflowers and insects of the locality.

PONDS: Adding water to a garden introduces a whole range of insects that cannot breed in a 'dry' garden. Dragonflies, damselflies, pond skaters, water boatmen, caddis flies, mayflies, water beetles, many flies and other insects are dependent on water and pond-side vegetation. Omitting fish from the pond will increase the diversity and abundance of insects. Even small bodies of water, such as a washing bowl with a thin layer of soil

Painted lady

Shield bug

under the water, will allow an insect community to develop.

LAWNS: Fine lawns that are frequently mown offer little to insects. However, lawns where clovers, daisies, dandelions, bird's-foot trefoil and other short-turf wildflowers are allowed to grow and flower can be attractive to both the eye and to insects. Where space allows, part of the lawn can be allowed to grow taller to accommodate meadow flowers. Long grass will suit grasshoppers, crickets, plant bugs, skippers and other meadow butterflies.

COMPOST HEAPS: Gardens generate grass mowings, autumn leaves, prunings, dead flower stems, leaf mould and weeds that need disposal. Taking such material to the council tip is a loss of valuable organic matter from your garden. It should be rotted down in a compost heap or bin so that the rotted compost can be used as a mulch or dug into the soil. Compost heaps teem with the larvae and adults of many beetles, flies, springtails and other invertebrate animals. They contribute to the composting process by breaking down the plant tissues. In the autumn, resist the temptation to cut down and compost all of the dead stems and foliage on herbaceous plants. Leave some until late winter or early spring to avoid flat, empty flower beds and to provide overwintering sites for insects.

HEDGES: Fences and walls support few insects so planting hedges should be considered where this is feasible. Broad-leaved hedging plants support more types of insect than conifer hedges, although the latter are good winter shelters. Hawthorn, privet, hornbeam, beech and holly are suitable for clipped hedges, but regular clipping will restrict the ability of the plants to produce flowers and fruits. An informal hedge or screen, where the plants are infrequently cut back, is better for most wildlife, including insects. Planting with a mixture of hedging plants, instead of a single plant species, enables the hedge to support a wider range of insects. An informal hedge can include some scrambling hedgerow plants, such as wild rose, honeysuckle, white bryony and bramble. If you haven't got space for a hedge, why not plant climbers against your wall or fence, for example ivy and honeysuckle.

DEAD WOOD AND ROT HOLES: Safety considerations may require the removal of dead trees or branches, but where possible, consider leaving dead wood in place.

Dead wood is far from lifeless in terms of value to insects. About 20% of woodland insects are directly or indirectly dependent on dead or dying trees.

A wide range of beetles and flies feed on decaying wood or associated fungi. Some solitary bees and wasps reuse beetle tunnels as nest sites, or make their own nest tunnels in rotten wood. When trees need to be felled or branches removed, the larger timber can be stacked, preferably in a shaded area, for the benefit of dead-wood insects and other wildlife. Standing trees sometimes develop rot holes.

Storm damage or bad pruning exposes the inner wood and allows colonisation by fungal decay that gradually results in a cavity forming in the trunk. These rot holes fill with rainwater, dead leaves and the corpses of birds and small mammals. The nutrient-rich sludge at the bottom of rot holes is home for some of Britain's rarest beetles and flies.

BEE NESTS: Many solitary bees and wasps nest in beetle tunnels in dead or rotten wood, or in hollow plant stems.

Artificial nest sites can be created by drilling holes of a variety of diameters, 2-9mm, in fence posts or blocks of wood. Hollow plant stems of herbaceous plants or bamboo canes can be pushed into plastic drink bottles from which the tops and bottoms have been removed.

Place the nests in sunny places under the eaves of a shed or on the rail of a fence in the spring. Boxes of nest tubes and drilled blocks of wood are often sold in garden centres.

They are also available by mail order from The Oxford Bee Company Ltd, Ash Business Centre, Gordon Road, Loughborough, Leicestershire LE11 1JP, Tel: 01509 261654 (www.oxbeeco.com); or Agralan Ltd, The Old Brickyard, Ashton Keynes, Swindon, Wiltshire SN6 6QR, Tel: 01285 8660015, (www.agralan.co.uk).

PESTICIDES: Insecticides used to control plant pests will also kill the insects that you are trying to attract. It is advised that any insecticides should only be used as a last resort. Avoid spraying all the plants 'just in case' they might have pests. Organically approved insecticides based on natural substances, such as pyrethrum, rotenone/derris, fatty acids or plant oils, have little persistence but even they will harm beneficial insects. If you do use an insecticide, make sure you spray at dusk when bees are not flying.

Biological controls, using predators or parasitoids, are available for many glasshouse pests, and for leatherjackets and chafer grubs in lawns. If used correctly, biological controls can be effective alternatives to pesticides.

Further advice on encouraging garden biodiversity is available on the RHS website, www.rhs.org.uk/biodiversity.

Red admiral

Beckoning butterflies

The Berkshire, Buckinghamshire and Oxfordshire Wildlife Trust advises:

Butterflies are well known as attractive insects but many others are worth a second glance. A close inspection of insects on plants, and watching their behaviour, can greatly add to the interest of a garden.

Butterflies such as red admirals and small tortoiseshells are also attracted to rotting fruit. Place a few bruised apples around your garden as an addition to nectar plants.

Avoid using insecticides in your garden as these may reduce insect numbers. Try to use alternative forms of control for example by encouraging natural predators such as frogs and hedgehogs.

Provide sheltered, undisturbed areas in your garden for adult butterflies and caterpillars to hibernate in over the winter months. These can include piles of logs and leaves and ivy.

Make a butterfly feeder! Stick a milk bottle top to a piece of brightly coloured card. Fill the bottle top with a sugar solution made from one teaspoon of sugar to 20 teaspoons of water. Place the feeder in a sunny, sheltered spot in your garden and watch the butterflies feed. Alternatively you could soak a piece of material in the sugar solution and hang from a tree or fence.

ME, MY GARDEN AND WILDLIFE

CHRIS BEARDSHAW

There can be few design features as variable and malleable as water. And there are certainly none that possess such magical powers to captivate and enchant a gardener. Water is perfect for highlighting the subtle changes in our plants through the gradually shifting seasons and for enticing wildlife into the garden. The flora and fauna find themselves perfectly reflected in a pool's mercurial surface. It is difficult to overstate the role that water plays in injecting life, energy and excitement into our gardens as it flows, splashes, gurgles and foams. It is, without doubt, the most valuable wildlife resource.

Great wildlife pools abound with life. They are the reflective surfaces over which pond-skating insects glide effortlessly as dragonflies and swallows dart overhead. In the water frogs, toads and newts thrive, taking time out to bask among muddy banks, also frequented by nesting and bathing birds. Inevitably such water bodies become the focal point of the garden and should be designed carefully. They are best placed in a natural hollow in the garden, or in low-lying sites where it is possible to suggest that water would naturally accumulate. For the most natural effects I opt for flexible liners (laid on a thick bed of compacted sand for protection) that follow the contours of the land. Ensure that the liner comes to the surface at the pond's edges and is then buried in the surrounding soil to prevent it moving. I also backfill the entire pond, and its submerged shelves with sub soil to allow the aquatic plants a generous

Chris Beardshaw is a writer, gardener and broadcaster who has appeared in *Gardeners' World*, *The Great Garden Challenge* and many other TV gardening shows.

rooting zone and insects or amphibians the opportunity to burrow and forage in the sludge. Try to ensure a variety of other habitats reach the margins of the pond, such as trees, shrubs and grass as this maximises the wildlife potential. Also create a beach for bathing birds and thirsty mammals. As the majority of artificial ponds are essentially static bodies of water it is vital that plenty of oxygenating plants are added. They may not appear the most glamorous plants in the garden, but they inject oxygen into the water without which the pond will stagnate.

This essential refuge for wildlife also uniquely provides an escape for gardeners, a calm pool into which our consciousness falls, drifts and meanders. Such a diverse repertoire means that a garden without water is a garden without a soul.

'It is difficult to overstate the role that water plays in injecting life, energy and excitement into our gardens.'

LADYBIRDS

The seven-spot ladybird is one of the commonest of the garden species of the family. It's an excellent destroyer of your aphid population, too.

Harlequin ladybird

● In 2004, a new species of ladybird first began to appear in the UK. Unfortunately the harlequin ladybird, as it is known, is a most unwelcome visitor. It not only out-competes our native species for food such as aphids, but when food is scarce, it even eats other ladybirds!

● The harlequin comes in many guises, as the guide (left) shows, so is very difficult to identify. They tend to be much larger than most of our native species, however, nearly 1cm in length, and their commonest form is orange with 15-21 black spots, or black with two or four orange or red spots.

● The harlequin has the potential to reduce our existing ladybird populations and represents a real threat. If you discover one in your garden, please contact the Harlequin Ladybird Survey at www.harlequin-survey.org, or email Dr Michael Majerus of the Genetics Department at University of Cambridge CB2 3EH at m.majerus@gen.cam.ac.uk.

John Ellis, Nottinghamshire Wildlife Trust, advises:

I would guess that most people recognise a ladybird when they see one, but how many appreciate that there are over 40 species to be found in Britain? Surprisingly many people are fond of ladybirds but totally abhor all other types of beetle or insect.

Ladybirds are voracious predators both in their larval and adult stages and should be welcomed in any garden, as they really will help reduce the aphid population. You can now buy ladybird hibernation houses but these are only really useful for a small number of species. Many species hibernate at ground level in leaf litter or plant litter and will not use these hibernation houses at all.

I have gardened organically for 30 years and one thing I always do is leave all the dead vegetation until the spring in order to provide hibernation sites for any insects including ladybirds. This means very untidy borders from September right through the winter and a lot of work in a short time period during the spring, but it also means I have a garden full of wildlife.

Some species of ladybird are unlikely to be found in your garden as their habitat preference may be specialised, such as heather heathland, deciduous woodland or marshland. However, there are still a good number to be found in the average garden.

Identification of some of the common species is easily accomplished by counting the spots but some are more problematic. The two-spot ladybird is probably the worst as it has many forms, mostly with more than two spots, and the 10-spot is not far behind as at least one form has only two spots! If you really want to get to grips with ladybird identification then there is an excellent publication to help, published in the *Naturalists' Handbooks* series, entitled *Ladybirds* by Michael Majerus and Peter Kearns (Richmond Publishing, Slough).

APHIDS

You said...

At the end of the garden, a nesting box has a blue tit pair. There was a lot of activity the day before, and yesterday I'm sure I heard tseeping from there. That evening, both parents were in and out of the nest incessantly – on the pear tree, at the bird feeder, on the clematis and on the rose – where one of them gathered up some aphids and flew off back to the nesting box. Thank you, blue tits! MoragS, Bristol

Life of an aphid

● The life cycles of aphids are varied and complex. Most species overwinter as small, shiny black eggs which are laid on trees and shrubs. These hatch in the spring into wingless female aphids which begin feeding on the new plant growth.

● At the beginning of the summer, winged aphids develop and these fly off to the herbaceous plants which act as their summer hosts. The colonies on the winter host die out at this time.

● All through the spring and summer, only female aphids are produced; these breed asexually and give birth to live young. At the end of the summer, winged males and females develop, and these fly back to the winter host where they mate and lay eggs.

John Hayward, Devon Wildlife Trust, advises:

Aphids are the curse of many a garden and are perhaps the best indicators of the futility of the chemical fight against nature that many gardeners engage. No matter how often you spray them, they often sometimes return in greater numbers than ever. Perhaps we should all have a sneaking regard for these tenacious little creatures.

These sap-sucking insects are members of the insect order Homoptera. In the process of feeding they can often transfer a number of viral diseases and kill the plant. They are about 1-5mm long with a soft body, long legs and antennae. Aphids come in a selection of colours, including the well-known greenfly and blackfly, and there are more than 500 species in Britain. Although they can't fly well, they can travel hundreds of kilometres on air currents. Unfortunately for us, aphids can produce many generations each year. Female aphids can give birth to live young as well as laying eggs, resulting in a rapid rate of reproduction as the temperature increases. They tend to cause leaf curl in plants which gives them shelter from predators (as well as insecticide sprays). Finally, they often form amazing associations with ants, who protect the aphids in return for access to sugary honeydew. Chemical solutions tend to potentially reduce the beneficial insects that can help with natural control of aphid populations. These include ladybird and lacewing larvae, earwigs and even bats and birds. Try hanging up pieces of fat in fruit trees and above rose bushes to attract blue tits which eat aphid eggs. A patch of nettles can encourage nettle aphids for hungry ladybirds. Nettle aphids will not attack other plants. Encouraging predators will help, but there's a lot more that can be done. Good plant husbandry is always crucial to fending off plant predators. Ensure strong plant growth through healthy soil, and try to choose resistant varieties. Barriers such as horticultural fleece are also good protection against aphids. You can hand-pick and squash aphids, and remove infested shoots and leaves. Water jets can also dislodge aphids.

Remember that a wildlife garden is all about balance and you can never expect to remove every last aphid. A combination of these approaches should, however, help to keep these creatures in their natural place.

ME, MY GARDEN AND WILDLIFE
RICHARD BRIERS

Richard Briers CBE, one of Britain's best actors on stage and screen, reached millions through TV for his role as Tom Good in the 1970s BBC sitcom *The Good Life*.

Our garden in Chiswick, West London, attracts its fair share of wildlife. I admit I'm not much of a gardener as I'm often away filming or touring, but I enjoy our little patch of greenery immensely and inviting in wildlife brings the place to life.

Watching the flurry of activity at our bird table every morning is a charming way to begin the day. My wife and I make sure we top-up the bird feeder regularly and keep fresh water on the go for our feathered friends. Scattering kitchen scraps onto the lawn can be a problem in the city as we don't want to attract rats but the birds get the crumbs from my morning toast and any other suitable offering from our table, so little goes to waste.

The only glitch in our suburban paradise is what I call the 'avian Mafia', the magpies and crows which swoop into our garden *en masse* sending smaller birds flying off in all directions. I'm worried that the smaller birds are reluctant to visit the bird feeders as much as they need to.

What's really amazing about garden wildlife is that you don't actually see most of it. The garden can look still and serene, yet invisible to the naked eye is a lively world of tiny invertebrates helping to make the garden look as good as it does. On a more leisurely day, I often stop to study the roses. If I spot a ladybird munching on a few unsuspecting aphids I'll think 'Good on you, girl! Keep doing the hard work for me...'

'The garden can look still and serene, yet invisible to the naked eye is a lively world of tiny invertebrates helping to make the garden look as good as it does.'

ME, MY GARDEN AND WILDLIFE

VAL BOURNE

I'd ask every gardener to consider conserving wildlife in their own gardens. But it's a very misunderstood topic. Plenty is written about the wildlife we can all see, the snuffling hedgehog, the spangled butterfly, the blue tit and his acrobatics at the bird table. And most gardeners are *au fait* with hedgehog houses, putting food out for birds and having plenty of nectar plants for butterflies and bees.

In its own way, this is important. However, generally the wellbeing of all these creatures is dependent on the lower orders of garden life. Track their food chains back and at the very bottom is either insect life (in some shape or form) or invertebrate life. And although the blue tit happily gobbles peanuts in winter, his fledglings will need a diet of grubs and small flies to thrive and breed. The hedgehog needs a high-protein diet of slugs and earthworms. The thrush needs a thousand snails to bring up a nestful of three or four. So we have to nurture this aspect of life, too, and avoid adding toxins to the garden. A truly natural gardener should eschew insecticides and slug killers, thus avoiding the inevitable build-up

Val Bourne is the author of the award-winning book *The Natural Gardener*, published by Frances Lincoln.

of toxins in bird and small-animal life. This chemical-free zone will be healthier for you and your family, too.

Preserving habitat is also highly desirable and one of the gardener's skills is beautifying these wilder areas. Leave some of your grass to move and sway in the wind, brown butterflies may lay eggs for you. Have a sunny bank with rough grass to help any nesting bumblebees to overwinter and breed. Stud it with red campion or cowslip. Leave leaf litter to float above your snowdrops and hellebores during winter — it's the equivalent of the insect duvet. In short, don't be too tidy.

Finally, stop trying to subdivide nature into good and bad wildlife. One depends on the other. Your good and saintly ladybird needs lots of colonies of those evil aphids to survive. Don't pull the individual pieces out. Conserve the lot and stand back and enjoy your own living jigsaw!

'Stop trying to subdivide nature into good and bad wildlife.'

MAY BUGS

You said...

Our annual invasion of may bugs started last night (16 May) which I think is a little later than last year. They fly around the outside light above our back door and end up on their backs on the doorstep. We have to remember to turn the lights off before we go out to try to ensure that none come into the house. Does anyone else get these visitors?
Tomofelstead, Elstead

By reducing your use of pesticides, you may help to encourage these magnificent insects into your garden.

 John Hughes, Shropshire Wildlife Trust, advises:

The may bug or cockchafer is a rather deliberate, and some might say clumsy, insect. Its large size, haphazard flight and droning buzz make it easy to recognise as it takes to the wing on early summer evenings.

They are attracted to light and can frequently be heard bouncing off windows in search of a mate.

Don't confuse them with delicate mayflies. May bugs are in fact closely related to dung beetles. At around 30mm long they certainly are big, but there's no need to panic as they neither bite nor sting. The adults eat leaves, but the larvae eat plant roots, especially grass, as they grow in the soil for three to four years. The larvae can be pests, but this tends to be localised.

Like so much of our wildlife they deserve a close look and you'll marvel at their beautiful fan-shaped antennae – males with seven 'leaves' and females with six. On the continent they have been something of a delicacy, too. They used to be eaten roasted or sugar-coated – delicious!

May bugs are more common in the south of Britain. In good years, adult beetles can appear in great numbers congregating at the tops of trees or on tall buildings.

ME, MY GARDEN AND WILDLIFE

CHRIS BAINES

It is more than 20 years since I wrote my book *How to Make a Wildlife Garden* and at the time it must have seemed like heresy. After all, in those days, garden wildlife was seen simply as a pest, a weed or a disease.

Now, gardening with wildlife seems like second nature. Good gardening has its roots in the changing seasons, and garden wildlife reinforces the natural rhythms. The spring's dawn chorus, the bees and butterflies of summer, the musty smells of autumn's fruit and fungi – even the winter frost on fallen flower stems – they all add to our gardening pleasure.

One reason that wildlife gardening has proved so successful is that each individual garden links into a complex neighbourhood habitat network. By planting wisely, providing food and water, safe shelter and a pesticide-free environment, even the smallest of inner-city gardens can provide a safe haven for a host of wild visitors.

Two things have made us value nature on the doorstep more and more in recent years. Most of us lead increasingly stressful, hectic lives and leafy green surroundings are the natural antidote. Scientists have shown that as little as three or four minutes in a garden filled with wildlife delivers measurable stress relief.

Many gardeners have also been motivated by the loss of wildlife in the wider countryside. The depressing decline of farmland birds, woodland wildflowers, wetland frogs and dragonflies has prompted a deep desire to make a positive difference. Between us we manage more than a million acres of domestic garden and the way we care for that resource can make a massive contribution to conservation – especially in a country which is more urbanised than most.

Chris Baines is a naturalist, author, TV presenter and environmental consultant. In 1985, he created the first wildlife garden to be presented at the Chelsea Flower Show.

Being able to make a tangible difference is undoubtedly empowering, and the nation's gardeners are becoming increasingly significant in the world of UK nature conservation. However, at the end of the day (and in my view that's probably the best time to enjoy it) most of us are now gardening with wildlife because it gives us so much personal pleasure. It simply seems the natural thing to do.

'One reason that wildlife gardening has proved so successful is that each individual garden links into a complex neighbourhood habitat network.'

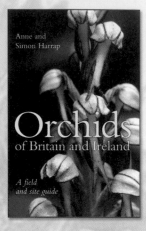

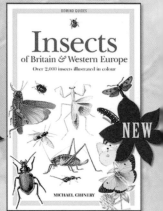

MILLIPEDES AND CENTIPEDES

You said...

Can anyone please describe the difference between a millipede and a centipede? I understand that one is very good for the garden and one is very harmful, but I don't know how to distinguish between the two.
Georgia, Redbridge

Millipedes have two pairs of legs per body segment, centipedes have one pair.
Selina, Chislehurst

Millipedes are also often tubular in shape and black in colouration whilst centipedes are often flatter and frequently brownish in colour. Both are relatively harmless in the garden to my knowledge.
Richard Burkmar, Horwich

These pictures are provided by Buglife, the charity committed to the conservation of all invertebrates. Buglife's website www.buglife.org.uk contains information about managing gardens and other habitats for bees, hoverflies, snails, ladybirds, spiders and other invertebrate inhabitants.

 Isobel Girvan, Surrey Wildlife Trust, advises:

Have you ever moved a log, a large stone or been rummaging in the compost heap and found a long, slender creature with lots of legs? It could be one of the species of millipedes (of which there are just under 50 species in Britain) or centipedes (there are a little over 40 species).

Millipede means 'thousand-feet', but whilst each body segment has two pairs of legs, segment numbers can vary from 20-60. Centipede means 'hundred-feet', and have one pair per segment, ranging from 15 to over 100 segments. They come in a range of different colours from yellow to orange through to dark brown.

Centipedes use antennae to feel for prey and have a pair of poisonous claws with which to kill them. But these are harmless to humans, as they cannot pierce the skin. However there are a number of predators that will eat them, such as spiders, frogs, toads, birds and small mammals.

Centipedes and millipedes both live in leaf litter, under logs and in compost heaps and come out during the night. They tend not to rest until their upper and lower body surfaces are in contact with surroundings; this helps to protect them and keep them moist. Large stones, logs and so on will encourage them as long as it is damp and dark. They lay eggs into the soil and the young emerge a few weeks later and can live for up to a few years (depending on the species).

ME, MY GARDEN AND WILDLIFE
ROGER LLOYD PACK

I live a lot of the time in a house which has a garden surrounded by woods and fields, so much of my energy is trying to keep the wildlife out of my garden! But we endeavour to grow flowers that attract butterflies, and all kinds of flying creatures are welcome, particularly birds, bees and dragonflies. Even though the birds may polish off some of the fruit, a decision has been taken in our household to share our garden with them because their company is such a joy. Each year there are at least two nesting pairs of tits and blackbirds and it's very soothing to monitor the routines of their day. I'm often alone there for several days, without seeing a soul, and I get a real feeling of comradeship from the birds, and when I answer their calls, it makes me feel part of the sweet world they live in.

Roger Lloyd Pack is an accomplished actor, as comfortable with Kafka as he is with *Only Fools and Horses*.

LACEWINGS

I like to garden organically, so last year we put up a lacewing chamber on a south-facing wall. This spring we were about to add the pheromone attractant when we saw a blue tit entering the chamber. It has now nested and is busy feeding its brood! This is all against the 'rules' as they don't usually like a south-facing nesting box. However this is what makes gardening so fascinating. In the meantime we have no lacewings to control our aphids! I wonder how this will affect our crops this year?
Angela, Norwich

The 14 species of British green lacewing can be seen, most often at night, between May and August.

John Hayward, Devon Wildlife Trust, advises:

Faced with an attack of aphids, most wildlife-friendly gardeners will reach for their local ladybirds. However, lurking in many gardens is another formidable aphid foe – the beautiful lacewing. This small flying creature is a really beneficial insect, eating not only aphids but also red spider mites, thrips, whiteflies, eggs of leafhoppers, moths, leaf miners and small caterpillars.

Lacewings belong to an order of insects called Neuroptera, and are easily recognised as they rest their highly-veined wings over the abdomen like a transparent tent. They are about 1cm long. The most familiar members of the group are the green lacewings (family Chrysopidae), which often come indoors or seek hibernation spots in outhouses and garden sheds during the autumn.

Although easily dismissed as small, green flies, they have a fascinating lifecycle. The larvae have well-developed legs, like ladybird larvae, but the pupae also have legs and working jaws, and may walk about before they become adults! Young ones have the delightful habit of covering themselves with the remains of their prey to camouflage themselves as little dirt balls. For loathers of aphids, it may be of interest to know that the lacewing larvae pierce the soft bodies of their prey with their hypodermic mouthparts and literally suck out the juicier parts. The larvae are sometimes called aphid lions, and have been reported to eat around 50 aphids a day.

To encourage lacewings in your garden, the young need damp places so that they don't dry out, so make sure there is plenty of shelter. You can also make a winter home for them by putting rolled corrugated card inside half a used drinks bottle and hang this from the bottle top in a damp shrubby area. Adult lacewings need nectar or honeydew as food before egg laying and they also feed on pollen. Make sure you have year-round nectar sources, and tolerate a few aphids for honeydew. Your lacewing army will be ready and on the march in the spring.

HOVERFLIES

You said...

Last year I introduced fennel into the garden primarily as an architectural plant. I was amazed at the variety of hoverflies it attracted and found myself gazing at its umbellifer heads for unnatural lengths of time. I have found that certain of the geraniums (cranesbill) are superb for bumblebees and yes, you guessed it, I do find myself lying in the grass when I get in from work, observing. sandj, Leyland

I grow fennel, too, Sandj. The hoverflies do love it – umbellifers in general are good for hoverflies and bees because they provide a nice landing platform as well as nectar and pollen.
Richard Burkmar, Horwich

I think ivy is one of the most essential plants to have in the garden if you want to attract bees and hoverflies. Hoverflies certainly seemed to be in abundance in 2004. Bunty, Ilford

To attract hoverflies, such as this marmalade fly, into your garden, have as many flowers as you can through the year. Compost heaps, a pond and decaying wood all help!

Want to know more?

● Hoverflies are important to gardeners because many of their larvae prey on greenfly, and the adults help with pollination. But with so many species of hoverfly to discover, how do you start? Here are two good books to help you get going: *British Hoverflies* by AE Stubbs & SJ Falk (published by the British Entomological and Natural History Society, 2002, 2nd edition) and *Hoverflies* by FG Gilbert (Naturalists' Handbooks No. 5, published by The Richmond Publishing Company Ltd, 1986).

● Having got to know this fascinating family of insects, you might like to help monitor them. For more information, visit the Hoverfly Recording Scheme at www.hoverfly.org.uk.

About 270 species of hoverflies occur in Britain. They are Diptera or 'true flies', with one pair of wings. Some species are commonly found visiting garden flowers and many people are familiar with those that look like honey bees (the drone flies) and the black and yellow species resembling wasps. Hoverflies are distinguished from Britain's 6,000 other Diptera by their behaviour, and a hazy grey line, the 'false vein', running through the wing between the dark veins. Many are excellent hoverers; males of the common *Syrphus ribesii*, a smart black and yellow fly, often hover waiting to pounce on passing females. A small dark hoverfly with broad femurs in its back legs, *Syritta pipiens*, visits cow parsley and garden flowers and is adept as 'helicoptering' among plants.

The hairy *Eristalis* hoverflies (drone flies) visit garden flowers and look rather like honeybees. They feed on nectar and pollen and are important pollinators, as they move from flower to flower. Their larvae live in wet, muddy ditches, manure pools and the like and have very long 'tails' – telescopic breathing tubes reaching the surface of water, hence the name 'rat-tailed maggot'.

Several species are migratory and in some years large numbers arrive in Britain from Europe. A dozen *Episyrphus balteatus*, the 'marmalade fly' can be seen on a dandelion flower in a good year. This medium-sized fly has double orange bands on the abdominal segments and its larva is a voracious aphid eater and an important pest controller in many garden plants.

The larvae of large hoverflies of the genus *Volucella* live in bumblebee and wasp nests. The larva of the common woodland species *Volucella pellucens* feeds on dead larvae and debris in wasp nests. *Volucella bombylans* larvae scavenge in bumblebee nests and the fly resembles small bumblebees. *Volucella inanis* (yellow and black) and *Volucella zonaria* (orange and black) are large, spectacular flies whose larvae are predators in wasp nests. After many years, these two species are currently extending their range from the South East into the English Midlands.

DEAD WOOD

You said...

I have an ancient pear tree. Just one branch is alive this spring. Should I fell it and make a log pile or leave it standing until it falls naturally? There is no public access or anything precious within falling range.
Bogweevil, Shaftesbury

The types of dead-wood habitats are as varied as the creatures that depend upon them. It is therefore important to retain as much variety as is possible, while obviously taking into account public safety.

 Sean Belcher, Surrey Wildlife Trust, advises:

The importance to wildlife of standing dead wood as well as fallen timber cannot be over-emphasised. Many organisms are completely dependent upon dead-wood habitats. There are fewer greater ecological resources than dead, dying and decaying wood. Woodlands that have had their decaying trees and dead and fallen timber removed show signs of a reduced diversity of animals and fungi, and the same goes for gardens. The wildlife that directly or indirectly depends upon dead wood is diverse and includes beetles, flies, solitary bees and wasps, insectivorous birds and mammals, fungi, lichens, mosses and liverworts.

Dead wood can consist of a single limb high up in a tree or a complete rotting trunk standing or fallen. The position of the dead wood in relation to the sun and wind is also important. Pieces of dry wood regularly exposed to the sun are utilised by fewer species than wood that is shaded and damp.

Across many of the Surrey Wildlife Trust's sites, where possible, dying and dead trees are left to decay naturally. These become important to larger animals such as birds and bats. Many old tree trunks are used by woodpeckers and other bird species as nesting sites and feeding stations. Owls will use them as territorial high points. Bats are also fond of old trees and will utilise holes as summer roosts. If the tree is in the correct position then it may be used as a winter roosting site.

It is the myriad of insects that use dead wood that is of interest. There isn't the space here to list all the creatures that depend upon dead wood; however, they all play an important role either as food for larger animals or breaking down the wood to release nutrients back into the environment. Along with fungi, the insects to be found in dead wood ensure the nutrient cycle continues.

LOG PILES

You said...

We are often told their virtues, but never told how to build them. Given that piles of logs do not occur naturally, there must be a best practice in log-pile construction to give home to the widest range of creatures and plants. ivy-tod, Reading

I've gone for the very scientific approach of just stacking them up like a pyramid. The bottom row has about six, the next five, etc. That way you get loads of little gaps for things to crawl into. Since then I've just left it alone. It seems to work but I never check to see what's in there. I leave it to its own devices. Paul, Leeds

I think it's more of an art than a science at the moment. In fact brush piles, although rather more unsightly than a nice neat log pile, may well provide more opportunities for wildlife – especially as nesting places for small mammals and birds. Trust your own judgement – take a bunch of logs and pile them up! See how the spirit moves you. Richard Burkmar, Horwich

Quick tips for a good log pile

● Wood from broad-leaved trees, especially oak, beech, ash, elm and sycamore, will attract the greatest range of species.

● Treated wood should be avoided.

● Place logs on or partly in the soil to retain moisture. Bury some vertically in the soil to increase the numbers of visiting insects, and help stag beetles.

● If the logs are in sunny places, drill holes of varying sizes in them for solitary bees to nest in, and as hibernation sites for other mini beasts.

● Log piles should be placed in partial shade. This could be under a tree or hedge. Logs look effective as edging for paths and borders, or as a feature in a shady corner.

● Gaps between logs can be planted up with spring bulbs, ground cover plants like bugle and wild strawberry, or such beauties as primrose and violets. These plants will quickly spread and partially cover the logs to create a really natural woodland garden effect.

Cath Knight, London Wildlife Trust, advises:

A log pile in the garden is one way of giving a helping hand to rarer species like the stag beetle, whose larval stage lives in rotting wood for up to seven years. It is also shelter to numerous mini beasts, most of which are beneficial to the gardener. Log piles attract a whole range of wildlife. Birds such as thrushes and blackbirds will visit for the food on offer. They are also a refuge for frogs, toads and newts, small mammals like mice, shrews and voles or even a hedgehog.

WILDLIFE TOWERS

You said...

We have started to build a round wildlife tower in our garden, inspired by an article in *The Garden* magazine in May 2004. It is loose-laid old bricks and can be 2m high and 800mm in diameter. What should I fill the centre with to encourage as wide a variety of insects etc as possible, but not rats?
rob thirlby, Loughborough

I reckon that the highest densities of invertebrates in my garden are to be found in my compost heap – especially the recently added stuff. So I would suggest filling it with some slow-rotting vegetable matter. Perhaps leaf litter mixed with lots of twiggy stuff to keep it relatively open with plenty of nooks and crannies for the insects. Mixing in some rubble might also be good.
Richard Burkmar, Horwich

We've built a much smaller structure, best described as a cairn made from pieces of sandstone, which we placed by our pond. We filled ours with rubble and dry leaves as we had discovered that our hedgehog house, which was also filled with dry leaves, was a magnet to a variety of small creatures. Sally, Belper

Mini-beast mansion: a wildlife tower for hedgehogs and other animals that will benefit your garden.

Why build a tower?

● Our gardens are home to a wide range of living creatures. An average garden can hold hundreds of different species of invertebrate. Many of these are very small, so are often overlooked. With all this diversity of life, it is good to know that very few creatures (ones that gardeners call pests) cause significant damage to our prized flowers, fruit and vegetables. Even better, there are many more creatures that help us control these pests. A wildlife tower can help you encourage these mini friends to your garden.

● By providing the right habitats we can greatly increase the number of beneficial insects in the garden. Some, such as bumblebees and solitary bees, are declining in numbers in the wider countryside, so by providing homes we can contribute to their conservation.

Sue Tatman, Cheshire Wildlife Trust, advises:

A wildlife or insect tower is a structure that provides homes for many different creatures. Our picture is a tower built from discarded pallets, but you could also build a wall, or place smaller structures all around the garden. Try to use recycled materials wherever you can. There are lots of things you can include:

● **Dead wood:** This is an increasingly rare habitat as we tidy our gardens, parks and amenity woodlands. It is essential for the larvae of wood-boring beetles, such as the stag beetle. It also supports many fungi, which help break down the woody material. Crevices under the bark hide small invertebrates.

● **Holes for solitary bees:** There are many different species of solitary bee, and all are excellent pollinators. The female bee lays an egg on top of a mass of pollen at the end of a hollow tube, she then seals the entrance with a plug of mud. Hollow stems, such as bamboo canes, or holes drilled into blocks of wood, make good nest sites for solitary bees.

● **Lacewing homes:** Lacewings and their larvae consume large numbers of aphids, as well as other garden pests. You can make a home for lacewings by rolling up a piece of corrugated cardboard and putting it in a waterproof cylinder, such as an old lemonade bottle.

● **Crevices:** Many garden invertebrates need a safe place to hibernate through the winter. Our habitat has many different types of crannies and crevices that different species of invertebrate can hide in over winter.

● **Straw and hay:** These provide many opportunities for invertebrates to burrow in and find safe hibernation sites.

● **Loose bark:** Beetles, centipedes, spiders and woodlice all lurk beneath the decaying wood and bark.

STAG BEETLES

You said...

Does anyone have any suggestions about how to encourage stag beetles, for example, what is a good habitat to provide for them?
Selina, Chislehurst

They like dead hardwood. You can also try an innovative technique recommended by the People's Trust for Endangered Species which involves sinking a bucket full of holes and woodchips into the ground! Look up 'Bury Buckets 4 Beetles' on Google to read about it.
Richard Burkmar, Horwich

We have occasionally found stag beetles in the garden. Are these good for the garden and should we try to protect them from frightened children?!
Farmers, Ringwood

Yes, the big white grubs are a sight! But please do not harm them; it takes four or more years to become a (proud) stag beetle.
John West, Petersfield

Would you like to help monitor stag beetles in your garden? Simply visit www.stagbeetlehelpline.co.uk to find out how to help this endangered and magnificent insect.

Fact file

Habitat: Broad-leaved woodlands, especially oak, but also parks and gardens where there are hedgerows, tree stumps and logs.

Lifespan: The larva lives three to five years. Adults live only between the months of May and August.

Breeding: Adult male stag beetles emerge in May or June, depending on the weather, followed shortly after by the females. The male has strong wings underneath the wing cases (elytra) and he flies at dusk in search of females. The flight can be rather erratic and the beetle sometimes flies indoors through open windows or doors, attracted by the light – and sometimes he bumps into things and crash-lands.

Feeding: Although it is known that the larva eats decaying wood, scientists are not certain whether adult stag beetles eat anything at all. Some think they use a special tongue to lick the sap from trees, but others believe they have no need to eat.

Mike Russell, Sussex Wildlife Trust, advises:

Stag beetles are an endangered species and gardens play a vital role in providing a safe haven for their survival. In a national survey undertaken by the People's Trust for Endangered Species in 1998, 70% of sightings came from gardens.

They are largely confined to southern England and there are particular hot spots where they can be found, even in very urban areas providing the conditions are right. You know when you see a stag beetle, they are Britain's largest beetle and the male has a magnificent pair of jaws that look like antlers, hence the name. They are likely to be encountered on warm summer evenings between May and August when they launch themselves into rather an unsteady flight and seemingly with no particular purpose, but actually looking for a mate.

You might also come across the larvae, especially if you are digging out an old tree stump, which is where the female lays her eggs. Once in the larval stage, they resemble a large white grub with an orange head and can take out up to five years before turning into an adult. So stag beetle survival depends on dead wood and little disturbance.

There are some simple things you can do to help them. Indeed, just by letting nature take its course and doing very little you can make a difference. First, don't keep your garden too tidy!

To encourage stag beetles into your garden, create some log piles using wood from broad-leaved trees such as oak, beech, or even fruit trees. They will need to be in some shady quiet corner if possible and the size of the log pile will depend on the size of your garden. The beetles will use small pieces of wood if that is all that is available, but if your garden is bigger, let your creative ideas flow in the construction of a larger habitat. Partially burying some of the logs will make the pile even more attractive. Leaving tree stumps will only add to the attraction.

And very importantly, cover your butts! Stag beetles are attracted to water, but once they've fallen into a water butt they can't get out again. In a recent survey, many beetles were found dead in water butts and buckets.

WORMS AND YOUR GARDEN

You said...

There were many raised eyebrows when people were told that my Mother's Day gift from my daughter last year was a wormery, but it gives me great pleasure lifting the top and seeing worms of all sizes happily turning kitchen waste into excellent compost!
Fuchsia Fanatic, Macclesfield

A robin is my constant companion when I am digging my allotment. I expect he eats all the earthworms, but whatever, he has to live.
Bogweevil, Shaftesbury

I also find that as soon as I start digging, a robin turns up, but they don't seem to eat the big earthworms, only the little centipede sorts of things. In fact, sometimes they struggle even with them. JJ, Bristol

I have also found that robins will only pick up very small worms but they are very partial to mealworms which can be purchased a lot more readily now. I know you probably shouldn't get them used to having food supplied but I like to think I am helping if there is not enough other food around for them to feed to their babies.
Bunty, Ilford

Starting a wormery

A wormery is relatively easy to establish. Worms are most active in warm, moist conditions, ideally between 18-25°C. Their activity noticeably declines below 10°C and above 30°C. Because of this wormeries are commonly kept in a shed or a sheltered area of the garden where it gets neither too cold in the winter nor too hot in the summer. Some people also keep wormeries in kitchens, utility rooms or on balconies. However, if neglected, wormeries sometimes produce odours. This should be considered before siting one indoors.

The environment within the wormery is also important. Composting worms prefer a pH of between 6.5-7.0, and well-ventilated conditions to live in. They will not tolerate extreme acidity and dislike being water-logged because this restricts their supply of air.

Before introducing the worms into a wormery an 8cm layer of moist 'bedding material' such as old compost or coir should be provided. This creates a humid layer in which the worms can burrow and begin to digest their food. To start with the wormery should be filled with no more than 8-10cm of kitchen waste and then left for about one week. This gives the worms time to settle into their new surroundings.

Maintenance

Some wastes have strong odours, which tend to attract flies. These are usually fruit flies and are harmless, but can be a nuisance. They can be avoided by burying new waste in the decomposed material or covering it with a layer of damp newspaper. Excess or unwanted food should be removed and disposed of as it can cause odours. If the wormery begins to smell it may be because it has become too wet. Excess liquid should be drained off and some shredded paper or card can be added to absorb excess moisture and increase air circulation.

Additional water should only be added if the wormery appears dry. Organic matter usually has a high water content and providing the lid is kept on the wormery, dry conditions are unlikely to occur.

An established wormery can be left without the addition of food for up to four weeks. However, during this period liquid may accumulate which needs to be drained off to avoid waterlogging.

Occasionally the compost can be forked over gently with a hand fork to verify that the worms are healthy and that compost production is underway.

The rate of composting can be increased by maintaining the right temperatures (especially during the winter), adding extra worms to the existing population, and avoiding overloading the wormery with waste. Wormeries with a greater surface area will also work faster.

Emptying the wormery

Most people do not empty their wormeries until they are full and this usually takes 8-12 months. Before using the compost the worms must be separated out. The worms tend to congregate in the area just below the top layer of food waste, so the top 20cm can simply be removed and used to restart the wormery again. The rest of the compost can then be used. Alternatively, if the weather is hot and sunny, the contents of the wormery can be spread out thinly over a sheet of polythene,

The worms used for composting are known as 'manure' or 'red' worms. These include the species *Eisenia foetida*, *Eisenia andreii* and *Dendrabaena veneta*. Composting worms live in decaying organic matter, whereas earthworms are soil dwellers. They are smaller and darker red than the common earthworm (*Lumbricus terrestris*), which is unsuitable for composting.

leaving a piece of wet newspaper lying on top of the compost in the centre. As the compost dries, the worms will move towards the cool, moist compost under the newspaper from where they can be collected.

Once emptied, and the worms separated, the wormery can be filled with a new layer of bedding, the worms returned and the cycle begun again. Many wormeries use stacking trays for the worms to work up through. The finished compost is in the bottom tray and can be removed. The tray is then emptied and returned to the top of the stack. This makes sorting the worms unnecessary.

Feeding

It is best to add small amounts of waste often to the wormery. Waste chopped into smaller pieces will be eaten faster. About 10-15cm of waste at any one time is sufficient to keep the worms going. If it appears that food is not being eaten, feeding should be stopped for a few days until the worms start to work through the top layer. If too much waste is added for the worms to cope with then it may start to smell and this could attract flies and possibly vermin.

Worms enjoy a varied diet eating any decaying organic matter. They will eat kitchen waste consisting of raw or cooked vegetables, (except for members of the onion family which are best fed in limited amounts or cooked first). All fruit can be included, except citrus peel, which again needs to be limited or preferably cooked. Fruit and vegetable scraps that contain seeds can be included but the seeds may germinate in the wormery. Dairy products, fat, grease, meat, fish and bones should not be fed, as these will attract unwanted pests and flies. Tea bags, eggshells, coffee grounds and small amounts of bread can be added to the wormery, as can small amounts of newspaper, shredded office paper and cardboard (not glossy magazines).

Worms will digest small amounts of garden waste such as annual weeds, leaves and other soft green material. Tough leaves and woodier material will slow the system down if fed in large quantities. If there is a lot of garden waste, which could overload the wormery, it is often best to have both a wormery and an ordinary compost heap.

 Rachael Tanner,
Royal Horticultural Society, RHS, advises:

Worm compost is an environmentally friendly method of recycling kitchen and garden waste. Composting worms are used to convert organic waste into a nutrient-rich compost and a concentrated liquid fertiliser. You can use a wormery to contain the waste material and worms: when diluted the liquid that results is excellent plant food. Wormeries are available from a number of sources, or they can be made at home. They often consist of at least two compartments: a lower collection sump for the liquid and an upper composting area where the kitchen waste goes and the worms actively work.

Worm composting

● Worm compost can be used as a general soil conditioner or as a constituent of home-made growing media. It is generally rich in nitrogen and potash. The liquid drained from wormeries can be used as a liquid fertiliser on garden plants after diluting with water at a rate of one part liquid to 10 parts water.

● You can buy wormeries and worms from:
Wiggly Wigglers Lower Blakemere Farm,
Blakemere, Herefordshire HR2 9PX;
Tel: 01981 500391/0800 216990; www.wigglywigglers.co.uk.

Worms Direct UK Drylands, Ulting, Nr Maldon, Essex CM9 6QS;
Tel: 01245 381933; www.wormsdirect.co.uk.

Original Organics Ltd, Unit 9, Langlands Business Park, Uffculme, Cullompton, Devon EX15 3DA; Tel: 01884 841515.

The Organic Gardening Catalogue, Riverdene Business Park, Molesey Road, Hersham, Surrey KT12 4RG; Tel: 01932 253666; www.organiccatalogue.com.

The Recycle Works Ltd, Unit 1, Bee Mill, Ribchester, Nr Longridge PR3 3XJ: Tel: 01254 820088; www.recycleworks.co.uk.

EARTHWORMS

Earthworms are nature's very own gardeners.

 Rosalind Cookson, Gloucestershire Wildlife Trust, advises:

The activity of earthworms is vital to life on earth. These industrious animals were considered to be sacred by the likes of Cleopatra and given the accolade of being the most important creatures in the history of the world by Charles Darwin. Today, scientists worldwide consider earthworms as one of the world's most crucial organisms in maintaining the sustainability of soils and advancing environmental and biomedical research.

The importance of the earthworm lies in its relationship to the soil. Neither could exist without the other. The earthworm consumes huge quantities of decomposed vegetation, manure and other organic matter, excreting a 'cast' containing nutrients. Earthworms also help reduce soil compaction by turning the soil as they burrow through it, improving permeability, and providing channels for root growth, water infiltration and gas exchange.

Depending on conditions, an area of natural grassland the size of a football pitch may contain five million worms. Their activity can process 15 tonnes of soil a year from the casts they leave on the surface.

Imagine the positive effect earthworms can have in your garden. Encourage worm activity and make the worm your most treasured garden friend! Put organic kitchen and garden waste in a compost heap, mulch it around flower and vegetable beds and earthworms will finish the job, producing a wonderful natural soil improver. This will reduce your visits to the recycling centre and the pressure on landfill, and also your reliance on soil improvers. To find out more ask your local council or county Wildlife Trust for help.

Worms are also important in your garden as primary consumers, in turn providing food for all of your favourite garden friends like the hedgehog and song thrush.

There's no need then to travel the world to see amazing wildlife. We have thousands of the most important creatures in our back gardens!

SLUGS AND SNAILS

You said...

My garden is connected to others by a series of largely overgrown alleys with lots of decaying wood piles and leafmould. It should be ideal for hedgehogs and I used to see lots of them but now they are rare. Some neighbours use slug pellets... are these the cause of their decline?
CC, New Malden

Could very well be as the pellets that are put down to poison slugs might harm birds or mammals that eat the pellets directly. There are varieties of pellets that are non-toxic, perhaps you could persuade your neighbour to use them (or if this fails buy a tub for them!).
Dizzy Bird, Petersfield

Has anyone else noticed how noisily snails eat after dark? They grind very loudly on our honeysuckle leaves. Can I prevent it from happening again this year without killing them? SAM, Penryn

Have you tried putting a ring of coarse sandpaper around the base of your plant? I've used this method this year after last year's young bean plants provided a yummy evening meal for the local snails. So far so good... patiostar, Cleveleys

Biological control: the Nemaslug

A non-chemical treatment is now available in the form of a microscopic pathogenic nematode or eelworm (*Phasmarhabditis hermaphrodita*). This is watered onto the soil, preferably in the evening, while the soil is moist and in the temperature range 5-20°C, usually March/April to September/October. The nematodes enter a slug's body and release bacteria that start attacking the slug. Affected slugs remain underground and stop feeding within a few days. The nematodes feed on bacteria generated in the decaying slug corpse. Newly hatched snails may also be attacked but older snails are less susceptible because they tend to live in comparatively dry situations above soil level where they are unlikely to get infected. The nematode only attacks molluscs; it has no effect on earthworms, insects, birds, mammals and other vertebrate animals.

The nematodes need damp conditions for survival and to enable them to move through the soil, so the soil should be kept moist for a week after application. If applied under suitable conditions, a significant reduction in the slug population can be expected for a period of at least six weeks. The nematodes are sold in pack sizes which treat between 40 or 100m^2. Since this is a living animal it has a short shelf life and the entire pack should be applied as soon as possible after purchase. If necessary it can be stored for a few weeks in a refrigerator, but it must not be frozen.

The nematode is available by mail order from the suppliers listed below or is sold from refrigerated cabinets in some garden centres. The nematode works best in light, well-drained soils; it may give disappointing results in heavy soils, such as clay.

Leopard slug

Mail order suppliers of Nemaslug include:

Biowise, Hoyle Depot, Graffham, Petworth, West Sussex GU28 0LR; Tel: 01798 867574.
Scarletts, Nayland Road, West Bergholt, Colchester, Essex CO6 3DH; Tel: 01206 242533.
Green Gardener, 41 Strumpshaw Road, Brundall, Norfolk NR13 5PG; Tel: 01603 715096.
Defenders Ltd, Occupation Road, Wye, Ashford, Kent TN25 5EN; Tel: 01233 813121.
Organic Gardening Catalogue, Riverdene Bus. Pk, Molesey Road, Surrey KT12 4RG; Tel: 01932 253666.
Just Green Ltd, Freepost ANG 10331, Burnham on Crouch, Essex CM0 8BF; Tel: 01621 785088.
Agralan Ltd, The Old Brickyard, Ashton Keynes, Swindon, Wiltshire SN6 6QR; Tel: 01285 860015.

The main period for slug and snail damage is March to October, and they feed in the greatest numbers during periods of warm, damp, still weather.

Herbaceous plants less likely to be eaten by slugs and snails

Bear's breeches (*Acanthus mollis*); gayfeather (*Liatris spicata*); ternleaf yarrow (*Achillea filipendulina*); yellow loosestrife (*Lysimachia punctata*); *Agapanthus* hybrids and cultivars; forget-me-not (*Myosotis* species); lady's mantle (*Alchemilla mollis*); catmint (*Nepeta* x *faassenii*); Japanese anemone (*Anemone* x *hybrida*); Ornamental grasses and sedges; Japanese anemone (*Anemone hupehensis*); oriental poppy (*Papaver orientale*); snapdragon (*Antirrhinum majus*); Iceland poppy (*Papaver nudicaule*); *Aquilegia* species; *Pelargonium*, *Armeria* species; *Phlox paniculata*; *Aster amellus*; obedient plant (*Physostegia virginiana*); *Aster* x *frikartii*; *Aster novae-angliae*; Michaelmas daisies; *Polemonium foliosissimum*; *Polygonum* species; *Astilbe* x *arendsii*; *Potentilla* hybrids and cultivars; *Astrantia major*; lungwort (*Pulmonaria* species); elephant's ears (*Bergenia*); *Rudbeckia fulgida*; *Centaurea dealbata* and *Centaurea montana*; *Salvia* x *superba*; *Corydalis lutea*; London pride (*Saxifraga* x *urbium*); globe artichoke (*Cynara cardunculus*); scabious (*Scabiosa caucasica*); bleeding heart (*Dicentra spectabilis*); ice plant (*Sedum spectabile*); foxglove (*Digitalis purpurea*); houseleeks (*Sempervivum* species); *Eryngium* species; *Sisyrinchium* species; spurges (*Euphorbia* species); golden rod (*Solidago* species); fennel (*Foeniculum vulgare*); *Stachys macrantha*; *Fuchsia* cultivars; pyrethrum (*Tanacetum coccineum*); *Gaillardia aristata*; *Thalictrum aquilegiifolium*; *Geranium* species; *Tradescantia virginiana*; *Geum chiloense*; nasturtium (*Tropaeolum* species); day lilies (*Hemerocallis* cultivars); mullein (*Verbascum* species).

One potato, two potato...

Potatoes vary in their susceptibility to slugs. Maris Piper, Cara, Arran Banner, Kirsty, Maris Bard, Maris Peer, Kondor, Pentland Crown and Rocket are frequently damaged, whereas Pentland Dell, Pentland Squire, Wilja, Charlotte, Golden Wonder, Kestrel, Estima, Stemster, Sante and Pentland Ivory are less susceptible. Damaged potatoes are more vulnerable to storage rots and the crop should be sorted into sound and damaged tubers, with the latter being stored separately for early consumption.

61

Top 3 reasons for choosing Páramo

1. Unique Nikwax Directional Fabrics

All Páramo garments use innovative fabrics engineered by our sister company Nikwax. Designed to actively 'Direct' water (liquid water as well as water vapour) to where you need it to keep you comfortable. This goes from our newest reversible, next-to-the-skin base layers to the outer weatherproof protection of Nikwax Analogy.

Thanks to Directionality, Páramo gear outperforms all other outdoor garments. Better than 'breathable', more comfortable than 'water-proof', as supple and silent as 'soft shell', Páramo continues to perform in a wide range of temperatures and in high humidity.

2. 'On the Hill' Design

All Páramo designs originate and are refined by our design team based in the Lake District. They are tested extensively in our labs and by our team of highly critical gear testers on the hill.

'Páramo style' emanates from function, comfort and safety – not just fashion. Each garment works superbly on its own but is also designed to be combined effectively with others in the range.

Through-to-skin ventilation sited for maximum impact, pockets in the sizes, shapes and places to be most useful, adjustable hoods and cuffs plus excellent articulation for unrestricted movement. Tell us what you think of our garments too – we listen to feedback.

3. Chosen by Outdoor Professionals

Rescue Teams, Outdoor Instructors and guides were among Páramo's earliest converts. Today, they remain the focus of our development – by satisfying their needs, Páramo can be sure that all outdoor enthusiasts gain from fabric and garment improvements.

Páramo gear is selected for its comfort and safety on the hills by such organisations as the National Search & Rescue Dog Association (SARDA), by English Nature, the Countryside Council of Wales and the National Trust for Scotland. It's the first choice of some 30 teams within the UK Mountain Rescue Community, who routinely use Páramo day in, day out across the wet and windy UK.

Why we use independent retailers

We've made a conscious decision to offer Páramo only through selected outdoor retailers – the reason is to ensure you get the best possible service and advice. Páramo is different and we think it's important that customers get a clear, well-informed picture of how it works and how Páramo garments can benefit them. All our independent retailers offer excellent advice, tailored to the individual's needs,

about the Páramo range and its suitability for your requirements. We know all of our retailers well and they all know Páramo well. Most are outdoor specialists with very useful insights to share.

To locate your nearest Páramo stockist, ring us on the number below, or go online at **www.paramo.co.uk**

PÁRAMO® – *Leaders in comfort and performance*

For our latest info pack please telephone **01892 786444** or email us at **info@paramo.co.uk**

Isobel Girvan, Surrey Wildlife Trust, advises:

There are about 125 species of terrestrial snail and slug in the British Isles, some native, others introduced, such as the Roman snail, a large edible snail. They live in a variety of habitats and a number of species are often seen in gardens, particularly after wet weather and at night, including garden snails, garden slugs, Budapest slugs and grey field slugs.

Ever wondered why there are so many snails in your garden? The garden snail lays about 80 round whitish eggs into the topsoil of the ground about six times a year. They hatch within two to six weeks and then take about two years to become adults and can live for several years. Slugs and snails will feed on rotted matter such as vegetation and fungi, which benefits the garden as it helps to return dead plant material back into the soil. But they will also munch away at garden plants – hence their bad reputation. However they are eaten by ground beetles, spiders, frogs, toads, slow-worms, birds, shrews and hedgehogs.

So how can you control them? There are a number of natural tried and tested methods. Recent research suggests that slug pellets do no harm to creatures that eat the poisoned slugs, but if animals eat the pellets directly, it may do them harm. The best bet is to look for alternatives: experiment to find out which works best in your garden.

Slugs can be controlled by introducing a minute pathogenic worm called *Phasmarhabditis hermaphrodita*, (see page 60), from garden centres. Be warned: this is only a temporary measure and you may have to reintroduce the following year. A traditional means of keeping slugs and snails away from plants is to surround them with a barrier of sharp sand. Proprietary slug barriers made from rock granules or crushed shells are sold under the brand names of Fito Slug Stoppa, Snail Ban, Bio Slug Barrier, Vitax Slug Off and Gem Slug 'n' Snail repellent. A copper impregnated material, Slug and Snail Shocka!, can be placed as a mat under flower pots or around the base of plants. Slug-tape made from copper carries a tiny electric charge and will act as a barrier – plants in containers can be protected by placing such a tape, (brand names include Fito Slug Stoppa Tape, Agralan Copper Snail & Slug Tape or Growing Success Slug Barrier Tape), around the pot. You can also try using bran or slug-resistant granules, which absorb the mucus.

'Slug pubs' are thought to at least provide slugs with an enjoyable boozy end. Put several saucers or commercially bought containers around the garden to increase chances of catching them. Empty them regularly and set them with the top 2cm above soil level so that ground beetles and other friendly invertebrates do not fall into them. You can try to catch slugs and snails by torchlight, or if you put old cabbage leaves down, or perhaps some cardboard you will find them underneath during the day. They can then be taken to a nearby wildlife area to be disposed of safely. Above all, try not to worry. You will never get rid of them completely, so you could invest in some slug-resistant plants.

FOCUS ON... PLANTS FOR INSECTS

Private gardens in Britain cover about 270,000ha, writes Andrew Halstead of the RHS, and, together with public parks, provide important feeding and nesting areas for bees and butterflies, the great pollinators of our gardens.

Habitat features, such as hedgerows, ponds, lawns and flower borders can be put into a garden to encourage insects. Some native wild plants are attractive enough to earn their own place in gardens and may help support bees and other insects that otherwise could not survive in urban areas. It should be remembered that bees like the sunshine and may ignore wild plants hidden in shady corners. Care should be taken to ensure that purchased wildflower seeds or plants are of native stock and not strains of the same plants obtained from other countries, as these may have different flowering periods and growth habits compared to native plants.

Many garden plants are of exotic origin or have been hybridised to produce flowers with different characteristics to the true species. These can be of value to bees with non-specialised feeding requirements but may be unattractive to certain wild bees which are restricted to a narrow range of flowers. These include monolectic species such as *Andrena florea* and *Macropis europaea*, which only take pollen from white bryony (*Bryonia dioica*) and yellow loosestrife (*Lysimachia vulgaris*) respectively.

There are also other bees (oligolectic species) which confine their pollen-collecting activities to a few closely related plants, for example *Andrena apicata* on willows (*Salix* species) and *Andrena lathyri* on vetches (*Vicia* species). Polylectic bees collect pollen from a wide range of flowers; examples of these are the honeybee and bumblebees.

Various annual and perennial wildflowers can be incorporated into flower borders and will not look out of place among the more conventional garden flowers. They will often make bigger plants than in their natural surroundings where competition with grass and other wildflowers restricts their growth.

Adult butterflies visit flowers to obtain nectar which they suck up with their long tongue or proboscis. They make use of a wide range of flowers and other sweet substances, such as the juices of overripe fruits. The plants listed (right) will generally attract butterflies but to get the best results they should be grown in sunny sheltered places. Clumps of plants are usually more attractive than single scattered plants. Nectar-providing flowers are also used by other insects, such as bees and moths.

Good plants for butterflies

WILD PLANTS: Angelica (*Angelica sylvestris*); bugle (*Ajuga reptans*); buttercups (*Ranunculus* spp.); clovers (*Trifolium* spp.); dandelion (*Taraxacum officinale*); fleabane (*Pulicaria dysenterica*); garlic mustard (*Alliaria petiolata*); hawkweeds (*Hieracium* spp.); hemp agrimony (*Eupatorium cannabinum*); hogweed (*Heracleum sphondylium*); knapweeds (*Centaurea* spp.); lady's smock (*Cardamine pratensis*); marjoram (*Origanum vulgare*); purple loosestrife (*Lythrum salicaria*); *Salix* spp., especially male forms of sallows (*Salix caprea*); scabious (*Knautia arvensis* and *Succisa pratensis*); stonecrop (*Sedum acre*); teasel (*Dipsacus fullonum*); thistles (*Cirsium* spp. and *Carduus* spp.); valerian (*Valeriana officinalis*); water mint (*Mentha aquatica*).

ANNUAL AND BIENNIAL GARDEN FLOWERS: African marigold (*Tagetes erecta*); ageratum (*Ageratum houstonianum*); alyssum (*Lobularia maritima*); candytuft (*Iberis amara*); China aster (*Callistephus chinensis*); cornflower (*Centaurea cyanus*); French marigold (*Tagetes patula*); heliotrope/cherry pie (*Heliotropium* cultivars); honesty (*Lunaria annua*); marigold (*Calendula officinalis*); mignonette (*Reseda odorata*); stocks (*Matthiola incana* and hybrids); sweet William (*Dianthus barbatus*); verbena (*Verbena rigida*); wallflower (*Erysimum cheiri*); zinnia (*Zinnia elegans*).

HERBACEOUS PERENNIALS: Alyssum (*Aurinia saxatilis*); *Agastache foeniculum*; arabis (*Arabis alpina* subsp. *caucasica*); *Asperula hexaphylla*; *Astrantia major*; aubrieta (*Aubrieta deltoidea*); blanket flower (*Gaillardia* cultivars); catmint (*Nepeta x faassenii*); *Centaurea* spp. eg *C. dealbata*, *C. montana*, *C. macrocephala*; dahlias – single flowered types; elephant's ears (*Bergenia* spp.); *Eryngium* spp.; garden mint (*Mentha spicata*); globe artichoke (*Cynara cardunculus*); globe thistles (*Echinops* spp.); golden rod (*Solidago*

spp.); hyssop (*Hyssopus officinalis*); ice plant (*Sedum spectabile* – dark red cultivars are less attractive); Jacob's ladder (*Polemonium caeruleum*); *Liatris spicata*, Michaelmas daisies (*Aster novae-angliae, A. amellus*); perennial candytuft (*Iberis sempervirens*); phlox (*Phlox paniculata*); red valerian (*Centranthus ruber*); scabious (*Scabiosa* spp.); soapwort (*Saponaria* spp., especially *S. ocymoides*); sweet rocket (*Hesperis matronalis*); thrift (*Armeria* spp.); *Verbena bonariensis*.

SHRUBS: Blackberry (*Rubus fruticosus*); butterfly bush (*Buddleja davidii*, also *B. globosa, B. alternifolia*); caryopteris (*Caryopteris x clandonensis*); cherry laurel* (*Prunus laurocerasus*); *Escallonia* hybrids; firethorn (*Pyracantha* cultivars); hawthorn* (*Crataegus monogyna*); heather (*Calluna vulgaris*); heaths (*Erica* spp., *Daboecia* spp.); *Hebe* spp.; ivy* (*Hedera helix*); lavender (*Lavandula* spp.); Oregon grape (*Mahonia aquifolium*); privet* (*Ligustrum* spp.); sallows (*Salix* spp., especially male forms of *Salix caprea*); thyme (*Thymus* spp.).

*These will not flower as young plants and flowering is inhibited by severe pruning, such as clipping to make a formal hedge.

WILDFLOWERS: common red poppy (*Papaver rhoeas*); wild candytuft (*Iberis amara*); mignonette (*Reseda lutea*); red campion (*Silene dioica*); white campion (*S. alba*); perforate St. John's wort (*Hypericum perforatum*); musk mallow (*Malva moschata*); common mallow (*M. sylvestris*); meadow cranesbill (*Geranium sylvestris*); sainfoin (*Onobrychis viciifolia*); tufted vetch (*Vicia cracca*); bush vetch (*V. sepium*); wild parsnip (*Pastinaca sativa*); teasel (*Dipsacus fullonum*); field scabious (*Knautia arvensis*); devil's bit scabious (*Succisa pratensis*); hemp agrimony (*Eupatorium cannabinum*); tansy (*Tanacetum vulgare*); ox-eye daisy (*Leucanthemum vulgare*); great knapweed (*Centaurea scabiosa*); hardheads (*C. nigra*); clustered bellflower (*Campanula glomerata*); nettle-leaved bellflower (*C. trachelium*); heathers (*Erica tetralix* and *E. cinerea*); ling heather (*Calluna vulgaris*); comfrey (*Symphytum officinale*); wood forget-me-not (*Myosotis sylvatica*); viper's bugloss (*Echium vulgare*); mulleins (*Verbascum thapsus* and *V. nigrum*); foxglove (*Digitalis purpurea*); marjoram (*Origanum vulgare*); English bluebell (*Hyacinthoides non-scripta*); meadow clary (*Salvia pratensis*); wood spurge (*Euphorbia amygdaloides*).

PONDS AND WET SOILS: Ideally the pond will have a variety of depths and at least one side should gradually slope up to an area of wet soil in order to accommodate a wide range of emergent and marginal plants. Water crowfoot (*Ranunculus aquatilis*); greater spearwort (*R. lingua*); marsh marigold (*Caltha palustris*); lady's smock (*Cardamine pratensis*); ragged robin (*Lychnis flos-cuculi*); purple loosestrife (*Lythrum salicaria*); yellow loosestrife (*Lysimachia vulgaris*); Jacob's ladder (*Polemonium caeruleum*); water forget-me-not (*Myosotis scorpioides*); water mint (*Mentha aquatica*); yellow flag iris (*Iris pseudocorus*); brook lime (*Veronica beccabunga*). These plants are also of benefit to bees (see page 68).

NECTAR PLANTS FOR BEES

You said...

I'm considering the possibility of replacing a lawn area with a mixed tapestry effect of nectar-rich flowering species which are also low-growing, for example clover or ajuga or sedums? The idea is to provide food for bees in particular. Has anyone tried these or other plants? Did you encounter or can you think of any potential problems? I'm not looking at meadow plants in this context, as the planting needs to be lower in height, to offset the border plants visually rather than compete with them.
Chris, Harrogate

Just today I got a catalogue from Wiggly Wigglers advertising 'Mrs Warhurst's Traditional Flower Shop'. It was full of plants and ideas that you would find really useful. See if you can request a copy from their website.
Richard Burkmar, Horwich

Various vegetables and culinary herbs can be of value to bees, as well as the gardener: examples include asparagus; brassicas left to flower; broad beans; hyssop; marjoram; mint; rosemary; runner beans; sage; and thyme.

Royal Horticultural Society

Andrew Halstead, RHS, advises:

Low-growing plants will be appreciated by insects, but you will have to remove grass weeds from time to time as these tend to take over. In winter, many plants die back, so be prepared for bare areas at this season. Also, only grass can bear traffic, so you might need to put in stepping stones for access. Watering and feeding are unlikely to be needed. Regular mowing is less necessary, but you will have to trim some plants, especially at summer's end.

Bees visit flowers to collect nectar and pollen. Some of the plants listed here provide pollen only but are valuable nevertheless to bees. Some may not always prove attractive to bees and this is particularly true of certain trees and shrubs which may not produce enough nectar to attract bees. See also pages 65-67.

TREES AND SHRUBS: Almond (*Prunus dulcis*); apple, incl. ornamental *Malus*; barberry (*Berberis* spp.); blackberry; blackthorn (*Prunus spinosa*); Boston ivy (*Parthenocissus tricuspidata*); box (*Buxus sempervirens*); brooms (*Cytisus* spp.); *Caryopteris*; *Ceanothus* spp. (Spring flowering types); cherry; cherry laurel (*Prunus laurocerasus*); Christmas box (*Sarcococca* spp.); *Cotoneaster* spp.; currants, (*Ribes* spp.); daisy bush (*Olearia* x *haastii*); *Daphne mezereum*; dogwood (*Cornus alba*); *Enkianthus campanulatus*; *Escallonia* hybrids; false acacia (*Robinia pseudoacacia*); firethorn (*Pyracantha* cultivars); *Fuchsia* spp.; *Gaultheria shallon*; gooseberry; gorse (*Ulex* spp.); hawthorns (*Crataegus* spp.);

Red-tailed bumblebee

Fact file

● Pollen contains proteins and fats and bees need large quantities, especially during the spring when many bee larvae are being raised.

● The extent to which nectar is secreted is influenced by factors such as temperature, humidity and soil moisture.

● Plants growing in sunny, sheltered places are more likely to be visited by bees than those growing in shaded or windswept situations.

● Low-growing plants, such as annuals and herbaceous plants, are more attractive to bees if the plants are grown in large clumps or patches, rather than being scattered and mixed up.

● Double-flowered or pollen-free varieties of plants are usually ignored by bees.

NB: Check your location first: some plants cannot be grown in all parts of the British Isles because of unsuitable climatic or soil conditions.

hazel (*Corylus avellana*); heather (*Calluna vulgaris*); heathers (*Erica* spp.); *Hebe* spp.; holly (*Ilex aquifolium*); horse chestnuts (*Aesculus* spp.); *Hypericum* spp.; Indian bean tree (*Catalpa bignonioides*); ivy (*Hedera helix*); Japanese quince (*Chaenomeles speciosa* and *C.* x *superba*); Judas tree (*Cercis siliquastrum*); *Koelreuteria paniculata*; lavender (*Lavandula* spp.); lime (*Tilia* spp. but *T. petiolaris* and sometimes *T. tomentosa*, *T. tomentosa* 'orbicularis' and *T. cordata* nectar is toxic to bumblebees); loganberry; *Lonicera* x *purpusii*; *Mahonia aquifolium*; maples (*Acer* spp.); mountain ash (*Sorbus aucuparia*); orange ball buddleia (*Buddleja globosa*); pear and ornamental *Pyrus* spp.; *Perovskia atriplicifolia*; plums; *Potentilla fruticosa*; raspberry; rock rose (*Helianthemum* spp.); rose – single flowered species types (*Rosa* spp.); snowberry (*Symphoricarpos* spp.); strawberry tree (*Arbutus unedo*); sycamore (*Acer pseudoplatanus*); sweet bay (*Laurus nobilis*); *Tetradium daniellii*; Virginia creeper (*Parthenocissus quinquefolia*); *Weigela florida* and hybrids.

LAWNS: Close mowing of lawns prevents most plants from flowering but in areas where the grass is cut infrequently there are a number of wildflowers attractive to bees that can be grown. Sowing seed direct into an established lawn often gives poor establishment; it is better to sow into cell trays and transplant the seedlings. Wildflower lawns should not be fed with fertilisers as excess nutrients encourage grasses at the expense of wild flowers. Good plants to choose include: creeping buttercup (*Ranunculus repens*); common rock rose (*Helianthemum nummularium*); violets (*Viola* species eg *V. riviana*, *V. hirta*); clovers (*Trifolium* species); bird's-foot trefoil (*Lotus corniculatus*); horseshoe vetch (*Hippocrepis comosa*); lawn daisy (*Bellis perennis*); dandelion (*Taraxacum officinale*); common eyebright (*Euphrasia nemorosa*); common thyme (*Thymus polytrichus*); self heal (*Prunella vulgaris*).

BUTTERFLIES

You said...

Early April was sunny (and breezy), but there didn't seem to be so many butterflies about. I've seen large whites quite a few times now, and a holly blue fluttered by. But I began to think that we'd had the first flush of speckled woods, then saw one (or two perhaps) briefly on one afternoon. Perhaps it wasn't quite warm enough? Although it was sunny, the air was quite cool. MoragS, Bristol

Lots of butterflies out this weekend, including several orange tips, attracted by the garlic mustard I've planted to attract them. Also several brimstones drawn in by the alder buckthorn. Garden butterflies spotted today include holly blues, speckled woods, peacock, comma, large white and green-veined white. With the right plants all of these (and more) can be attracted into an average-sized garden. I had 20 butterfly species in my garden last year. Malcolm Hull, St Albans

Comma

For further advice on how to attract butterflies to your garden, such as this comma, and how to identify them, visit Butterfly Conservation at their website www.butterfly-conservation.org.

Which plants for butterflies?

Although many species of flower are good for nectaring butterflies, their caterpillars, or larvae, are far more particular, requiring very specific foodstuffs to be able to survive. The following plants will provide food for the larvae of those species that might breed in gardens, although some butterflies tend to fly in restricted areas and will not readily colonise a new suitable habitat unless it is very close to existing butterfly colonies.
STINGING NETTLES: Used by peacock, red admiral, comma and small tortoiseshell. Needs to be grown in a sunny position to encourage egg laying. Prevent seeding by cutting down in midsummer after the first brood of the small tortoiseshell has developed.
THISTLES: Painted lady lays eggs on plants such as welted thistle and creeping thistle.
CABBAGES, OTHER BRASSICAS AND NASTURTIUMS: Large cabbage white and small cabbage white.

GARLIC MUSTARD AND LADY'S SMOCK: Orange-tip and green-veined white.
MIXED GRASSES: Various grasses are used by speckled wood, wall butterfly, meadow brown, gatekeeper, marbled white, ringlet, small heath, large skipper, small skipper and Essex skipper. The habitat requirements of these butterflies vary, particularly regarding the types of grass, the height of the sward and whether it is dry or damp grassland. Generally the grass should be left uncut during the growing season and scythed in the spring, leaving a good basal growth on the tussocks.
HOLLY AND IVY: Holly blue lays eggs on holly flowers in spring and on ivy flowers in late summer.
ALDER BUCKTHORN AND PURGING BUCKTHORN: Brimstone.
BIRD'S-FOOT TREFOIL: Common blue.
DOCKS AND SORRELS: Small copper.

Mike Russell, Sussex Wildlife Trust, advises:

Whatever the size of your garden and wherever you live in the UK, you can do something to attract butterflies and bring some extra colour and beauty into your lives!

Even if you have only room for pots in a backyard, fill them with nectar-rich plants such as buddleia, sedum or lavender, put them in the sunniest position and at some point you may well be rewarded with a visit from a red admiral, small tortoiseshell or a peacock. Regarding warm weather, a sunny day in a sheltered garden in February might entice a brimstone to take an early flight, while on similar days in November you may well still see the last of the year's red admirals. Butterflies need sun and preferably little wind to get them out and about.

When planning a garden to attract butterflies, think too about food plants for the caterpillars to encourage breeding and, in addition, plan for both food sources to be available from spring right through to autumn. By planting primrose, sweet rocket, hebes, thyme or Michaelmas daisies, you are providing opportunities for butterflies to feed for over half the year.

Think about turning part of your garden into a mini-meadow and sow with grasses such as meadow grass, Yorkshire fog and false broom to attract species like meadow brown, gatekeeper and skippers. Add bird's-foot trefoil and you might encourage breeding common blues. Nettles are common in the wild, but if you can find room for a decent-sized patch of them in a sunny position, you may attract red admirals and small tortoiseshells, among others.

Gardens that have mature trees and hedgerows might attract more woodland species such as speckled wood or orange-tips, the latter laying its eggs on lady's smock or garlic mustard. Plant an alder buckthorn and you may well be treated to the sight of a brimstone in March or April.

Butterflies can be attracted with just a little bit of thought given to the planting and management of the garden and will help create your very own little nature reserve.

Small tortoiseshell

MOTHS

You said...

We get hummingbird hawk moths into our garden every year, feeding from red and white valerian. The books say they only come this far north in exceptional years, but that does not seem to be the case. kate, Stockton-on-Tees

We were astonished and fascinated to see a hummingbird hawk moth feeding from a large lychnis plant in our small urban container garden last weekend, whilst we were enjoying a late evening barbecue with friends. None of us had ever seen such an insect before, and were very excited and entranced. Reading up after its departure (it only stayed for a brief couple of minutes), we were surprised that a resident of the south of France had flown all the way to Wrexham, North Wales. Presumably this is a result of general climate change caused by global warming. It was incredible to observe the very birdlike hoverings of this reasonably large moth, and would love to observe it again. We are also keeping eyes peeled for a convolvulus hawk moth, almost twice the size, and the largest insect to visit these shores. Evidently they originate in the Mediterranean, and can travel 1,000 miles in a few days. Impressive! treaclechops, Wrexham

We were pleased to find elephant hawk moth caterpillars three years ago, so we have kept a small patch of great willowherb and have seen them each summer since then. JackieP, Winchcombe

Trapping in your garden

Putting a moth trap out in the garden at dusk, and going through the catch in the morning is an easy and enjoyable way to study the range of insects visiting your garden. Even urban gardens should attract well over 100 species during the year, with more favoured gardens easily achieving lists of 200-300 species. The peak months are July and August when nightly catches of several hundred moths can be expected, and for the beginner the range of species is at first sight daunting. However, an hour or two with a good guide book – try British Wildlife Publishing's *Field Guide to the Moths of Great Britain and Ireland* – will usually sort out the majority, and having seen the species once things can only get easier!

● In small gardens, traps should not be run every night unless the moths can be released elsewhere. Running traps on successive nights in small areas will result in re-trapping a small proportion of the moths you released that day. This prevents the moths from feeding and from mating. By running the trap every other night, moths are given a chance to 'do their own thing' every so often.

● When releasing catches, think about the release site. Ideally you should provide a site which is relatively overgrown, giving the

The hummingbird hawk moth, hovering as it feeds from nectaring plants, is truly a magnificent sight.

moths somewhere to hide during the day. Concentrating large numbers of moths in one area on release should also be avoided. It's good for the local bird population, but not so good for the moths!

● If the trap has to be left before unloading, for example because you don't have time to unload before going to work, the trap should be moved into a cool, shaded position. The addition of a small piece of damp cloth or sponge to the bottom of the trap will also help prevent casualties from dehydration.

● Perhaps the easiest way to begin moth trapping is to suspend the light source over a large white sheet. This is also great fun as you can watch the moths arrive at the trap. Obviously no attempt is made to hold the catch, and hence you must stay with the trap, potting the moths for inspection as they arrive.

The above advice is kindly provided by Anglian Lepidopterist Supplies (ALS), who offers a range of moth traps and other equipment for the knowledgeable professional and enthusiast beginner alike. You can contact ALS by calling 01263 862068, or visiting www.angleps.btinternet.co.uk.

Burnet

Do YOU love seeing butterflies in your garden?

Sadly seven out of 10 butterfly species in Britain are in decline. Butterfly Conservation is the UK charity taking action to save butterflies, moths and their habitats. We need your support!

YOU can help us save butterflies and moths in 2 ways:

1. By gardening for butterflies – we can provide you with information about nectar and food plants that enable butterflies and moths to thrive in your garden. To obtain your free gardening pack send an A5 stamped addressed envelope marked "Gardening Pack - RHS" to Butterfly Conservation, Manor Yard, East Lulworth, Wareham, Dorset, BH20 5QP.

2. By becoming a member and supporting the vital conservation work we are undertaking: telephone **0870 7744309** or join online at **www.butterfly-conservation.org**

Butterfly Conservation is a registered charity and non-profit making company, limited by guarantee
Registered office: Manor Yard, East Lulworth, Wareham, Dorset, BH20 5QP
Registered in England No 2206468 –
Registered Charity No 254937

Butterfly Conservation

Phil Porter, Lincolnshire Wildlife Trust, advises:

One of the most rewarding natural history interests that I have ever developed is to record moths. There are such a lot of different species. Dozens at least, maybe hundreds, can be found in gardens depending on the latitude and the quality of the surrounding habitats. Compared to butterflies (about 60 British species), moths represent riches indeed. Moths can be found during every single month of the year and the cast changes with the seasons, so there is never any reason for interest to flag. Some even migrate to this country from the continent. One of these, the hummingbird hawk moth, has been occurring further north in recent years, even reaching as far as the Shetland Islands.

As a matter of fact many of the winter flying moths have a curious strategy for surviving during this harsh time of year. Species such as the pale brindled beauty and the winter moth absorb all the food for their lives as caterpillars, which can thrive on almost any tree and shrub foliage. This means that they can devote all their energies as moths to finding a mate. The females of many winter species are flightless and lay many eggs to compensate for the high risk of failure in the next generation of moths if

Privet hawk moth

icy weather prevents them from achieving any of their goals. Because of their catholic tastes, these species can be found in most gardens sheltered from the worst of winter winds, but they usually go unnoticed.

People perceive moths to be dull and somehow repellent, due mostly to the mystery surrounding many nocturnal animals, and the panic that ensues when one gets into lit rooms at night. But really, there is no worthwhile distinction between butterflies and moths, and scientists organise the Lepidoptera with primitive and tiny moths early in the list, more advanced larger moths at the end, and butterflies in the middle!

There are some fantastically vivid moths such as the garden tiger, with orange hindwings spotted with deep metallic blue; species marked with metallic wings like the burnished brass; very large specimens such as the privet hawk moth; camouflage experts like the buff-tip resembling a broken birch twig, or the pale prominent which is easy to pass over as a chip of broken wood. There are green moths such as the common emerald and the green carpet. Even the large brownish or greyish majority are usually intricately patterned and repay close observation.

Live trapping is quite simple and your local Trust will be able to supply details. Get to know moths – you won't regret it.

Mother Shipton

HOMES FOR BUMBLEBEES

You said...

Has anyone had success with artificial bumblebee nests? Which designs and situations worked?
Richard Burkmar, Horwich

The BUGS project (Sheffield University) found the occupancy rate of artificial bumblebee boxes to be very low. This is probably because the bees are very fussy about location, temperature etc. Why not concentrate on 'natural' nest sites – a drystone wall, pile of old flower pots or overgrown bank? Last year I had a bumblebee nest beneath my greenhouse and a friend had one in an abandoned guinea pig cage! I have even found a nest in a discarded polystyrene hamburger wrapper! So do not give up hope.
ST, Crewe

I have had bees nesting in the garden, but more by accident than design. I put in two submerged pots for bumblebees and they did not use them. However they did nest in the base of an old rubbish bin that I had put a drainage hole in the bottom of and filled with old prunings. They moved in after these had composted for a year. loulall, Glenrothes

I make mounds of earth from lawn sods, arranging them upside-down like an igloo. These habitat homes have proved popular with amphibians. Bees might be attracted to something similar. I have seen them nest in hollows under a concrete driveway so it might help to prop an old paving slab in the shade and seal the edges with soil, leaving access holes. sandj, Leyland

Queen bumblebees often build their nests underground in old mouse nests in places like hedge bottoms and compost heaps but some species prefer to nest on the surface in grass tussocks. Bumblebee nests reach peak strength in mid to late summer, after which they die out, with only young queens overwintering in sheltered places away from the nest. If a bumblebee nest develops in an inconvenient place in a garden, it should be left alone until bee activity has finished in August to October, after which there will be no harm done in disturbing the nest site.

Plants for bees

Favourite bee plants through the seasons include:
Spring: berberis, bluebell, bugle, flowering currant, lungwort, rhododendron, rosemary, dead-nettle, heather

Early summer: aquilegia, borage, campanula, clover, comfrey, geranium, foxglove, honeysuckle, stachys, thyme

Late summer: cornflower, delphinium, lavender, fuchsia, scabious, sea holly, teasel, thistle

Sue Tatman, Cheshire Wildlife Trust, advises:

Bumblebees need our help! The gentle buzz of bumblebees working their way along a flowery border is a sound which typifies the British summer. But this sound is becoming rarer, as even the most common species have become increasingly scarce in recent decades; and two species have disappeared altogether. This is due to loss of suitable habitat in the countryside. However, a number of species can live in our gardens, so we can easily contribute to their survival, by growing plenty of suitable flowers and providing nest sites.

Bumblebees have bodies that are covered in fur. This helps them retain heat, so they are active at lower temperatures than other insects. Bumblebees appear in our gardens and start pollinating flowers, much earlier in the year than most other bees.

Bumblebees collect pollen to take back to the nest as food for the developing larvae. To do this they have special structures on the hind legs called pollen baskets. These are concave areas surrounded by stiff bristles. As the bee forages it uses its other legs to pack pollen into the pollen baskets; when full they can easily be seen as yellow or orangey blobs on the hind legs.

Worker bumblebees will forage from dawn to dusk. On each trip a bumblebee will visit several hundred flowers and can fly several

hundred metres from the nest site. As they fly such long distances they can visit many different gardens. So even if your garden has only a few bee plants, it can still attract bees.

Bumblebees need a supply of nectar and pollen to feed themselves and the growing larvae, from early spring to the first frosts of autumn. Bees have long tongues, so are able to reach nectar in tubular flowers such as clover, which are inaccessible to butterflies. Different species of bumblebee have different length tongues, so they prefer different flower species. Aim to plant a variety of flowers, to cater for as many bumblebee species as possible.

A bumblebee colony lasts only for a single summer – the queen is the only bumblebee to hibernate through the winter. In spring the queen looks for a suitable site to build her nest and start a new colony. A favoured site is an old mouse or vole hole (they are attracted to the scent of mouse urine!), but they can also find places in tussocks of grass or under dry debris. Sadly, scientific research has shown that artificial nest sites are rarely used, but natural nest sites in the garden are ideal. An area of permanent long grass along a hedge bottom, an overgrown stone wall or even an abandoned log pile are all likely to provide suitable sites.

SOLITARY BEES

You said...

I have a mason bee nesting kit in my garden which was very successful last year.
Maggi Pryce, Warminster

I have had mason bee nest kits in my garden since 2001, now with 330 tubes. Last year about 100 of these were completely filled compared with 25 in 2001. One of the boxes containing 100 tubes was supplied free by the Oxford Bee Company when they were looking for volunteers to help with their research projects. Each year I return 75% of their tubes which have been filled and they analyse the larvae for sex/ parasites etc and supply a recording update each spring and also replace your tubes free of charge. I don't know whether they still want new helpers.
Jeff Davis, Leatherhead

One year some similar bees started boring into my limestone walls, but seemed to do little damage. However, a woodpecker started having a go at the walls to feed on them. I am afraid I had to resort to humming tape to see him off. He bears no grudge however and visits the bird feeders.
Bogweevil, Shaftesbury

Bamboo sections, bound together horizontally, or stored in an old piece of piping, can make excellent nesting sites for mason bees in your garden.

Which bee?

About 20 species of solitary bees have been found nesting in soft mortar in Britain, of which six are the most frequently seen. Here's a quick guide:

● **Wool-carder bee (*Anthidium manicatum*):** Length 9-12mm. Flies from late May to early September. Locally common in England and Wales, rare in southern Scotland.

● **Hairy-footed flower-bee (*Anthophora plumipes*):** Length 14-17mm. Flies from mid March to the end of May. Found only in England and Wales (especially in the south).

● *Colletes daviesanus*: Length 8-10mm. Flies from mid June to mid September. Occurs commonly in England and Wales; local in Scotland and Ireland.

● *Lasioglossum smeathmanellum*: Length 6-7mm. Flies from March to early September. Common in southern Britain, rarer in the north. Absent Scotland and Ireland.

● *Megachile centuncularis*: Length 9-12mm. Flies from May to the end of August. Found throughout England and Wales; uncommon in Scotland and Ireland.

● **Red mason bee (*Osmia rufa*):** Length 7-14mm. Flies from April to June. Very common bee in southern England; occasional in southern Scotland.

Mason bees are excellent pollinators of many kinds of flowers, fruit trees and herbs.

Robin Williams, Somerset Invertebrates Group, advises:

Solitary bees are among the most important pollinators for wild and garden plants, so it is vital that their numbers are encouraged. Fortunately, this is easy with one important group – the mason and leaf-cutter bees. They both look for holes in which to nest and it is easy to supply their perfect needs. To understand how, it is best to explain how their nests are constructed and used.

Both types are solitary bees; they make a nest, provision it with nectar and pollen, lay an egg and then close the cell up. After that they go off and die, leaving the emerging larvae to fend for themselves. The cells are made of mud in the case of mason bees, or leaves for the leaf-cutter bees. The bees look for a deep hole and make a series of cells. By some special mechanisms, the bees emerge in sequence, the males first, followed by females.

The perfect nest site may be provided by hanging bunches of bamboo sections horizontally on the hottest wall of the house and just leave them to be occupied. Cut the bamboo cane with the node in the centre, leaving a tube just under 30cm long, with an end open at each end. This will hold around eight cells and provide endless interest to anyone caring to watch.

The first mason bees (*Osmia rufa*), will appear in late April and the females will buzz in and out looking for their ideal nesting space, then bring materials and you will be able to watch them constructing the cells with great skill. Leave the canes in place over winter and the new generation will emerge the next spring. Logs drilled with varying sized holes (2-8mm) will also attract these insects, as well as many other species.

Our 'bee flats' have been visited by over 40 species in 10 years or so.

ME, MY GARDEN AND WILDLIFE

RICHARD BURKMAR

I think the world of my garden. It lies somewhere between my home and the wider countryside; not just physically, but also in the emotional response it evokes from me when I spend time there. Like my home, it's a haven – a place where I can unwind and shut out intrusions from the outside world. But like the countryside, many animals and plants also lay claim to it, exciting and delighting me with their frequent and often unexpected appearances. It's the unpredictability of gardening for wildlife that I relish most of all: you never know what's around the next corner.

I change the world with my garden. I aim to make it as attractive to visiting animals as possible. A useful rule of thumb has been 'take care of the invertebrates and the rest will take care of itself'. I like to use plants that attract insects, spiders and other mini-beasts. The traditional cottage garden plants with plenty of accessible pollen and nectar serve me well, but just as importantly, I use lots of structural plants – climbers, shrubs and trees. By attracting invertebrates, larger animals like birds and mammals have inevitably followed: it's a simple ecological maxim for wildlife gardeners.

I find the world in my garden. As the years of looking at garden wildlife go by, I find that I am more and more attracted to the invertebrates for their own sake. I learned to look at things differently and really appreciate the environment on their scale. Perhaps I should say relearned because I think it's a skill we

Richard Burkmar is the editor of Space for Nature, an online wildlife gardening forum that can be found at www.wildlife-gardening.org.uk. Many of the comments in the 'You Said...' sections of this book were provided by Richard.

all have as children but lose as we get older. Now my eyes are tuned in to their world and everywhere in my garden I see amazing biodiversity – a constant source of beauty, delight, wonder and creative inspiration.

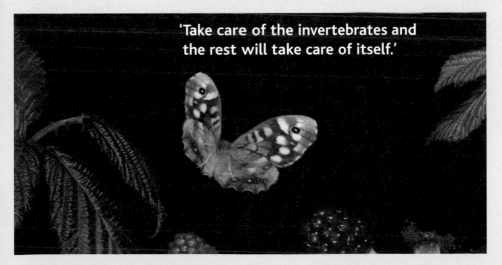

'Take care of the invertebrates and the rest will take care of itself.'

FOCUS ON... GOING NATIVE

Wildflower gardens can consist entirely of native plants, writes Helen Bostock of the RHS, replicating a natural plant community. Alternatively, a wildflower garden can be designed to create a certain effect, without being too purist about whether the plants are native or not, and there are many steps in between.

The establishment of native wildflowers in gardens requires some thought about the mode of introduction and the management regime throughout the year, to be successful.

When planning a wildflower area, assess the site, taking into account climate, soil type, drainage and the degree of shade and shelter.

The growing conditions largely determine the plants that will thrive and look natural in the setting. It is better to adapt the selection of plants to the site rather than the other way round.

Observing the local wild flora will indicate which species to grow.

Seeding new sites

Drifts of wildflowers can be created in the garden but many gardeners want a traditional flowering meadow of grasses intermixed with wildflowers.

If this is the aim it is important to avoid vigorous grasses such as rye grass and cocksfoot. Proprietary seed mixtures are available related to the type of soil and situation. A mix containing around 85% grasses and 15% wildflower seeds is suitable.

Prepare the seedbed as for a new lawn, removing stones and breaking up large clods of soil. Allow four to six weeks for the soil to settle and for weed seeds to germinate.

Spray or hoe these off before sowing.

It is important not to fertilise the soil in any way. Many wildflowers colonise poor land and it will upset the balance and encourage excessive vigour in the grasses if extra nutrients are added.

On very fertile soils it may be an advantage to remove the topsoil but, for anything other than the smallest area, this requires machinery. Subsoil sites will retain an open sward for several years with bare patches of ground ideal for natural colonisation. An alternative approach, on soils other than clays and those with high organic matter, may be to put the land down to mustard for a season to reduce fertility, removing the crop at flowering time.

Once the ground is prepared seed can be broadcast and raked in, following standard lawn-seeding practices. Sowing thinly at a rate of $5g/m^2$ for grass seed mixes and $1g$ for pure wildflower seed will suit most sites and allow the establishment of the slower-growing species.

To achieve even sowing, mix the seed with a carrier, such as dry silver sand or barley meal (available from pet shops), and sow at half the rate in two directions.

Water thoroughly after sowing and if conditions remain dry.

The best time to sow wildflower seed is in September. Some seeds will germinate almost immediately, but some may require low winter temperatures to break dormancy and initiate germination the following spring.

On heavy soils, which become waterlogged in winter, sowing in spring is advisable, as some seeds may rot in wet soil. If sown in spring, germination of some species may not occur until the second year.

Simon Milne,
Scottish Wildlife Trust, advises:

Giant rhubarb

Our private gardens, the great collections and municipal plantings are packed full of exotic delights from all over the world. But beware! An increasing number of imported invasive species are on the rampage and present one of the greatest threats to our native plant life by damaging our precious habitats and countryside. Every gardener should be alert to this problem and play a role in helping to halt the offensive march of non-native plants. To be a responsible gardener, follow the advice of the experts. For further information, please turn to pages 92-3.

We recommend you do not use the plants listed below (source: PLANTLIFE), although the RHS considers there are circumstances when you can use those not marked * (see pages 92-3).

LAND PLANTS	WATER PLANTS
Cotoneaster microphyllus and C. simonsii	Australian swamp stonecrop (Crassula helmsii) *
False acacia (Robinia pseudoacacia)	Canadian pondweed (Elodea canadensis)
Few-flowered leek (Allium paradoxum)	Nuttall's pondweed (Elodea nuttallii)
Giant hogweed (Heracleum mantegazzianum) *	Curly water weed (Lagarosiphon major)
Giant rhubarb (Gunnera tinctoria)	Fanwort (Cabomba caroliniana)
Hottentot fig (Carpobrotus edulis)	Floating pennywort (Hydrocotyle ranunculoides) *
Indian (Himalayan) balsam (Impatiens glandulifera) *	Giant salvinia (Salvinia molesta)
Japanese knotweed (Fallopia japonica) *	Parrot's feather (Myriophyllum aquaticum) *
Rhododendron ponticum	Water fern or Fairy fern (Azolla filiculoides) *
Shallon (Gaultheria shallon)	Water hyacinth (Eichhornia crassipes)
Spanish bluebell (Hyacinthoides hispanica) and its hybrid	Water lettuce (Pistia stratiotes)
H. hispanica x non-scripta	

If you already have one or more of the above in your garden or if you believe a plant is spreading out of control, remove it (safely) and create a new planting opportunity for wildlife-friendly plants. Burn Japanese knotweed. If in any doubt, seek advice on the safest and most effective techniques (see right).

● Only buy plants that are suitably labelled (in Latin).
● If you see an invasive non-native plant for sale, alert the management to the dangers.
● Reduce the risk and plant suitable native plants (that, ideally, have been locally sourced) or those which you are sure are non-invasive. Native plants tend to be best for native wildlife.
● Adhere to legislation and follow the horticultural code of practice on invasive and non-native plants.

● For further information and advice, contact Defra Helpline 08459 335577 or visit www.defra.gov.uk. A fact sheet on invasive species can found at www.plantlife.org
● For the Scottish horticultural code of practice, visit www.scotland.gov.uk
● For a list of suppliers who stock seeds of local provenance, visit www.floralocale.org
● For information from the RHS, visit www.rhs.org.uk and search for 'invasive'.

WILDFLOWER MEADOWS

You said...

I'd like to plant a wildflower meadow in my garden but the area concerned is around fruit trees and under large oaks/chestnuts. Would I be able to grow anything in this sort of area? The patch is not in shadow by the trees but the soil is clay. Any help appreciated.
catandsplat, Heathfield

Under the dense shade of oaks and chestnuts, I suggest you just go for spring bulbs and wildflowers. Nothing much will thrive once the leaf canopy closes up. Fruit trees are much easier – you may be able to incorporate them into a larger meadow or just allow the grass to grow long around the base of trees and plug plant with suitable wildflowers. I have stripped off the turf and sown a wildflower/grass mix from scratch in my own garden but never thought it was a great success (also on clay). I concentrate on good 'cottage-style' planting and incorporate wildflowers that are not too rampant into this. Those that take over, I use in specific areas that you can leave to take care of themselves except for spot-weeding and tidy-ups. My 'woodland' edge at the bottom of my garden has a hedgerow underplanted with white dead-nettle; yellow archangel; wood avens; red campion and under other hazel and guelder rose shrubs we leave wild garlic and red campion to fight it out. In a grassier area we use wild daffodils and leave the grass uncut here until about mid-August for the froglets from the pond to disperse into.
Jeff Davis, Leatherhead

Suppliers of wildflower seeds and plants

- **British Seed Houses Ltd**
Bewsey Industrial Estate, Pitt Street, Warrington WA5 5LE; Tel: (01925) 654411.
- **John Chambers**
15 Westleigh Road, Barton Seagrave, Kettering, Northamptonshire NN15 5AJ; Tel: (01933) 652562 (also bulbs).
- **Chiltern Seeds**
Bortree Stile, Ulverston, Cumbria LA12 7PB; Tel: (0129) 581173; www.chilternseeds.co.uk.
- **Emorsgate Seeds**
Limes Farm, Tilney All Saints, King's Lynn, Norfolk PE34 4RT; Tel: (01553) 829028.

- **Landlife Wildflowers Ltd**
National Wildflower Centre, Court Hey Park, Liverpool L16 3NA; Tel: (0151) 737 1819; www.wildflower.org.uk.
- **MAS**
4 Pinhills, Wenhill heights, Calne, Wiltshire SN11 0SA; Tel: (01249) 819013; www.meadowmania.co.uk.
- **Naturescape**
Wild Flower Farm, Coach Gap Lane, Langar, Nottinghamshire NG13 9HP; Tel: (01949) 851045/860592; www.naturescape.co.uk (also bulbs).

Although the deliberate use of native plants in gardens is not new, wildflower gardening has recently become more popular, and is excellent for our native species of wildlife, too.

● **Natural Surroundings**
Bayfield Estate, Holt,
Norfolk NR25 7JN;
Tel: (01263) 711091;
www.hartlana.co.uk/natural
(also bulbs).

● **Really Wild Flowers/
HV Horticulture Ltd**
Spring Mead, Bedchester, Shaftsbury,
Dorset SP7 0JU; Tel: (01747) 811778;
www.reallywildflowers.co.uk
(including bulbs).

● **Suffolk Herbs**
Monks Farm, Coggeshall Road,
Kelvedon, Essex CO5 9PG;
Tel: (01376) 572456;
www.suffolkherbs.com.

● **Mike Thorne Wild Seeds**
Branas, Llandderfel, Nr. Bala,
Gwynedd LL23 7RF
(also bulbs).

● **YSJ Seeds**
Kingsfield Conservation
Nursery, Broadenham Lane,
Winsham, Chard,
Somerset TA20 TJF;
Tel: (01460) 30070

● **Yellow Flag
Wildflowers**
8 Plock Court, Longford,
Gloucester GL2 9DW;
Tel: (01452) 311525;
www.wildflowersuk.com
(also bulbs).

The following are
suppliers of plants only
● **British Wild Flower Plants**
31 Main Road, North Burlingham,
Norwich, Norfolk NR13 4TA; Tel:
(01603) 716615;
www.Wildflowers.co.uk.

● **Conway Valley Plantations**
'Fron Francis', Llanrwst, Gwynedd
LL26 0TY; Tel: (01492) 640259
(bluebells).

● **Hardy Orchids** New Gate Farm,
Scotchey Lane, Stour Provost,
Gillingham, Dorset SP8 5LT.

● **John Shipton**
Y Felin, Hellan Armgoed, Whitland,
Dyfed SA34 0DL; Tel: (01994) 240125;
www.bluebellbulbs.co.uk (British
native bulbs including bluebells).

Tony Dickerson, RHS, advises:

● **Seeds:** Wildflower seedsmen supply mixtures of wildflowers and grasses suitable for various soil types and situations. Choose according to local conditions. Woodland plants such as bluebells, primroses and violets thrive under the shade of deciduous trees. ou should be aware that special regulations apply to collecting seeds and bulbs of bluebells. The RHS discourages the removal of plants from the countryside and repeated seed collecting would, over time, be likely to have a destructive effect on many species. Where possible, obtain seed of British origin, raised by wildflower seedsmen on their own land.

● **Sowing time:** Sow during September, ideally early September. Some seeds may germinate quickly, others not until the following spring. Sow in spring on heavy soils which become waterlogged in winter.

● **Ground preparation:** Dig or rotavate, then firm and rake to make a seedbed as for a new lawn. Don't incorporate manure or fertiliser. Many wildflowers colonise poor land; feeding would encourage excessive vigour, particularly in grasses. Broadcast the seeds, half lengthways, half widthways. Rake in lightly, water thoroughly then leave to natural conditions.

● **Converting a lawn:** Stop feeding and weedkilling. Continue mowing weekly to weaken the grass. Some wild species will establish and thrive. Raise others from seed, introducing as sturdy one- to two-year-old pot-grown plants.

● **Maintenance:** Once established, a wildflower meadow requires annual maintenance to allow the more desirable species to flourish and to reduce the vigour of some of the more rampant species. Using long-flowering, clump-forming perennials, grasses and annuals is a practical way to create a meadow-like effect in small gardens.

● **Watering and feeding:** A wildflower area doesn't require any additional watering or feeding. This regime could alter the natural balance of plants in the area. Many native flowers colonise poor land and the addition of extra nutrients and water will encourage excessive vigour in grasses, which will out-compete the more desirable native plants.

● **Mowing:** This is one way gardeners can manipulate the range of wildflowers growing in a chosen area. For a mixed meadow with plants flowering at various times, cut the area down to 5-7.5cm in autumn, after the majority have flowered and seeded. The mowings should be allowed to dry on the ground for a few days, thus allowing any seeds to drop to the ground. To encourage spring-flowering species, mow from July onwards, leaving the area unmown from March to early July. Alternatively encourage late summer wildflowers by mowing from mid to late September and again in spring (picking up the spring mowings before they have time to drop their seed).

Plants & Garden Art

We now offer a special range of individually created stationery & other useful gifts (with horticultura & other themes) to compliment ou mail order herbaceous perennials, which you may already be familiar with.

These 2 designs are in our pack of 6 different notelets/greeting cards supplied with envelopes in a decorative wallet
for £4.99 *including P&P* GB mainland

Gifts for keen gardeners

Larger planting schemes grown to order

Bespoke stationery also commisioned

ANTONY WORRALL THOMPSON

A garden without wildlife is a bit like a dish without seasoning – I see it as absolutely integral in making all the elements work. I grow fruit, herbs, vegetables and salads for their wonderful flavour – and the wildlife in my garden loves it. Bees, hoverflies and butterflies dart between the flowers – five minutes of watching them busily collecting food helps me unwind from my own hectic day! What creatures do you love watching in your garden?

Antony Worrall Thompson is a chef and broadcaster.

Raymond Blanc is chef patron of Le Manoir aux Quat' Saisons.

This year is Le Manoir aux Quat' Saisons' twenty-first birthday; as a treat I will present myself and all of my guests with a creation of a field of wildflowers. As a child, (40 years ago), these most enchanting and colourful fields were natural companions; unfortunately, with today's pollution and intensive agriculture, the fields are still there, but minus their colourful companions, so this year in our orchard, cornflowers, cowslips, buttercups, forget-me-nots, poppies, the ragged robin and many others will be abundant and, of course, be the delight of our guests, and also the butterflies, bees and seed-eating birds.

RAYMOND BLANC

YELLOW RATTLE

Yellow rattle is often included in grassland wildflower seed mixes, in part because it helps in the establishment of other species, although swathes of yellow rattle create an attractive spectacle in their own right.

You said...

Does anyone know anything about yellow rattle? I've planted some and just wondered when it might start to flower? Noel, Okehampton

I understand yellow rattle is semi-parasitic on grass roots, and therefore needs grass around it. An annual and autumn sowing in pre-cut grass is recommended. DEREK, St Andrews

I was successful with sowing yellow rattle last September. I vigorously scarified some patches in my 'meadow' (old lawn, really) and sowed the seed in the bare soil sections. You're supposed to keep the grass short until March in order not to compete with the new seedlings (I didn't worry too much as I've cowslips in that part). The seedlings appeared in March and look very similar to verbena seedlings. My plants are just starting to come into flower. For small quantities of seed try John Chambers Wild Flower Seed, Tel: 01933 652562. HB, Abingdon

Graham Peake, Staffordshire Wildlife Trust, advises:

Yellow rattle (*Rhinanthus minor*) is a native plant of grassy meadows and pastures, which is semi-parasitic on various grass species. In late summer its dry seed pods rattle loudly, and this used to be taken as a sign that it was time to harvest the hay. The *Flora Britannica* also records other locally used names for yellow rattle including hay-rattle, rattlebaskets, pots and pans and tiddibottles.

Yellow rattle is a widespread and relatively common annual growing to around 45cm in height. Plants have black-spotted stems, toothed oblong leaves and yellow flowers which can appear any time between May and September. The flowers are characteristic of the foxglove family of which yellow rattle is a member.

The semi-parasitic habit of yellow rattle makes it a great plant for recreating flower-rich meadows. Its roots fix to those of grasses, sapping their energy and helping to reduce the competition with other meadow flowers.

Yellow rattle seed can be used to over-sow existing grassland although the technique only works well on land where there is low fertility. The successful introduction of yellow rattle will control grass growth, reducing the need for mowing and improving the viability of other wildflowers.

To sow seed directly cut the grass short (3cm), scarify the surface and sow with yellow rattle seed by hand on to short grass before January so that it overwinters and vernalises naturally in moist conditions. It does not need to be worked into the soil surface. As a rough guide $1/2$-1g/m^2 will be required. It is important to ensure that the grass is fairly short (maximum 2-5cm) by the beginning of March so that the seedlings can more easily push up through the sward in early spring.

The grass should then not be cut from early March through at least until the end of July to allow the yellow rattle seed to ripen. (Grass that is heavily summer-grazed by rabbits will not be appropriate.) It is important that the grass is then cut quite short and the cuttings removed. This will also help spread the yellow rattle seed around.

PLANTS TO AVOID

You said...

I have Japanese knotweed. Is it right to get rid of it, and how should I do it?
naj, Caernarfon

Knotweed is notoriously difficult to get rid of, as its roots reach down to remarkable depths. Once you have got it all out (if you can – it's notoriously difficult to remove completely) you can only dispose of it at a licensed landfill site. Ask your council where you can find one. Never just throw it away, as it can regrow from the smallest stem sections.
Suzig, Norwich

You've got to be really careful with this stuff. If you allow Japanese knotweed to spread, it's actually an offence. Once you have dug it out, you need to let it dry out completely before you dispose of it.
Gardengnome, Newbury

Japanese knotweed is one of several introduced plants that have put pressure on our native habitats.

Removing knotweed

● Japanese knotweed (*Fallopia japonica* syn. *Polygonum cuspidatum*) is a strong-growing, clump-forming perennial, the stout annual stems growing to upwards of 2m in one season. Stem growth is renewed each year from the stout, creeping, deeply penetrating rhizomatous rootstock.

● Chemicals, such as glyphosate, will help destroy the plant, but as they are not selective, they will damage other plants that they touch. It is possible to dig the plant out, but this can take a long time to achieve, and is generally discouraged, due to the depth to which the rhizomatous root can penetrate, and because it is classed as 'controlled waste' under the Environmental Protection Act 1990. This requires disposal at licensed landfill sites. On no account should it be disposed with normal household waste or dumped in the countryside.

● To dig the plant out, remove as much root as possible, then repeatedly destroy regrowth. In this way the energy reserves in the remaining underground parts will be gradually exhausted – a process which will, however, take several seasons. Dug roots and stems can be burned.

Tony Dickerson, RHS, advises:

Our gardens have been greatly enhanced by the introduction of plants from abroad but a small number have proved invasive in the wider environment, threatening natural habitats and native species (see page 83). Several of these are so invasive that gardeners would not wish to grow them. These include giant hogweed (*Heracleum mantegazzianum*) and Japanese knotweed (*Fallopia japonica*).

Invasive non-native tree species such as evergreen oak (*Quercus ilex*) and false acacia (*Robinia pseudoacacia*) are very large trees and unsuitable for gardens. With climate change these species are establishing in the countryside as native oak and beech come under increased environmental stress. Evergreen oak is, however, a useful evergreen hedging plant and, kept trimmed, does not set seed.

Rhododendron ponticum has established in the countryside in areas of acid soils and in moister upland areas where it shades out native flora. Today, with many more ornamental species and cultivars available to gardeners, there is little reason to grow it.

Low-growing cotoneasters (*Cotoneaster microphyllus* agg, *C. horizontalis*) and

Gaultheria shallon are tough, reliable groundcover shrubs – ideal for difficult situations and poorer soils. However, the seeds are spread by birds. If you live in the countryside near downland or hill country try to avoid them.

Some introduced annuals and perennials also cause problems in the countryside. Himalayan balsam (*Impatiens glandulifera*) readily self-seeds into the wild and grows so rapidly that it shades out native vegetation, especially alongside rivers and lakes in both towns and countryside. It is a serious threat to our rare wetland species and should always be avoided by gardeners. In our milder coastal areas Hottentot fig (*Carpobrotus edulis*) has clothed cliffs pushing out native plants. Gardeners in these areas should not grow this plant.

While Spanish bluebells (*Hyacinthoides hispanica*) and their hybrids (*H. hispanica* x *H. non-scripta*) are tough bulbs ideally suited to the poorest soils in towns and cities; they hybridise readily with native bluebells and should not be grown by gardeners in areas where our native species is found. Most gardeners would also wish to avoid the weedy few-flowered leek (*Allium paradoxum*) that so freely self-seeds in gardens that it becomes a nuisance.

COMPOST

Composting provides a means of converting waste materials from both the kitchen and garden into a free, environmentally friendly source of organic matter which can be used throughout the garden to improve soil fertility, conserve soil moisture and enhance plant growth. It also helps the community as a whole by diverting organic refuse away from the dustbin and ultimately reducing landfill.

You said...

My compost bin provides a habitat for many creatures and insects. I have even had some mice raising a family. My compost includes kitchen waste, garden waste, eggshells, egg cartons, torn-up newspaper, grass cuttings and even some seaweed. I never ever put cooked food in so I am not sure what attracted the mice, apart from the heat and the vegetable waste.
Composter, Stoborough

Here's an idea that I wanted to share: knock buddleia trimmings into the ground in two loose lines and put your other plant prunings between them (eg like a cheap compost heap).
loulall, Glenrothes

Royal Horticultural Society

Paul Alexander, RHS, advises:

In garden composting, the very best compost is made by accumulating a large quantity of raw, undecomposed organic material, building a heap, and maintaining a supply of air by turning the material periodically to encourage aerobic conditions as far as possible. However, in most households, composting materials tend to be added in small amounts and easily become compacted. Turning is also often neglected because of the labour involved. The result is that most garden compost is produced by a combination of both aerobic and anaerobic decomposition with perhaps some temperature increase occurring at the centre of the heap. This type of composting is quite acceptable, and should be persevered with, even though the compost is unlikely to be 100% free from weeds and seeds.

The most important aspect of any compost heap is the raw waste material initially accumulated for composting. The best composts contain a mixture of both woody, carbon-rich waste such as prunings, wood chippings, straw or dead leaves and softer, more nitrogen-rich materials such as grass clippings, annual weeds, vegetable kitchen waste, or horse manure. In an ideal world, the amount of soft green nitrogen-rich materials added to a heap would occupy between 25-50% of the volume, the remainder being made up of tougher, drier woody materials. In practice few gardeners have access to a wide range of materials throughout the year and have to simply add whatever waste they have at a particular time. This is acceptable providing you observe the following rules:

1. Avoid letting one material dominate a heap – try to restrict the addition of single ingredients to layers less than 10cm deep. This is usually only a problem in the summer when grass mowings predominate, or when a large hedge is trimmed.

2. If woody material or leaves are added, chop them up or shred them beforehand. It is unlikely that twigs thicker than a pencil will rot down in one season, but these can still be added, as they will help to maintain an open structure within the heap. When the compost is used these can be sieved out and re-composted.

3. Materials that have been wrongly labelled as unsuitable for composting include rhubarb, laurel leaves (*Prunus laurocerasus*), potato peelings, citrus, tea bags and egg shells. These can all be composted safely, provided they are chopped up, well mixed in and the compost given adequate time to mature.

4. Avoid diseased plants, perennial weeds and seed heads containing mature seeds. It is much easier to sort out what goes into the heap than to try and clean up the end product.

5. Avoid composting grass mowings recently treated with herbicide. Although the composting process is very effective at breaking down most organic chemicals, some residues can persist, especially if the composting process is inefficient. Check on the herbicide label for directions.

Garden compost can take between six months and two years to reach maturity. This variation is due to a number of factors, for instance, a heap will require longer if conditions are cold and dry and less if the heap is kept moist and warm. Similarly if the heap contains a mixture of materials it will mature more rapidly than if only one or two raw materials are used. Mature compost will be dark brown, with a crumbly soil-like texture and a smell resembling damp woodland. It is unlikely that all the material in the heap will be like this; usually the top will be dry and undecomposed while the base will be wet and have a bad odour. Separate these portions so they can be re-composted and use the remainder.

On the whole, composts look after themselves. The main thing to watch is that the composting organic matter has a supply of air, and that the material gets neither too wet nor too dry. Air is circulated by 'turning' the heap periodically. It involves emptying the heap out, and thoroughly mixing it so the material, which was previously on the outside, is moved to the centre. If a heap contains a large quantity of waste all added at the same time, try to turn as often as possible. At least once will help! If the heap has been built up in layers it should be turned once when the heap is finally full and then once again after two to three weeks.

Starting to compost

Some people compost their garden and kitchen waste in an open heap. This is satisfactory if a reasonable quantity of waste is available and tidiness is less important. However, with small quantities of waste, some form of container or bin is beneficial. It not only keeps the heat insulated, but it also prevents the wind blowing rubbish around. There is a wide range of containers available in which to compost organic waste. The important characteristics to look for are:

1. SIZE: The container has to fit into the space available, but, generally speaking, the larger the better. The best garden compost is made from large initial volumes of waste and a good minimum size to aim for is 1m³.

2. MATERIALS: Manufactured compost bins tend to be either made of plastic or wood whilst construction of home-made containers will depend upon whatever materials are available. A brick-built heap will be expensive but lasts considerably longer than one made from wood. Wood is relatively cheap, easy to use and insulates well, but over time it will rot. Wire-mesh containers are cheap and easy to make but provide little insulation against heat and moisture loss. Choice depends on cost, and how long the compost heap is required for.

3. DESIGN: The best designs are sturdy, being able to withstand strong winds and should include both a lid to keep the rain out and easy access for turning and emptying. They should not have a sealed base, because this will restrict drainage and prevent access of soil organisms. Air spaces may be present in the walls but this is not critical, because the main method of keeping the heap aerated is by using the right mix of materials and turning the contents. If air spaces are present, care should be taken to avoid excessive drying of the outer layers of compost during hot weather.

Hedgehogs are one of many species that will enjoy the shelter and safety of your compost heap.

4. PREPARATION: On a soil base, the site should be dug over to encourage maximum drainage beneath the heap. During composting moisture is released, and if it cannot drain away, anaerobic conditions quickly develop. Some people put bricks or branches at the bottom of the heap to lift the lower material up and allow air in. Organic matter can then be added to the heap, either premixed or in thin layers of woody carbon-rich materials and soft nitrogen-rich waste.

Ideally the heap should contain between 25% and 50% soft green nitrogen-rich materials to balance the tougher, woody waste added. As the heap is built up, water should be added to moisten (not soak) the mixture. It doesn't matter if insufficient waste is available to fill a whole container, but it is better to add as much waste as possible at any one time to encourage the heap to heat up. Waste can be accumulated next to the heap in a tightly folded plastic sack if materials only become available intermittently.

Where to site your compost heap

The selection of a composting site will be strongly influenced by the layout of a garden and choice may be limited, but it is worth taking the following points into consideration:

● A direct pathway from the house simplifies the despatch of kitchen waste.

● Sufficient space around a heap allows stockpiling of excess materials.

● An earth, rather than concrete base under a heap is recommended to allow drainage and access to soil organisms.

● In colder districts a sunny site encourages composting during cold weather, but in hotter, drier areas the shade of a tree or wall will help prevent the heap drying out.

● A compost heap built on an area of ground to be planted the following year will enhance soil fertility due to the nutrients leached from the compost into the underlying soil.

PEAT

You said...

What is peat?

● Peat is formed from incompletely decomposed plant remains, mainly sedges, grasses, reeds and mosses.

● It forms when the natural processes of decay are arrested by waterlogging and the exclusion of oxygen, with the remains of succeeding wetland plants becoming compacted to form peat. It is a slow process with the layer of peat increasing by an average rate calculated to be no more than 1mm depth per year.

● Existing peatlands cover about four million km² of the land and freshwater surface of the planet and are found throughout the world. Currently though, peat formation is occurring mainly in the northern temperate zone.

● In the UK, peatlands cover 1.6 million ha, 95% of which is upland blanket bog and the remainder is lowland raised bog. Not all peat types are suitable for commercial extraction and it is the lowland raised bog, composed of deep sphagnum moss peat, that gives rise to most of the product destined for horticulture.

● Of the 70,000ha of lowland raised bog in the UK, estimates suggest that only 3,800-8,000ha remain in pristine or near-natural condition. Suitability for commercial extraction is determined by many factors, such as its proximity to market, ease of access to the peat itself and peat quality. It is these factors which make lowland raised bogs attractive to commercial extraction operations. It is also for these reasons that the global volume of peat suitable for commercial extraction is much lower than the figures presented as the remaining peat reserves; replenishment figures have to be looked at closely. Global replenishment rates are based upon the global peat reserves and not the reserves that are commercially extractable. Peat that is growing beyond commercial reach cannot be said to replenish a renewable resource. According to the Environment Agency, 'over human timescales, the loss of peat is irreversible due to the slow rate of natural regeneration'.

According to the Environment Agency, 'over human timescales, the loss of peat is irreversible due to the slow rate of natural regeneration', such as the Thorne Crowle And Goole Moors Site of Special Scientific Interest at Humberhead Peatlands National Nature Reserve (right)

Paul Alexander, RHS, explains:

Peatlands are important for four main reasons. Firstly, they form a unique natural habitat that supports important biodiversity and species at risk (plants, birds and insects). Secondly, peatlands are an important carbon sink, they contain one third of the world's soil carbon. This carbon pool exceeds that of the world's forests and equals that of the atmosphere. The removal of peat not only leads to the release of this carbon but also removes the carbon sink, exacerbating global warming and climate change. Thirdly, they contain vital geochemical and palaeological archives offering unique historical evidence on the area and its inhabitants. Finally, they play an important role in the global hydrological cycle helping maintain both water quantity and quality: they contain 10% of global freshwater resources. In the UK, peatlands are thought to play an important role in flood prevention.

The effects of extraction are irreparable as peatlands take thousands of years to form. Reclamation schemes at previously worked sites have succeeded in creating attractive wetland areas, but they have not recreated peatlands. Peat forms at a rate of only 1mm per year, while peat extractors remove up to 22cm a year. A 10m-deep peat reserve, which took around 10,000 years to form, will be cleared in less than 50 years. Bearing these timescales in mind, it is impossible to illustrate rehabilitated and restored peatlands. Even if peatlands could be restored, it is important to remember that preservation is cheaper than restoration.

As a result, peat alternatives are now being developed using materials such as bark, woodchip, coir, biosolids, bracken and green waste.

Many of these alternatives work well in certain circumstances.

NatureProducts
Catalogue

Ernest Charles has been associated with The Wildlife Trusts for five years. During this time, much has changed, both for the Trusts and for U.K. wildlife.

In this time, membership of the Trusts has grown from 335,000 to 580,000, which means more people have pledged to help wildlife in their local areas than ever before and the membership continues to grow.

Whether you buy birdseed, nesting boxes or greeting cards you will be helping to secure the work of the Wildlife Trusts for the future.

*Stephanie Hilbourne - **Chief Executive of The Royal Wildlife Trust***

SUPPORT YOUR LOCAL **WILDLIFE** TRUST

Remember to order your Ernest Charles catalogue today!

PAM LEWIS

Teasels are superb nectar- and seed-producing plants – a special favourite for bumblebees and goldcrests. They are statuesque plants that often self-seed in incongruous situations where their towering height can sometimes be an embarrassment. I recommend cutting the stems to the base in June whence a burst of several shorter stems will proliferate and provide even more thistle-shaped flower heads on multiples of shorter, more stable stems. Leave the handsome seed heads for winter and you are likely to be rewarded with visits from charming, multi-coloured goldfinches.

For my own pleasure, I harvest a bunch of stems from outlying parts of the garden in autumn and bring them close to the house to attract the birds so that I can watch them from indoors. Most birds flit swiftly from one food source to another, but goldfinches linger for several golden moments at a time.

In recent years, the damp, warm autumns have provided conditions where premature germination of seed occurs on the seed head; pretty to look at but useless for a hungry seed-seeking bird. To pre-empt this occurrence, I store a few stems in a cool,

dry place so I can present my goldfinches with a feast around Christmas-time when food sources may be scarce. I arrange the stems in pots or set them into shrubs where they can be held in firmly in place and look decorative – especially when dusted with a festive icing of frost or snow.

Another trick is to purchase some niger seed – a favourite with many seed-eating birds – and sprinkle a pinch or two into the bristly seed heads when their natural seed content is depleted. I imagine our local birds must believe Sticky Wicket

Pam Lewis is the author of *Making Wildflower Meadows and Sticky Wicket – Gardening in Tune with Nature*, which tells the tale of how she converted her 2ha property in Dorset into a wildlife garden haven.

garden to be a magic place where Nature's larder is constantly replenished!

'I store a few stems in a cool, dry place so I can present my goldfinches with a feast around Christmas-time when food sources may be scarce.'

FOCUS ON... MULCHES

Paul Alexander of the RHS provides a comprehensive list of the characteristics and performance of a wide range of organic mulches that you can use in your garden to encourage growth and keep the wildlife happy.

PROCESSED CONIFER BARK

This is a by-product of the timber industry which is composted for several weeks before marketing in order to disperse substances that are harmful to plant growth. It is an acidic material suitable for lime-haters. Pine bark is used mainly as a container and potting compost medium, whereas bark marketed for mulching and soil improvement is usually derived from a mixture of pine and/or spruce.

SAWDUST

Sawdust has been used for many years in the United States as a mulch for a wide range of plants, including rhododendrons and azaleas. Coarse sawmill material has sufficient porosity to allow the passage of air and water but finer carpenters' sawdust may pack down and 'cake' on drying and is better composted for at least 12 months before use. Mulches of fresh sawdust may deplete soil nitrogen due to the action of bacteria. Well-composted sawdust utilises little soil nitrogen, although the annual spring fertiliser dressing may need to be slightly increased. Experiment with sawdust for a time rather than use it immediately on a large scale.

WOOD CHIPPINGS

Wood chippings, from coppice growth or unwanted saplings, can be purchased for use as a garden mulch but if you have large quantities of prunings or hedge trimmings you may find it worthwhile to buy a garden shredder and produce your own. Some nitrogen can be lost from the soil if fresh wood chippings are used so compensate for this by applying a moderate dressing of a nitrogenous fertiliser in spring. Fresh material, particularly if coniferous, may contain toxins harmful to young plants so this is best composted for three to four months before use to avoid risk.

STRAW

Straw is often used with strawberries for weed suppression and to lift the fruit off the soil. It is sometimes used for mulching cut flower crops such as dahlia and gladiolus and is generally considered effective. However, it can look untidy and may deplete soil nitrogen levels when dug in after cropping.

LEAFMOULD

Leaf mulches tend to blow around unless netted so may prove more satisfactory if shredded or composted for one to two years prior to use. Oak and beech leaves make the best leaf mould and are usually suitable for mulching lime-hating plants. Most leaves should break down to provide a neutral to slightly acid material, but leaves from trees growing on chalk soil may have a more alkaline content and be unsuitable for use with lime-haters.

PINE NEEDLES

Pine needles are used quite widely in the United States as a mulch for rhododendrons, azaleas and camellias. Some growers maintain an 8-10cm layer by 'topping up' annually; others apply the mulch, allow it

to settle for several months, then level off to leave a 5cm mulch which may persist for three to four years before needing attention. Litter accumulated under old conifer trees or hedges can be similarly used as a 5cm mulch.

COCOA SHELLS

Cocoa shells are a by-product of cocoa production. The material is lightweight and becomes heavier and more compacted as it begins to decompose under moist conditions. It has a noticeable 'chocolate' odour once wetted and supports a grey mould which appears shortly after application. Both the odour and the mould (which is harmless) disappear in time leaving an effective, moisture retentive mulch.

Please be aware that dogs are attracted to cocoa shell mulch when it is fresh as it contains theobromine and is known to be potentially fatal to dogs. Cocoa mulch has been known to attract rodents.

FARM MANURES

Animal droppings mixed with bedding material (straw or wood shavings) provide some plant nutrients but may damage foliage by the release of ammonia if used fresh. Composting the manure for several months before use overcomes this potential problem. Horse and cow manure are most satisfactory but

avoid pig manure, which has an unpleasant and persistent smell when fresh.

SPENT MUSHROOM COMPOST

This material comes from the mushroom industry where it is used as the substrate on which mushrooms are grown. It is made from rotted horse manure and straw and has some nutrient value but usually contains a considerable amount of chalk. In consequence it is strongly alkaline and unsuitable for use around lime-hating plants.

Mushroom compost is useful on acid soils, where it will give some reduction in acidity, but its regular use on neutral or alkaline soils may raise soil pH to undesirably high levels of alkalinity.

POULTRY MANURE AND SPENT HOPS

There is usually a high ratio of droppings to litter in poultry manure, resulting in a nutrient content which is too high for mulching; it is also quite alkaline. Sometimes poultry manure is composted at a rate of 10% by volume with straw to provide a better mulching material.

Spent hops are now only occasionally available in the vicinity of small independent breweries. Grape pomace like spent hops is occasionally available in the vicinity of small vineyards.

STOP SLUGS THE NATURAL WAY
with Nemaslug from Green Gardener

Safe for children,pets, birds and wildlife.
Easy to use-just water onto soil.
Protects all plants. Now you can grow hostas, lettuce and
potatoes without holes!
We also supply ladybirds,lacewings,butterfly breeding
kits,wormeries and much more!

www.greengardener.co.uk
Phone for our free 70 page green guide HELPLINE 01603 715096 (7DAYS)
or drop a line to Green Gardener, Brookhill, Brundall Rd, Blofield, Norfolk NR13 4LB

Green manuring

Green manures are plants grown from seed whose foliage is useful for providing ground cover to smother weeds and to store soil nutrients, thus preventing leaching during non-crop periods. When the land is needed again, the green manure plant is dug back in so that it rots down releasing nutrients and adding organic matter to the soil.

The main period for growing green manure is in winter, although these plants can also be grown between crops during the main growing season. Although rarely possible, a vegetable garden would benefit even more from a whole year under green manure, allowing the soil to rest from intensive cropping while improving soil structure and fertility.

Green manures are characterised by their fast growth rate, absorbing water and nutrients and converting them to plant material. Leguminous plants have the additional capacity of fixing nitrogen in root nodules. Once the land is needed for cropping, the plants are dug into the top 20cm of soil, where they decompose, and their stored nutrients are gradually released.

Seed type	Type	Cropping	Sowing	Best soil type or conditions
Alfalfa (*Medicago sativa*)	L/P	1,3	April-July	Alkaline soils. Soils must be inoculated with nitrogen-fixing bacteria in order to fix nitrogen
Bean, winter field (*Vicia faba*)	L/A	1	September-November	Heavy soils
Buckwheat (*Fagopyrum esculentum*)	HHA	1	April-August	Light soils, acid soils
Clover, alsike (*Trifolium hybridum*)	L/P	1,3	April-August	Will tolerate wet soils
Clover, crimson (*Trifolium incarnatum*)	L/A	1	March-August	Light soils
Clover, Essex red (*Trifolium pratense*)	L/P	1,2,3	March-August	Loamy soils
Fenugreek (*Trigonella foenum-graecum*)	L/A	1	Spring/summer	Unlikely to fix nitrogen in the UK, any soil
Lupin, bitter blue (*Lupinus angustifolius*)	L/P	1	March-June	Light, sandy, acid soils
Mustard (*Sinapis alba*)	A	1	March-September	To discourage clubroot, do not follow on with brassicas
Phacelia (*Phacelia tanacetifolia*)	A	1	April-August.	Later sowings may overwinter in some areas
Rye, grazing (*Secale cereale*)	A	2	August-November	Good for soil structure
Trefoil (*Medicago lupulina*)	A/B/L	1,2,3	March-August	Tolerates some shade, useful for underplanting tall crops, eg sweetcorn. Light, dry alkaline soils
Tare, winter (*Vicia sativa*)	L/A	1 2	March-August July-September	Will tolerate heavy soils

KEY:

A = Annual; B = Biennial; HHA = Half hardy annual; L = Legume; P = Perennial; 1 = from sowing, leave for two to three months up to flowering; 2 = overwinters well; 3 = can be left in for one to two years to provide cover on uncropped land.

The green manures listed above are available from:

The Organic Gardening Catalogue, Riverdene Business, Park, Molesey Road, Hersham, Surrey KY12 4RG; Tel: 01932 253666; Email: chaseorg@aol.com; www.organiccatalog.com.

Tuckers Seeds, Brewery Meadow, Stonepark, Ashburton, Newton Abbott, Devon; Tel: 01364 652233; Email: seeds@edwintucker.com; www.edwintucker.com

SEAWEED

In addition to fresh seaweed there are a number of other seaweed products available via mail order. These include seaweed meal, calcified seaweed and a range of liquid fertilisers containing seaweed.

Seaweed collection

Please be aware of the potential illegality of removing seaweed from beaches. Much of the coast is designated as SSSI, SAC etc. and seaweed forms an important part of the marine ecosystem. In these areas removal of seaweed may therefore be controlled by statutory regulations, thus any request for large-scale removal would be unlikely to gain the necessary approval.

According to the Coast Protection Act (1949) it is illegal to remove seaweed if it is protecting the beach. Otherwise the general position is that there is no public right to collect seaweed (although such rights are possibly capable of being acquired by custom or prescription). We would not recommend removal of any seaweed that is still alive and attached to the beach or rocks. We suggest you contact the owner of the beach (and possibly the local council) where you intend collecting the seaweed and ask for their permission. Some councils actually pay contractors to remove washed-up seaweed so there may not be a problem.

Paul Alexander, RHS, advises:

Seaweed is a very useful material for soil improvement and has been used in coastal farming for many years as a substitute for farm manure. Where digging is carried out, it should be incorporated fresh before it has had time to dry, at 5-10kg/sq.m. It can be used when preparing land for crops, such as potatoes and brassicas and is reportedly acid in reaction.

Seaweed is similar to farmyard manure in nitrogen content, with considerably more potash, but is low in phosphate; it also has a useful magnesium content. As with farmyard manure, it only goes a short way towards supplying the nutrients required by crops and, in site preparation, general fertiliser such as Growmore should be added at 90-120g/sq.m as a pre-sowing or pre-planting dressing, forked well into the top layers of soil without disturbing the dug-in seaweed.

Seaweed contains sodium chloride (common salt) but this is not usually present in sufficient amounts to be harmful, and as it is water soluble, it would not build up following annual applications.

Seaweed can be composted but as it contains little fibre it is best mixed with other garden refuse. The resultant material can be dug in or used for mulching purposes when well decomposed. If fresh seaweed is spread over the surface of the soil it may, depending on type and species, pass through a rather glutinous stage before becoming desiccated, and is probably not a very effective material for mulching purposes. It can also smell unpleasant as it decomposes.

Suppliers of seaweed products include:
Garden Direct, Unit 4, Hillgrove Business Park, Nazing Road, Nazing, Essex EN9 2BB; Tel: 01992 890550.
The Organic Gardening Catalogue, Riverdene Business Park, Molesey Road, Hersham, Surrey KT12 4RG; Tel: 01932 253666; www.organiccatalog.com.
Suffolk Herbs, EW King & Co Ltd, Monks Farm, Coggeshall Road, Kelveden, Essex CO5 9PG; Tel: 01376 572456; www.suffolkherbs.com.

H**O**STAS

Bowden Hostas
for all your Hosta needs

A Mature Hosta garden to visit with a wide range of Hostas for sale

36 page fully illustrated catalogue available

Also available 'Slug Busters' our guide to a slug free garden

Close to 5 National Trust properties in Cornwall and Devon

Visit us any time between March 1st - September 30th Our Opening Times Are: **Mon – Sat from 10am – 4pm**

RHS Gold Medal Winners Chelsea 2005 for an exhibit of Hostas

Follow the tourist signs

Call us now on:
01837 840 989
sales@bowdenhostas.com
www.bowdenhostas.com

ASH FOR YOUR SOIL

Wood ash from your barbecue can be of great benefit to your soil, without having to add any chemicals.

You said...

We have just built a barbie in our garden in time to capitalise on the imminent long summer (don't laugh – we're optimists). Which ways are there of reusing the ash to benefit the garden afterwards?
Preston Peat, Preston

We have a woodchip burner here at work and I use the resultant ash to 'feed' our newly planted hedging plants and flowering/berrying shrubs. It contains useful amounts of potash which ought to be beneficial, but make sure that you do not use too much of the stuff in a confined area otherwise it may begin to affect the pH of your soil. Also, you should apply it dry since it's very water soluble. You could add small amounts to your compost but don't rely on this to get rid of all your ash.
sandj, Leyland

Royal Horticultural Society

Paul Alexander, RHS, advises:

Wood ash is sometimes recommended as a source of potash. It contains potassium in the form of potassium carbonate and also traces of other elements. The percentage of potash may vary from 4-15% depending on the source material. Ashes from young, sappy wood and small twigs may contain up to 15% potash, whereas heartwood, wood from thicker limbs and from sawdust may contain as little as 4%. Fronds of young bracken may contain up to 50% potash. The potassium in wood ash is in a very soluble form, easily washed out in the rain. If the ash is not for immediate use, collect it and store it under cover.

Sulphate of potash (potassium sulphate) contains 48% potash and is normally used at 34-68g/sq.m. Equivalent dressings of potassium from wood ash will need much greater quantities, depending on the origin of the material.

Wood ash is alkaline and tends to raise the pH level of soils. Do not use it among roses, fruit and vegetable crops, rhododendrons and other plants needing acid soil conditions. Use sulphate of potash instead, reserving wood ash, particularly if its origin is uncertain or mixed, as a general dressing to soils known to be deficient in potassium. All wood ash will provide some liming effect, but only the fresh material will also supply potassium.

Alternatively it can be added to the compost heap, in place of lime, and to provide some extra potassium. A suitable rate of application would be 800g/sq.m of compost heap surface area, repeated in layers 15-20cm apart.

Solid fuel ash (from anthracite etc) has little or no nutritional value to plants and because of its fine particle size, it is of little help in soil improvement. On clay soils fine particle ash may even be detrimental, increasing their glutinous nature when wet. Coarser types of ash, such as clinker, are sometimes useful for pathways or for surfacing in other non-cultivated parts of the garden.

HERBS

You said...

I've cleared an area in my garden to plant some herbs for a spot of home cooking, and I was wondering whether there are any types that are particularly good for wildlife.
Brian, Hull

Thyme is a real winner, because its flowers attract bees and butterflies, and it's a good all-round cooking herb into the bargain, too. You should find that rosemary is a pretty good addition to your patch, too.
Starman, Dumfries

Lots of flowering herbs are really good for nectaring insects, but you might want to think about planting some angelica in particular. The flowers seem to attract all sorts of hoverflies as well as bees in my garden, and the seed heads are excellent for visiting birds, such as finches, who are looking for a quick snack.
Fiveways, Stroud

Choice herbs

Herbs are the perfect all-purpose garden plants, says Philip Precey of the Derbyshire Wildlife Trust. Attractive foliage, wonderful scents, colourful flowers, and they're useful: roast lamb wouldn't be the same without rosemary and a good dollop of mint sauce. All that, and they can be fantastic for wildlife, too.

● **Marjoram** may be more well known as oregano, without which no pizza would be complete. On a warm summer's day, the flower heads can be particularly attractive to large numbers of butterflies, particularly gatekeeper and common blue.

● **Fennel flowers** are a fantastic nectar source for late summer insects, particularly favoured by garden hoverflies, the larvae of which are voracious predators of aphids.

● No wildlife garden should be without a big clump of **lavender**. During the summer months, lavender bushes are literally buzzing with a constant traffic of bumblebees.

● The flowers of **thyme and mint** provide a rich source of nectar for solitary bees, while both also support the handsome purple and gold micromoth (*Pyrausta aurata*).

● And last but by no means least, **borage**, a favourite nectar source for bees, but more importantly, a vital plant to have close at hand for those lazy summer afternoons: it goes so well in a hard-earned glass of Pimms.

No matter how small your garden, there's always room for herbs. Familiar herbs such as thyme and marjoram originate from dry, calcareous grasslands and will do well in pots on a patio or even in a hanging basket. Mint is so easy to grow that it would quite happily spread throughout the garden if they weren't picked and trimmed with some regularity!

The Northumberland Wildlife Trust advises:

Herbs have been cultivated in gardens for at least 2,000 years. Many of the familiar herbs grown today were introduced into the country at some point in time. Many garden escapes have now become naturalised and are treated as native. We all know of their use in cooking and health treatments, but they are also extremely decorative and some can be used in the garden to attract wildlife.

Quick guide to herbs and wildlife

HERB	TYPE	WILDLIFE VALUE
ANGELICA (*Angelica archangelica*)	Biennial	FLOWERS: hoverflies and bees; LEAVES: leaf-mining fly SEEDHEADS: greenfinches and blue tits
BORAGE (*Borago officinalis*)	Annual	FLOWERS: bees
CHIVES (*Allium schoenoprasum*)	Perennial	FLOWERS: bees and butterflies
COMFREY (*Symphytum x uplandicum*)	Perennial	FLOWERS: bees; LEAVES: moths
FENNEL (*Foeniculum vulgare*)	Perennial	FLOWERS: bees, wasps and hoverflies; LEAVES: caterpillars
HYSSOP (*Hyssopus officinalis*)	Perennial	FLOWERS: lacewings and bees
LAVENDER (*Lavandula angustifolia*)	Shrub	FLOWERS: bees and butterflies
MARJORAM (*Origanum vulgare*)	Perennial	FLOWERS: bees and butterflies
MINT (*Mentha*) – all types	Perennial	FLOWERS: bees, butterflies and moths
ROSEMARY (*Rosmarinus officinalis*)	Shrub	FLOWERS: bees, butterflies and moths
THYME (*Thymus*) – all types	Perennial	FLOWERS: bees, butterflies and hoverflies

WORMWOOD

You said...

I have noticed starlings gathering leaves of wormwood for their nests this week (early April), something I have seen in previous years also. What are they doing this for?
MT, Maidenhead

Wormwood was once used as a deterrent of clothes moths, but some animals have found it has housekeeping advantages, too. Starlings (below, left), can sometimes be seen collecting it to fumigate their nests.

Nick Brown, Derbyshire Wildlife Trust, advises:

Wormwood (*Artemesia absinthium*), is not the most obvious plant to grow in your wildlife garden but read on and you'll discover why I wouldn't be without it.

An attractive, silver-leaved perennial, wormwood grows into a small bush no more than 1m in height. Botanists doubt if it is truly native or whether it was brought here for its medicinal properties many centuries ago. Its current stronghold is in the Midlands, though it can also be found along the south coast, in Wales, in the home counties and up the east coast. It grows mostly in urban wastelands, pushing up through tarmac and between paving slabs.

Wormwood was once used against intestinal worms and clothes moths. It is

Starling

still an important constituent of absinthe, giving this liqueur its bitter taste (rub the leaves between your fingers and smell their spicy pungency). Starlings, among others, have also discovered that this plant will protect their nests from parasitic invasion. Each spring they deliberately pluck wormwood leaves and carry them off to fumigate their nests, a remarkable piece of behaviour in itself!

Then, in summer, the plants become infested with blackfly. Most gardeners, even organic ones, would be reaching for the spray or the soapy water whereas I'm cock-a-hoop to see these insects massing round the upper leaves and insignificant flowers.

The reason is that this high-protein food supply attracts a stream of migrant birds to the garden. The main beneficiaries are willow warblers and chiffchaffs pausing temporarily with us as they put on body weight before flying off to Europe and beyond. Sitting over a lazy weekend breakfast, watching them busily feeding, is a real pleasure. Their agility and speed is a delight and sorting out the willows from the chiffs adds a touch of challenge to the whole exercise. August wouldn't be the same without them... all thanks to the wormwood!

IVY

You said...

Ivy is often, for very sound reasons, held up as a great plant for a wildlife garden. I grow ivy in my garden, but I see very few flowers and berries. I have two questions: firstly, what factors (eg age?) are important in determining how well ivy flowers/fruits? Secondly, are there any varieties that are particularly good flowerers and therefore particularly suitable for a wildlife garden? Richard Burkmar, Horwich

Have you tried the shrubby ivy *Hedera helix* 'arborescens'? It's been brilliant in my garden, producing masses of flowers followed by some very large berries? I planted mine about four years ago and the flowers attract lots of bees and the odd late butterfly. Malcolm Newland, Hemel Hempstead

The ivy we plant is in its juvenile form and doesn't bear flowers. Ivy will not put out adult growth until it is ready, usually when it is quite large and has reached the top of its support. The leaf shape will change from juvenile to adult, which is usually more rounded. It will also lose its self-clinging habit. The adult form is 'aborescent'. The variety 'Aborescens' is a cutting from this adult aborescent form and grows a lot more slowly but it does produce flowers and berries. I have a specimen growing in moderate to heavy shade that produces berries each year. It is now some six years old and is about 1m high and across. Peter, Middlewich

Comma

Ivy will not kill an otherwise healthy tree (it is not parasitic), but it might hasten the end of a dying one. If you are removing ivy, try at least to keep some of it – it's a brilliant plant for insects, and birds, too (for nesting and feeding). Be sure there are no nesting birds before you remove any.

Good for wildlife

● Ivy has much wildlife value. As ground cover in woodland, ivy greatly lessens the effect of frost, enabling birds and woodland creatures to forage in leaf litter during bitter spells. Growing on trees it provides hiding, roosting, hibernating or nesting places for various animals, birds and insects, including butterflies, particularly during the winter months, and in areas where there are few evergreens.

● It will often grow part-way up the stems of trees, but usually only grows into the crowns where the trees are in decline or are diseased and slowly dying. If the branch canopy becomes thin and allows sufficient light to enter, the ivy will develop into its arboreal form. Ash, a naturally thin, open-crowned tree may, however, suffer heavy infestation. With ornamental trees grown for their stem or bark, such as birch and some acers, the stems or trunks should be kept free from ivy.

● Ivy is not a parasite – the short, root-like growths which form along climbing stems are for support only. Its own root system supplies it with water and nutrients and is unlikely to be strongly competitive with the trees on which it is growing. You should, however, treat ivy with care. One problem is that ivy may hide cavities which, in time, could gradually enlarge and possibly affect stability.

Leigh Hunt, RHS, advises:

Any of the native common ivies, (*Hedera helix*) will flower well, but variegated forms are less effective than fully green ones. They take some years to settle down and flower, and pruning will delay this, so let them grow in a space where they are free to expand.

Although ivy is not really a problem for healthy trees, it's worth making sure that it's not damaging any of the brickwork of your house or garden walls. Ivy supports itself with aerial roots and if these are able to penetrate cracks or open joints, they may in time cause serious structural damage. It would therefore be advisable to make a careful structural survey if considering planting ivy against older buildings, and better to avoid planting it to grow on walls of ancient and historical buildings. In addition, its dense growth could hide defects in the fabric of the building, or hinder maintenance and repair work.

Where brickwork is sound, the main problem is to keep growth away from gutters and from attaching itself to paintwork around windows and doors, as otherwise the self-clinging shoots will need to be removed when routine repainting is done. Even on sound brickwork it is still advisable to carry out a structural check from time to time.

It has been suggested that vegetation attached to walls could lead to dampness resulting from slower drying conditions following rain. This may be plausible on a south-west facing wall where the rain is driven by prevailing winds. However, other sources suggest such plants will have a slight drying effect on mortar, and provide some insulation in winter, particularly evergreen ivies covering north and east-facing walls.

In terms of security, well-established ivy or *Parthenocissus* can provide a climbing frame for intruders. A further point sometimes raised is that climbers may pose a risk to house foundations due to the drying action of their roots on shrinkable clay soils. Reference to ivy in this context is given in the book *Tree Roots and Buildings*, by DF Cutler, and IBK Richardson (published by Longman, 1989, 2nd edition).

FUNGI

 John Hughes, Shropshire Wildlife Trust, advises:

Misunderstood or what? 'They appear overnight, they'll kill my trees and, worse still, they'll kill me!' That seems to be the general level of knowledge (or ignorance) on fungi. The truth is that they are fundamental to the survival of wildlife – and our gardens.

Fungi are everywhere, but we seldom see them. Thin, white fungal threads permeate the soil extracting any available food. The toadstools you see in autumn are simply fruit, their sole purpose to produce seeds, fungal spores, which they do by the billion.

Nature's recyclers

Fungi are fantastic at absorbing nutrients. And nutrients are everywhere, locked up in plants and animals. As soon as something dies fungi get to work rotting, digesting and recycling; ultimately keeping the soil healthy and nutritious. This absorbing ability is put to good use by many plants, particularly trees. Fungi live on and even inside roots giving nutrients to the plant in return for a share of the sugars from photosynthesis. Trees and fungi have evolved together for the last 130 million years. They are so close that the majority of a tree's nutrient gathering 'equipment' is actually fungal threads.

Oak butt rot

Pests, diseases and certain death?

Yes, fungi can be the cause of devastating diseases – Dutch elm disease and potato blight for example. Most diseases occur at a low level causing little harm to other species: they're just fungi eking out a living! And as for fungi killing trees, they will, but normally only when the trees are stressed and ready to die.

And, of course, some fungi are edible. 'Oh, but some are poisonous'. This is true and your identification must be accurate. But very few species are deadly and we Brits are one of the only countries not to take full gastronomic advantage of fungi.

So, please learn to live with fungi; because one thing's for certain, you can't live without them. If you'd like to discover more, why not contact the British Mycological Society at www.britmycolsoc.org.uk.

Shaggy inkcap

THISTLES

You said...

We managed to attract goldfinches to our small suburban garden this year for the first time by hanging out a thistle seed feeder. It worked a treat! John, Glasgow

 Dr Lizzie Wilberforce, The Wildlife Trust of South and West Wales, advises:

Thistles have traditionally been regarded as weeds in gardens, and for many gardeners the idea of deliberately allowing them space is unimaginable. But for wildlife gardeners, they are invaluable.

Most native thistles have purple flowers and produce seed heads that are a valuable food source for seed-eating birds like goldfinches. In fact for goldfinches they are particularly valuable, because they provide a source of seed that even other seed-eating birds cannot access.

Thistles are also extremely important for insects. They produce a great deal of nectar, which means they will attract a lot of bees, bumble bees and butterflies. For example, the marbled white, a butterfly that occurs in south England and parts of south Wales, shows a particular preference for purple flowers, and makes particular use of thistles.

Thistles are also important as a food plant for caterpillars. It is worth remembering that most caterpillars are very fussy about what they eat and will often prefer a native thistle to other garden plants – even those in your vegetable patch! The painted lady, a beautiful orange, black and white butterfly that migrates to Europe from north Africa and the Middle East, lays its eggs on welted and creeping thistles.

Gardening tips for thistles:
1. Try growing native thistles. You may already have them in areas of bare soil in the garden. Because thistles seed heavily they can be prone to spreading, especially creeping thistle. Try growing them in a pot to limit this spread. Positioning a few pots together has benefits because clumps are often more attractive to wildlife than individual plants.
2. If you really don't like the thought of natives, try globe thistle *Echinops ritro*. This herbaceous perennial is easy to grow, and likes full sun or slight shade. It can grow up to a metre tall, with spiky leaves, and blue flowers in late summer. Plant the seeds late spring to early summer in quite well drained soil. It will do well in sunny borders and provide lots of seed for birds.

Globe thistle *Echinops ritro*

LAWN CARE

You said...

This is more a query and a request for help rather than anything else. Does anyone have any suggestions for treating a mossy, increasingly weed-laden lawn organically (to remove said weeds and moss) without using any of the products that are available in garden centres and which seem to harm insect life and by extension everything else up the food chain?
Old Composter, Cardiff

Spiking (or stabbing the ground with a fork) could benefit poorly drained areas – which I believe could help on the moss situation.
whitewolf, Cardiff

Autumn, with the arrival of cooler, moister conditions, is the time to examine the lawn for signs of summer 'wear and tear' or general deterioration. Any necessary treatment is best carried out during September when there is time for the grass to respond to treatment before, with falling soil temperatures, growth terminates for the season.

Mowing tips

● Frequency and cutting height depend on lawn quality and time of year. Start the season on a high setting and gradually lower the cut. For high quality, well-managed turf cutting height may be as low as 6mm up to 13mm. For ornamental lawns heights vary from 13mm up to 4cm.

● For fine quality lawns mow twice weekly in summer and once a week in spring and autumn or dry spells in summer. Aim to remove up to one third of the shoot at each cut. During mild spells in winter, an occasional cut at a high setting can be carried out if conditions allow.

● The highest-quality cuts are achieved with cylinder mowers with a large number of blades. Rotary and hover mowers are suitable for ornamental rather than fine lawns.

● Remove clippings except in spells of hot dry weather, when they can help reduce water evaporation. Leaving clippings may return nutrients to the soil, but spreads weeds, impedes aeration and encourages worms and disease.

● Scalping can occur on soft ground and from mowing too fast when turning. Also where ruts form from not varying direction of cut and if the height of cut is too low. Tearing occurs when cutting surfaces are not sharp or incorrectly set. Ribbing can occur when cylinder mowers are operated too fast, reducing the number of cuts or when cutting long grass.

Maya Albert, RHS, advises:

SCARIFYING: Between the roots and the foliage of all established lawns will be found a layer of living or dead fibrous material – stems, stolons, rhizomes, together with miscellaneous debris. This accumulation of material is termed 'thatch'. Routine raking will keep it in check in most cases and, in moderation, it acts as a mulch, reducing the surface from drying out, and gives a resilience to turf, protecting against heavy wear.

An accumulation in excess of about 1cm can, however, impede penetration of moisture and fertilisers and the turf can become increasingly less resistant to disease and drought. To remove a build-up of thatch, scarify (rake vigorously) with a spring-tine or rubber-toothed rake. Powered tools are available and can usually be hired on a daily basis. Use with care as over-enthusiastic use can seriously damage the turf. Where there is no thatch problem lightly rake the lawn in autumn to remove any surface debris, repeating at intervals as necessary to prevent accumulation of dead leaves. Repeat in spring before the first mowing.

AERATING: This is the process of spiking a lawn to relieve compaction. Under such conditions grass growth deteriorates. Areas of turf may die in hot, dry weather and become moss-infested in wet conditions. Few lawns require annual aeration and spiking every two to three years should be sufficient. Most lawns will have some areas that need regular attention, for example, where deckchairs are used regularly or short-cuts are taken over the grass. Aerate wherever the turf appears to be lacking in vigour, particularly children's playing areas and areas where there is moss or the turf turns brown during dry weather.

For small areas a garden fork is quite satisfactory, spacing sets of holes 10-15cm apart. If buying or hiring, choose tools which give at least 7.5cm penetration.

On heavy or waterlogged soils hollow-tine tools can be used. These extract plugs of soil. After hollow tining, sweep up the plugs, then top-dress with a sandy mixture. This will fill the holes, the grittier medium improving air and moisture penetration and stimulating new root growth. Repeat every third or fourth year, as necessary.

Aerate deeply in the autumn after scarifying or raking, when the soil is moist. In spring and summer spike localised areas of heavy usage every four or five weeks.

TOP DRESSING: This is the application of loam, sand and well-rotted organic matter to a lawn in order to correct surface irregularities. Top dressing also improves poor soils encouraging better rooting of stoloniferous grasses and thickening of turf. The term is also applied to the mixture itself.

A simple formula is three parts sandy loam, six parts sharp sand (not builder's sand) and one part peat or peat substitute or sieved leaf mould, (all parts by volume, not weight).

An average dressing is about 2kg/sq.m but on irregular turf, this can be increased to 3kg. Work the dressing in well with the back of a garden rake. Excessive amounts can smother the finer grasses. Do not attempt to correct major irregularities in a single season by top-dressing. Apply top dressing after scarifying and aerating.

You said...

The hot summer of 2003 was most enjoyable, but I have to say, my lawn suffered somewhat. Partly my fault, I didn't pay enough attention to it. As a result, I don't seem to get as many birds and insects visiting. How can I make sure, if we have another hot summer, that it doesn't happen again.
LauraT, London

It sounds as if you're going to need to resow. Give your lawn a gentle raking first before sowing, to get rid of the debris that has probably accumulated.
DS, Leicester

Seeding bare patches of turf.

Lawn treatment after drought

Where the grass is sparse, or has been killed, weeds and moss will establish with the onset of autumn rains. It is therefore essential to carry out remedial treatment in the autumn with the arrival of cooler, moister autumn weather.

1. Rake lightly to remove debris, but only where really necessary. Heavy raking or scarification would be harmful in most cases.

2. Spike or aerate the whole lawn to a depth of at least 10cm. Even with free-draining sandy soils there may be some areas of compaction.

3. Apply a proprietary autumn lawn fertiliser.

4. Overseed any sparsely grassed areas using an appropriate mixture. Do so when the weather and soil conditions are suitably cool and moist for germination, usually in September. If drought continues to the end of September, defer sowing until late March or April, as results are often unsatisfactory from late autumn sowings.

Maya Albert, RHS, advises:

A well-managed lawn has good drought resistance. The first sign of stress is when the grass no longer springs up after it has been stepped on. Grass can then turn brown and stop growing in dry spells. Although unsightly, this is not serious as grass regrows strongly once the rain resumes. In most gardens lawns are not a high priority for watering. However, where green grass is required it is essential to water the lawn.

It is important to apply the right amount of water. Too much water is wasteful, encourages shallow rooting and the weed annual meadow grass, which is an undesirable constituent of lawns. Also when it is no longer possible to water, during a hosepipe ban for example, the lawn is more susceptible to drought.

A sufficient amount of water should be given at each watering to wet the top 10-15cm of soil. Use a trowel to open a small test hole to find out when the soil is sufficiently damp. By noting the duration of watering required, future waterings can be more accurately applied. Early morning, evening or even night irrigation will lessen water wastage from evaporation.

The average hosepipe will deliver through a sprinkler up to 900L of water per hour. If it is assumed that the sprinkler covers 9m², in one hour it will deliver about 100L/sq.m. Even in June or July, 1sq.m will need only 20L every seven days. On that basis, need will be satisfied by 12 minutes of steady sprinkling.

However, sprinklers may vary considerably in area of coverage. Check, marking out the area of spray coverage with canes, referring to the rate of delivery and recommended 20L/sq.m: for example, 24 minutes for coverage of 18m²; 37 minutes for coverage of 28m². By spacing jam jars over the lawn or using a rain gauge, water usage can be measured. Each 2.5cm of water collected equals roughly 20L of water to 1m².

As this picture shows, a well-managed lawn will be able to withstand periods of drought that can devastate other lawns.

THE WRONG TYPE OF GRASS

You said...

I've got little clumps of meadow grass growing in various patches around my lawn, and I'd rather it wasn't there. Presumably it was dropped there by birds. Does anyone have any ideas for the best way that I can remove it, without affecting the grass that I do want to see there, or am I going to have remove the whole topsoil and resow later?
Fiveways, Stroud

The trouble with this type of grass is that it thrives particularly well when you water your lawn during the summer months. If you can, minimise the amount of watering you do during this time, feed well in the spring, and top-dress the lawn once the summer comes to an end.
Gardengnome, Newbury

Coarse grasses in turf

Coarse grasses may be introduced in the form of seed by birds, or in loam soil used as a top dressing. They may, on occasion, be present in the original seed mixture and come into prominence as the condition of the finer grasses deteriorates following compaction and drought. In a new, or fairly new lawn, the seeds may have been present in the soil and were not eliminated beforehand. Whatever their source of origin, there is at present no chemical means of control – chemicals that would kill the coarse grasses would be equally damaging to the finer lawn grasses. There are several ways of checking the coarser grasses in lawns:

1. Feed in spring (early April) with a proprietary spring/summer lawn feed to encourage vigour in the finer grasses and combine with regular mowing (constant defoliation weakens the coarser species).

2. Light wire-rake or brush before mowing to lift up the coarser grasses.

3. Completely remove coarser patches by digging out in early September, work in a light dressing of fertiliser and add soil to re-establish the level, then re-sow with a fine lawn grass seed mixture. By the following spring the new grass should have become well-established. This is perhaps the most satisfactory approach.

Royal Horticultural Society

Maya Albert, RHS, advises:

Poa annua, commonly called annual meadow grass, is a small native grass which seeds freely, even when turf is mown very close. It is frequently found in established lawns and being a grass, there is no selective means of control although it is regarded as a lawn weed.

Although it is basically an annual grass, there are strains which tend to be biennial, or even perennial. The best approach for small patches is complete removal in October or November, replacing them with new turfs.

If infestation is extensive, control is much more difficult. Measures to reduce the vigour of the infestation are light wire-raking before mowing to lift up the grass and, particularly, the seed heads so they can be cut by the mower. Avoid the introduction of fresh seed by using sterilised loam when top dressing.

The grass is shallow rooting and is encouraged by frequent watering in dry summers. Regular feeding in spring, aeration and if necessary, top-dressing of the lawn in September will help to encourage good cover of the more desirable grasses and keep *Poa annua* in check.

Some types of creeping grasses tend to become more apparent in periods of drought, particularly on lighter, quick-drying soils, as the leaf sheaths rapidly turn brown, giving the turf a rather burnt appearance.

On heavier and moister soils, the long creeping stems root into the soil much more readily and this problem seldom occurs.

The long creeping stems can be substantially reduced by regular raking with a wire rake during the summer and autumn before mowing. This lifts up the stems so they are more easily cut by the mower.

Do not rake vigorously in the spring, as at this time of year new shoots are rooting into the soil and disturbance could result in turf becoming sparser and more open to weed infestation.

Combined with wire raking, a light top-dressing of either a good loam soil and sieved leaf mould mixture with added sharp sand, or a proprietary top-dressing product, can be given in September.

Annual feeding in the spring will also encourage better growth in other grasses present in the lawn.

It may be necessary to relay lawns completely in order to ensure you have the right grass type

FOCUS ON... GARDEN PONDS

During the past 100 years, the UK countryside has lost almost 70% of its ponds, resulting in the critically damaging reduction of a major form of habitat. As Helen Bostock of the RHS explains, the creation of new ponds, therefore, has never been more important for wildlife, and this is where the nation's gardens can really make a difference.

There is a wealth of wildlife that depends heavily on ponds for its success, and most of it will not only make a welcome addition to the diversity of your garden, but will be of great benefit to it, too. Small inhabitants of your pond will be numerous. You are likely to discover in and above its waters pond skaters, water beetles, snails, mayflies, caddis flies, damselflies and dragonflies.

Where there are insects, amphibians are not far behind. Frogs, toads and newts are all quite happy breeding and living in small bodies of water, as long as it's deep enough – around 60cm – for their purposes. Several bird species will enjoy drinking and feeding from your pond, too, and if it's large enough you might attract swallows and house martins that swoop across the water's surface plucking off insects, and using its mud to build their nests.

WHAT TYPE OF POND WORKS BEST?

Wildlife doesn't make any distinction between natural and man-made ponds, shape being far more important. Try to build in a long, shallow slope on at least one side of your pond; it will allow easy access for wildlife into and out of the water, and creates a vital damp habitat for beetles, bugs and flies. If space is at a premium and steep sides cannot be avoided, place a stone or wooden ramp in one corner to help amphibians – or unlucky hedgehogs that have lost their footing – to find a way out. Try to minimise fish stocks – they tend to keep wildlife levels down.

HOW BIG SHOULD IT BE?

No matter the size of your pond, it will attract wildlife – although of course the larger you can make it the better. If you can vary the depth across the pond you will suit a good variety of plants and creatures. Make sure, too, you have a shallow end for amphibians to crawl in and out. Allow the pond should be in a sunny spot, shade over part of it helps keep down algae and is tolerated by many pond plants and animals.

WHAT SHOULD I PLANT?

First, you do not have to plant up your pond at all. Natural colonisation by plants and wildlife usually happens quicker than expected, though may take longer in sites isolated from other ponds. Most people however

prefer to control the look of their ponds.

Marginal plantings provide important areas of cover, and plant stems at the water's edge are needed for emerging damselfly and dragonfly nymphs. Aim to achieve 65-75% surface coverage with floating aquatics. Some submerged planting (often called oxygenators) is equally important. Use native plants where possible and avoid known invasives such as fairy fern (*Azolla filiculoides*), New Zealand pygmy weed (*Crassula helmsii*), parrot's feather (*Myriophyllum aquaticum*) and floating pennywort (*Hydrocotyle ranunculoides*). Don't forget that you'll need landowners' permission if you're collecting plants from local ponds and ditches.

Dead branches in the pond will enrich the habitat considerably, as do tree roots growing into the pond. Resist removing overhanging branches that naturally dip or fall into the water.

HOW OFTEN SHOULD I TOP THE POND UP?

Don't be too hasty to top up the pond during dry weather in late summer. Seasonal ponds are a natural feature in the UK, filling up in winter and occasionally drying out in long, hot summers. This seemingly inhospitable environment can actually favour certain animals. Newts,

for example, are able to survive in the mud during dry months, unlike fish who predate on newt larvae. Where additional water needs to be added try to use rainwater. Tap water should be a last resort.

IS SILTING UP A BAD THING?

The natural progression of a pond is to fill in until it becomes wetland and each stage of this process has its own unique wildlife. If you wish to remove sediment to maintain your pond, try to remove only half at one time to minimise the loss of mud-dwelling creatures and their habitat. There is no ideal time for such a job, though late summer when the water is naturally at its lowest is considered the most practical period (see page 137).

HOW CAN I FIND OUT MORE?

Turn the pages for much more detail on pond-building, care and maintenance. If you'd like to find out even more, try to get hold of *The Pond Book: A Guide to the Management and Creation of Ponds* (published by The Ponds Conservation Trust, 1999), or visit their website www.pondstrust.org.uk.

Whatever type of pond you decide to create, make sure you enjoy it. The wildlife certainly will.

POND CONSTRUCTION

You said...

I have a large plastic container about 1m x 70cm. Would it be possible to sink it in the ground and make a temporary pond for the next year or so? Do ponds need pumps to keep the water fresh, or do I just use tap water? Won't it go green and smell or flood or evaporate? In which case, do I fill it up with more tap water? And as it's quite deep, won't things fall in and drown? Help! Any advice gratefully received.
Jane, Barton upon Humber

The main problem with using a container for a pond is that you need to fill it with enough rocks, rubble etc to make it shallow enough at the edges (or at least one of them) to enable animals to easily get in and out. Don't use garden soil to fill it because it's too fertile and you will just get green water. With a small pond like this, you don't need any great depth of water, so if your container is very deep, you may find that you need to fill most of it with rubble/rocks.
Richard Burkmar, Horwich

When I built my pond, I sloped one edge and laid turf upside-down to cover the edge. I have the same all the way round the pond but on the other sides I have shelves for marginals. I have planted creeping bog plants which do very well. The other benefit is that the birds come down to collect the mud.
Wenda, Newark

Before you start:

● The size of a garden pool and its position within the garden needs to be assessed to obtain a balanced and harmonious relationship with other garden features. Try to choose a site that at least in part benefits from the sun to obtain maximum value from reflections of sun and sky, and from water lilies whose flowers only open in direct sunlight. Position carefully in relation to deciduous trees, whose leaves may otherwise fill the pool in autumn.

● Algae will form in the initial stages, but once the balance of the pool is established, should cease to be a problem. In practice, a small, shallow pool soon becomes algae infested or overcrowded. it is therefore important to have an area of deeper water in small ponds to reduce such problems.

● The easiest way to mark out any proposed site is to lay rope to form the outline, and mark the area of any associated plantings then look at the site from all angles. When satisfied, draw a rough plan of the site, then cut around the rope marker with a spade before removing the rope. Avoid extreme shapes. Also avoid precise geometrical shapes unless the surroundings are formal.

Before and after: the evolution of a garden pond

Helen Bostock, RHS, advises:

Even shallow containers make useful ponds. Ensure there is some form of ramp to allow creatures to access and exit the pond. With some water plants the water should be reasonably wholesome. Be aware that even shallow water can pose a threat to young children. A shallow bog is safer than a pond.

Concrete pools: These are most durable of pool-lining materials when soundly constructed and are particularly effective for pools in formal settings. Paving stones cemented on top of the vertical walls make a stable and attractive surround. Concrete pools are also easy to clean. If cracks develop, concrete pools can be difficult to repair. Concrete must be treated or allowed to season before introducing fish or plants.

Excavate the pool area, allowing an extra 15cm all round for the walls and 15cm extra at the base, to accommodate the thickness of the concrete. Walls angled outwards by 20 degrees from the vertical are less vulnerable to winter ice pressure but shuttering is more difficult than for vertical walls. Remember, however, that at least one shallow side is needed to assist easy access for wildlife. Reference can be made to DIY publications if you are not familiar with the construction of shuttering and the handling of concrete.

For larger pools the concrete may need reinforcing and expert help is advisable. Plan construction so the actual laying of the concrete floor and the pouring of the concrete into the wall shuttering is completed in one day, to ensure that the finished pool is waterproof.

Where the concreting is done in winter, cover all concrete surfaces against frost for four days. In summertime, or when it is very warm and dry, water the concrete, soaking shutterings and concrete together each day. The setting of concrete is a chemical reaction and the slower the concrete sets, the harder it will be and the more resistant to cracking. The supports can be removed two days after concreting, and the shuttering removed from four days afterwards.

Soften the sharp edges of the concrete with a trowel or similar tool to make the pool safe, then sweep out the pool to clear it of all bits of concrete and cement dust, and fill with water. Leave the water for two days, then empty the pool.

At this stage there are two options. The first is to fill and empty the pool at least twice. This will get rid of the impurities harmful to plant and animal life, but it is best left filled for at least a week each time before emptying to allow the concrete to become fully set, to clean the pool and to neutralise the alkalinity. Alternatively, thoroughly clean the pool, allow it to almost dry, then apply a bitumen paint, which will seal the concrete or a proprietary neutralising or sealing product.

Lined pools: Plastic liners are variable in longevity, and dependent on quality and cost. 500 gauge black polythene could be used but may need replacement after as little as three or four years. PVC liners, single, double-layer or reinforced are more durable. A drawback is that exposed margins degrade and deteriorate from the effects of the sun's ultra-violet radiation. The best safeguards are to keep pools well filled and to plant masking marginal plants, particularly along the south-facing edge of the pool. Repair kits are available if accidental damage occurs but repairs can be difficult to carry out.

Butyl is a rubber material, heavier and more expensive than PVC but easy to install and with a life of 25-50 years or more. It can be successfully patched if accidentally pierced. It is available in black only, the most suitable and natural colour for a pool liner.

To calculate the size of liner required, measure the maximum length and width of the marked-out area. To each measurement add twice the depth, then allow an overlap of at least 15cm all round so the liner can be held firmly by paving or tucked under turf. The liner can be laid directly into the smooth, stone-free excavation, with its slightly sloping sides. Draw it over the hole, positioning it and carefully hold it in position with bricks. Then let water from a hose gradually weigh down the liner into the hole, smoothly and with a minimum of creasing or wrinkling.

Commercially available underfelts should be used beneath liners. Fibreglass roll, as used for loft insulation, can also be used. Pools where the floor is flat and there are no sharp obstructions, can be stepped into with reasonable care, and even have stone rock-work laid in them to continue a rock garden. Set any rocks or statues on polythene or butyl offcuts to make future removal possible without damaging the liner.

Clay pools: The method of lining pools with clay is an acceptable approach where there is underlying clay. The drawbacks are the difficulties in obtaining a sufficiently plastic clay uncontaminated with sand or stones and the degree of skill needed in applying and working the clay until it is completely free of air pockets and forms a uniformly deep cover (of not less than 15cm).

Preformed pools: Cast in various shapes and sizes from plastic or fibreglass, these are rigid, lightweight and easily installed. Fibreglass is very durable but the edges of rigid liners can be difficult to mask. The exposed edges of plastic models can become brittle and crack with age. Choose darker internal colouring, as it is more natural in appearance and more aesthetically pleasing. Few preformed ponds are a good shape for wildlife, lacking gently sloping sides. A flexible liner will always give better scope for designing a pond with wildlife in mind.

When to plant: Mid-spring through to early summer is the best time to purchase new plants. At this time the water is warming up and plants should start to grow. Choose an appropriate container for the size of the plant. For stability, ballast in the form of large bricks or stones may be needed in the base of containers for taller plants. Part fill the container with compost and plant to the same depth as in the original container, or plant rhizomes at the surface. Plants should be firmed in and a layer of shingle, or heavier pebbles.

Containers and compost: In smaller ponds, aquatic plants benefit from being grown in containers as this prevents them becoming too large or invasive. Proprietary containers usually have lattice sides to allow water and gas movement. All but those with a finer mesh need lining with hessian or polypropylene materials to prevent soil washing from the container.

Compost suitable for planting aquatic plants should be a medium to heavy loam. Garden soil can be used if it is suitable and free from fertiliser and herbicides. Otherwise proprietary aquatic compost should be used which may also contain a slow release fertiliser.

Feeding: Hungry plants such as water lilies, benefit from regular dividing and repotting

in fresh soil. They may benefit from a supplementary feed in the spring of a specialist aquatic feed, when not being potted on, to encourage better flowering.

Deep water aquatics: These are either bought as container-grown or bare-rooted plants. Due to their vigour, deep-water aquatics such as water lilies require potting into larger containers. Bare-rooted plants should have old roots and large leaves removed before planting. Place containers on raised bricks lowered in stages as their leaves reach the surface, until the appropriate depth is reached.

Submerged aquatics: Submerged oxygenating plants are vital to pool hygiene and balance. They can be purchased as bunches, which can be planted into baskets to keep them under control. They will need anchoring firmly in place. Approximately four to five bunches, each containing three to four stems, per square metre of water surface should be sufficient. Avoid invasive species such as *Myriophyllum aquaticum*. See page 83 for a detailed list of these species.

POND MAINTENANCE

You said...

I have a small pond (about three years old) created using a PVC liner. About a year ago, small round holes started appearing near the waterline, now the waterline is halfway down the pond. Can anyone tell me what could have caused these holes and how do I prevent them in a new pond? Paul, Kegworth

It could be the exposure to light has rotted the liner. My first pond had a butyl liner that some helpful fox stuck a claw through! Replaced it with a preformed rigid liner. Irene, Derby

I had couch grass growing through my plastic liner. I replaced the pond using a butyl rubber liner and weeded all the grass around it and planted wildflowers to shade any out that was left. Still no probs after six years. Sunlight damages liners also, so I have wildflowers all over the edge. nature boy, Croydon

 Helen Bostock, RHS, advises:

Pond repairs: Plastic liners can degrade under the influence of light. If the holes are above the water line and worse on south facing areas, suspect light. Foxes and other creatures with claws might be involved, but you can usually see scratches as well. Ideally use turf to ensure no liner is exposed to light. Butyl rubber liners are easier to repair than PVC although they can be difficult in the area of any folds.

A kit is available for each type of liner consisting of a special glue and patch. Before applying the patch, the area to be repaired must be thoroughly cleaned and dried. Follow the instructions on the kit, but make sure the glue has set before filling the pool with water.

In concrete pools, where the leak is very slight, it will usually be at the level to which the water drops each time the pool is topped up, but there may also be others above this level. First mark this level clearly then lower the water by a further 10-15cm and allow

Problems with freezing

● Gases such as methane and hydrogen sulphide that result from the decomposition of decaying plant material are poisonous to fish if levels build up. This occurs in winter if the pond freezes over, trapping gases under the surface.

● Never smash the ice as the shock waves can kill the inhabitants. Instead install a heater before the winter, so it can be switched on when a frost is expected, to melt a hole in the ice. Alternatively stand a pan of hot water on the surface to melt a hole.

● Expanding ice can damage a pond by putting excessive amounts of pressure on the walls of the pond. A float made from polystyrene or an inflatable ball, absorbs some of this pressure. After removing the float it is possible to siphon out some of the water to create an air pocket below the ice.

● Running a fountain can prevent the water freezing in an area large enough to allow gases to escape. If a pump is left in over winter it is worth running it on a weekly basis to keep it operating efficiently.

the sides to dry. Then rub with a wire brush, rubbing the surface of an area around the leak and the whole area at the same level and above it right round the pool. Brush off all the dust until the whole area is free from debris. Mix one part cement to two parts sand and four parts gravel, with some added waterproofing compound, and mix to a stiff but moist consistency. After filling the crack, leave for up to a week and apply a sealing compound. If repairs are not effective, the pool may need to be lined with a butyl liner.

Where the cracks are more severe, it may be possible to use a liner to cover the whole pool, if there are no sharp obstructions. Otherwise it is more satisfactory to completely demolish an old pool and start again from scratch.

When to clean: Avoid cleaning out wildlife ponds in spring when frogs, toads and newts are breeding. Ideally, remove a third of the water and accumulated debris every few years rather than a complete overhaul. Maintain plant habitats but thin out over-vigorous plants in late summer.

POND WEEDS

You said...

I have the dreaded New Zealand pygmy weed *Crassula helmsii* in my lovely pond. I spend time every year dragging it out as best I can and putting it in the compost. It has rooted around half the edge of my otherwise pretty naturalistic pond. The pond is otherwise edged and filled with lots of native plants. We have newts and frogs, bathing birds, lots of mini-beasts and even a grass snake. Is there any reason, apart from the danger of it spreading outside the garden, that I should try harder to get rid of the *Crassula*? Helsbels, Martin

Eventually I got so sick of the *Crassula* in my pond, and so worried about it spreading to other places on birds' feet, that I tore my pond up and started again. I saved every species of plant and at least a few of every animal visible to the naked eye by keeping them in a paddling pool over winter while I did the work. It nearly killed me but I checked every bucketful of plant matter out and in, and it seems I've got rid of the stuff. Some people also have problems with blanket weed, and to deal with this you need to reduce nutrients in the water. So in the short-term, shade the surface, and in the medium-term remove the blanket weed and other excess plant growth whenever there's too much. This strips the nutrients from the water. Fish, tap water and rotting vegetation all increase nutrients, so no fish and harvesting of excess plant growth is a good plan. Rainwater is best for topping-up. Rupert Paul, Oundle

Specialist tools for clearing water weeds can be obtained from BTCV, Tel: (01302) 572244, website: www.btcv.org.

Dealing with unwanted water plants

These types of weeds are rooted in mud, usually with only the flowering shoots appearing above the surface. Among the most troublesome are New Zealand pygmy weed (*Crassula helmsii*), Nuttall's pondweed (*E. nuttallii*), curly waterweed (*Lagarosiphon major*), curled pondweed (*Potamogeton crispus*) and non-native species of water milfoil (*Myriophyllum*). See page 83.

● In garden ponds, control by frequent thinning using a rake. In larger, shallow ponds and lakes it may be possible using a long handled scythe to cut weed by hand. Because *Crassula helmsii* regrows from stem fragments, cutting is not recommended for this weed.

● In deeper water use a chain scythe. For large areas engage specialist contractors with weed-cutting boats or weed-bucket attachments. Cutting will probably be required twice during the growing season.

● Most water weeds float when cut. Prompt removal is essential to avoid deoxygenation as it decays.

● Chinese grass carp (*Ctenopharyngodon idella*) can be used to control some submerged species in enclosed situations in the UK. Licences are required from the Environment Agency and Defra before introduction. Bottom-feeding fish such as carp are an alternative as they stir up sediment, which inhibits the growth of submerged water weeds.

Royal Horticultural Society

Tony Dickerson, RHS, advises:

Marginal or emergent weeds: Emergent plants, such as rushes, reeds and sedges grow in shallow water and along the margins. They increase by means of spreading rhizomatous roots. Some of the most invasive species in larger areas of water include reed sweet-grass, common reed, bulrush, branched bur-reed and reedmace.

In garden ponds species such as yellow flag iris may need lifting every three to four years and dividing before replanting. For small natural ponds and the margins of larger lakes, hand-pulling or digging is effective, but try to ensure the roots are removed. Cutting in July or August limits the time available for regrowth before the end of the growing season, but has to be repeated annually. Livestock can be used to manage bank-side growth of some rushes and reeds.

Most emergent weeds are restricted to water less than 1m deep. The creation of a bank descending steeply into water more than 1m deep by dredging will therefore limit growth to a narrow band. There are no weedkillers approved for the control of aquatic weeds in gardens, but there are a small number approved for use by professionals. Because of the danger of water pollution their application is very carefully controlled and prior approval for their use must be obtained. The National Association of Agricultural Contractors can provide details of suitably qualified contractors to carry out spraying of aquatic weeds.

Free-floating weeds: Duckweed and fairy fern are common problems. In garden ponds raking, netting or hosing to the side of the pond allows removal. Using a fountain to disturb the water surface may reduce infestations. Duckweeds compete poorly with other floating-leaved plants, so planting water lilies and similar plants can help. Some domestic ducks and other wildfowl may provide a degree of control. Whatever methods are used, complete control is usually impossible. Regular inspection is necessary to prevent re-establishment.

Floating-leaved weeds: Floating pennywort roots in the margins and forms floating mats. Plants capable of rooting in deeper water include yellow water lily, white water lily, broad-leaved pondweed and amphibious bistort. They can be cut and cleared in the same way as submerged water weeds. With water lilies, however, cutting only gives short-term control as new leaves will regrow from the rhizomes. In garden ponds, plants can be lifted out every two or three years, thinned and replanted. The use of planting baskets may make the job easier. Wildfowl can be useful in controlling water lily growth.

Cultural control: Many aquatic weeds are intolerant of shade. This can be created by planting taller marginals or trees and shrubs on the south side. In still waters with heavy weed infestations, black polythene sheet weighted at the corners can be used to shade out water weeds. It should remain in place for at least four to six months. Typically, no more than 30-50% of the surface area is covered, allowing fauna to later recolonise the treated area and reducing the risk of deoxygenation from decaying weed.

Health and safety issues: When hand-pulling weeds, wear gloves, as many emergent plants have leaves that can cut. It is prudent to wear waterproof gloves to guard against Weil's disease in places where there are rats.

POND CLEARING

Although a silted-up pond can be an excellent wildlife habitat, it can get too much, and you need to clear space.

Helen Bostock, RHS, advises:

It is best to carry out regular maintenance to keep the pond healthy. Cleaning may be necessary occasionally to remove decaying debris at the bottom of the pond and provides a chance for repairs, propagation and planting. Small ponds may be cleaned out after four to five years, larger ponds after 10 years or longer. In a wildlife pond there is no ideal time for clearing it out as it will always affect some creatures. To remove excess vegetation and take advantage of the low water levels, the end of summer is probably easiest.

Start by preparing a holding tank in a shady spot for deep-water plants. Marginals will survive out of the pond as long as they are kept moist and shaded. Use some pond water in the holding tank as it can be reused when refilling the pond, reducing the use of tap water. Draining the pond using a pump is easiest (hired if necessary). If your pond has a submersible pump use the return pipe to empty the pool. Bear in mind that after cleaning out a pond it can take months or years to return to a balanced ecosystem. Pond clearing is mainly done for aesthetic

reasons, as a silted-up pond can be an excellent wildlife habitat in its own right.

1. Start removing fish and other animals as the water level falls and they become more visible.
2. Remove plants to the holding areas as the water level falls.
3. Remove decaying plant material once the water is drained and heap it beside the pool for later removal. This will allow hidden creatures to return to the pool.
4. Remove remaining fish to the holding tank. Remove one third to one half of the silt in the base, spreading it on neighbouring borders.
5. By leaving the remainder of the silt undisturbed it will have much less harmful impact on pond wildlife.
6. Clean and inspect the liner taking care not to damage it and make any repairs.
7. Return the saved silt and pond water.
8. Refill with water and replant in stages.
9. Repot or divide plants before returning them to the pond, where necessary.
10. Finally, return marginals before completely refilling.

WATER USAGE

Soil moisture deficit

● This is the amount of water needed to bring soil back to its full moisture-holding capacity, beyond which point drainage occurs. The estimated average soil moisture deficit (SMD) in southern and central parts of the country is:

April	5cm
May	7.5cm
June	10cm
July	10cm
August	7.5cm
September	5cm

Further north the SMD is about one third less.

● So, if in April there is 2.5cm of rain, at the beginning of May there will be a 2.5cm deficit. If there were only 5cm of rainfall in May, then June would begin with a 5cm deficit. If, however, there is 2.5cm of rain in April and in May 12.5cm, there will be a total of 15cm, which is 2.5cm more than the seasonal average. This would mean that the April deficit was rectified, and June would begin with no deficit, the surplus being lost to drainage.

● To ensure economical use of mains supplies, use a rainfall gauge and check and record the quantity after each period of rain, before there is any evaporation loss. A square-sided plastic container can be suitably marked with a waterproof felt-tipped pen. With this information a continuous check can be kept as to whether a deficit is developing.

Make sure that your water butt has a lid on it to keep debris and birds from falling in.

Royal Horticultural Society

Leigh Hunt, RHS, advises:

Using stored rainwater is the best advice for filling ponds, but what do you do when the rain is so sparse that the rest of your garden becomes short of water? In periods of drought when there are bans on the use of domestic water supplies for garden watering, it is often suggested that domestic waste or used water may be utilised to avoid plant loss, and is known as 'grey water'. The most suitable waste water would be that in which there are few or no additives and no bleaching agents, such as water used for washing and preparing vegetables.

While it is unlikely that moderate use of domestic waste water would have a serious detrimental effect on soil structure, soil organisms or plant life, frequent and prolonged usage of water containing detergents may give rise to an increase in pH reaction and phosphate levels and also in total salinity of the soil, and this could cause some harm.

There may be more risk of accumulating harmful effects in some soils than in others, but it would certainly be advisable when planning to use bath water or other domestic waste water in the garden to restrict the use of additives such as bath salts and bath oils and to avoid excessive use of water containing detergents, particularly with lime-hating plants.

Some plants are more drought-tolerant than others, particularly the deep-rooting members of the family *Leguminaceae* such as *Cytisus*, *Genista* and *Laburnum* together with many of the grey-leaved aromatic shrubby or herbaceous plants native to drier climates such as the Mediterranean region. Once well-established, leeks, carrots, parsnips, marrows, onions and spinach beet are among the most drought-tolerant of commonly grown vegetable crops.

The term 'little and often' is sometimes recommended but this encourages the development of a shallow root system and plants may become more susceptible to any interruption in supply. Less frequent but more thorough watering is a better policy.

Basic priorities with most people would be certain vegetable crops and in particular recently planted trees and shrubs where roots are not sufficiently well-established to support themselves. Keeping such plants well-mulched, or planting them with a surround of black polythene to conserve soil moisture is particularly helpful with all newly planted woody-stemmed plants. Avoid disturbing the soil of unmulched areas, as hoeing encourages moisture loss.

TADPOLES

You said...

We have hundreds of frog and newt tadpoles in our small pond, far more than last year. Why is this, and will many of them survive? Jenny, Wigston

I think the large number is just because it was a good year in your area. Survival of the frog tadpoles depends firstly on how many adult newts are left in the water (they love frog tadpoles), and other predators such as dragonfly nymphs and water beetle larvae. As it's a small pond you might not have many of these. Newt tadpoles can be eaten too of course. If they're not ready to come onto land they sometimes stay in the water over their first winter. But the main way to help the babies survive is to give them the right habitat when they emerge onto land around June or July. They need cool, damp edge areas such as long grass and log piles with big, chunky logs (smaller logs dry out). Finally, in winter, they will need hibernation places – tumbledown walls, rock piles overgrown with ivy or turf, or a big log pile. Rupert Paul, Oundle

Having lots of plants will help, but you can also add stones etc to the pond to make nooks and crannies where they can hide. I made a couple of small wire cages from wire netting and filled them with broken bricks, small logs, stones etc. Then I put these into my pond – they give small creatures somewhere to retreat from predators. Richard Burkmar, Horwich

Get your pond habitat right, and within two years on average, you should find amphibians have started breeding in it.

Spawn answers

● In the spring, some small garden ponds can be almost choked with spawn. The first impulse is to transfer some of it elsewhere, but this could be a mistake. Moving spawn from one pond to another brings with it the possibility of transferring unwanted pond weeds, or even disease. The best thing is to leave the spawn where it is – the excess will make a fine meal for predators, keeping your garden richer in wildlife.

● If there really is so much spawn that the surface area of the pond is becoming choked, and you need to remove some of it, then the best thing to do is put some in a bowl by the back door so you can watch it develop in comfort.

● Different types of amphibians may lay eggs in your pond. If the spawn is clumped and bunched together, it comes from a frog. Toad spawn is joined together in long strings. Newt spawn, however, is unlikely to be seen – they lay their eggs on the undersides of plant leaves.

Rosie Woolley, Gloucestershire Wildlife Trust, advises:

On a warm evening between December and April, frogs and toads will awake from hibernation and indulge in an orgy of mating in which eggs are laid and fertilised. Occasionally spawn will be lost in a late frost, but predators are repelled by a special chemical. Don't worry about too much spawn: on average a female frog lays 2,000 eggs of which only five survive to adulthood. Juicy tadpoles are the favourite food of many kinds of garden wildlife, including birds, mammals, grass snakes, newts and invertebrates like dragonfly nymphs. Only the strongest (and luckiest) will survive, leading to a healthy population.

If the water is warm enough, spawn should hatch in four to six weeks and tadpoles start to feed on jelly and then algae. At around six to nine weeks, the hind legs emerge, gills are replaced by lungs, and their diet changes to invertebrates. Around 11 weeks, by which time most frog tadpoles are larger and brown, unlike the small black toad tadpoles, the front legs emerge and tails begin to disappear.

With huge loss of natural and farm ponds, garden ponds are vital habitat. An ideal pond slopes gently from the edge to the middle, with no steep sides. Submerged plants provide oxygen and tadpole refuges, while marginal plants allow safe and shady routes for froglets and toadlets to launch themselves onto land in June or July. Provide an area of vegetation beside the pond for shelter and food, and watch where you walk and mow, to avoid mass slaughter! Give them a shady log, stone piles and a compost heap – shelter from which they can emerge to hunt for slugs, snails and other invertebrates. They may travel further afield, but in three years, when sexually mature, hopefully they will return to your pond!

HOMES FOR FROGS

You said...

As a newcomer to encouraging wildlife into my garden – do I need to have a pond to encourage frogs and toads to visit my garden?
Georgia, Redbridge

Not if there are other ponds in your vicinity. Frogs and toads (especially) spend most of their time out of water – often a long way from a pond. You can encourage them by having lots of vegetation and dark, damp places where they can hang out. Log piles are good.
Richard Burkmar, Horwich

If your garden has nooks and crannies out of the way of your favourite view, you could help the frog community by leaving some old paving slabs for them to hide under. Corrugated tin sheeting is great but make sure it is out of the direct sunshine for obvious reasons.
sandj, Leyland

Fact file

Habitat: The common frog (*Rana temporaria*) can be found in woods, hedgerows, fields and gardens, generally not too far from water. During the winter frogs hibernate, normally under cover such as logs, although some males hibernate under the mud at the bottom of ponds, taking in oxygen through their skin, so as to be ready for the next breeding season. Frogs can leap up to six or seven times their own length.

Lifespan: On average, five to six years in the wild.

Breeding: Males arrive first at breeding sites and begin croaking around February or March to coax females into mating. Frogs begin breeding at the age of two, and try to return each year to the breeding site of their own birth. If you discover a new frog-breeding site, do contact your local wildlife trust to let them know.

Feeding: Insects, slugs, snails and worms.

Frogs and toads, unlike humans, depend on their external environment for their body temperature. They need maximum protection from direct sunlight to prevent overheating and drying out in summer, as well as cover and shelter from frost in winter.

Dave Garner, Scottish Wildlife Trust, advises:

The common frog is Britain's best-known amphibian. During spring, it frequently visits the humble garden pond to breed, and in summer it acts as a natural pest controller on your slugs and other garden plant munchers! As the future of many rural ponds may be uncertain, which may be due to pollution or neglect, the correct design and maintenance of these garden havens provide the frog with an important refuge.

If you want to attract frogs to your garden the provision of a pond is the most important feature, but you also need to ensure that the pond and your garden are both attractive and safe for frogs.

When designing your pond try to incorporate the following features:

1. Create it in a sunny area. Shaded ponds tend not to have many plants and remain cold longer in spring.
2. Make sure it has a varying depth and profile. Shallow gentle slopes are good in the spring for spawning and deep (1m) areas with steep sides tend not to freeze in winter.
3. Make sure the pond is watertight. Use a butyl or polyethylene liner or create the base and sides from clay.

4. Make sure there is good native plant cover in and around the pond's edges.

The garden is important to provide these features as terrestrial homes for frogs:

1. Make sure you leave a small area of uncut grass around the pond to provide damp cover for frogs entering/leaving the pond.
2. Minimise the area of mown lawn. Large areas of manicured lawn mean the frog's water-permeable skin is more likely to dry out and they will have nowhere to feed or hide from predators when out of the pond. If your lawn must be mown during summer months, make sure you mow it regularly so that you are able to see hiding froglets before you start.
3. Designate a wild area, preferably with a compost heap or log piles, for the frogs to feed and seek refuge in May to September and to hibernate in October to March when their body temperature decreases.
4. Make sure the feeding and hibernation areas are in sunny south-facing parts of the garden to provide winter protection from the cold and encourage the frogs to become active earlier.

NEWTS

You said...

Our pond attracts many frogs in the spring where they lay their spawn. Unfortunately it all gets eaten by newts. How do we re-establish the balance so that some tadpoles survive?
Sandra, Dursley

I had a similar problem – so I removed two ice-cream containers full of the spawn – took one indoors and left one under a seat in the shaded sun. When the spawn had grown into tiny tadpoles I released them into the pond and, hey presto, I now have many wonderful tadpoles with the beginnings of back legs. Give it a try next year.
Ann J, Wareham

My understanding is that some ponds are good for newts and some for frogs. It's probably not an easy one to change so I would just try to accept that yours is a good newter and hope that some of the neighbouring ponds are good froggers!
HB, Abingdon

Palmate newt

Which newt?

Smooth or common newt: Adults grow to 8-10cm long. The skin is smooth and may look slightly velvety outside the breeding season. The male can be distinguished from the female by his larger throat spots and large swollen cloaca (reproductive opening). During the breeding season, the male acquires a high wavy crest along the back and tail, and is marked all over with black spots. In both sexes the belly ranges in colour from yellow to orange, marked with dark blotches which are finer in the female. The female lacks a crest and is drab compared to the male.

Palmate newt: This is the smallest of the three species. The total length of a fully grown adult male is about 8cm, the female being slightly larger. Palmate and smooth newts look similar. However, they can be distinguished by inspection of the throats: the smooth newt has a white-spotted throat whereas the palmate's throat is pinkish and unspotted in both sexes. Like the male smooth newt, the male palmate newt has a crest during the breeding season but it is straight-edged and much less obvious.

Great crested newt: This species is the largest of our native species and grows up to twice the size of the former species. Adult males reach 14-15cm while females grow to 16cm. This species has a warty skin which is rough and dark in colour. During the breeding season, the male develops a high spiky crest running down the body and a conspicuous silver stripe along each side of the tail. This stripe is present outside the breeding season but it is not obvious. Both sexes have orange-yellow bellies blotched with black.

Smooth newt

The great crested newt is the largest species in Britain, although rarely encountered in garden ponds.

Neil Wyatt, Birmingham and Black Country Wildlife Trust, advises:

Newts are amphibians – the juvenile or 'tadpole' phase is dependent on water, whereas the adult is land-living. The transition from tadpole to adult involves a complete reorganisation or metamorphosis of the body form. The newt tadpole looks like the adult form, unlike frog or toad juveniles, which do not. (Newts, incidentally, do eat tadpoles. Generally speaking, ponds tend either to be good frog ponds, or good newt ponds, rarely accommodating both amphibians.) The tadpole has frilly gills, which are absorbed during metamorphosis. The fin on the tail is also absorbed and there are slight changes in the shape of the head and body. Adult newts have elongated bodies, well-developed tails and short slender legs for crawling. During the breeding season the males develop crests on their backs, flaps of skin on the hind toes, and brightly coloured skin on their underparts.

There are three species of newt native to the British Isles, all of which may be found in gardens: the great crested newt (*Triturus*

cristatus), the smooth or common newt (*Triturus vulgaris*) and the palmate newt (*Triturus helveticus*). Britain has 3-4% of their global populations.

Habitat: When they are on land, newts occupy a diverse range of damp habitats, which range from woodlands and pastures to gardens. During the summer in hot, dry spells, newts hide in damp locations until the weather cools. In October or November they find somewhere to hibernate that will be frost free, and relatively warm and sheltered. Shaded piles of logs or rocks can provide safe hibernation sites.

Breeding: Newts migrate to ponds to breed in February or March as the spring temperature rises. The males reach the pond before the females and feed well to develop their breeding crests and toe webs. Newt eggs are laid singly and are usually folded into the leaf of a water plant. The 200-300 eggs laid by the female hatch after two to three weeks.

DRAGONFLIES: ABOUT THEM

You said...

I have two ponds in my garden, both quite small and no more than 3ft deep. I was very excited last year to see emperor dragonflies laying eggs in one of them. Does anyone know anything more about these amazing creatures? I have an identification book but it's not very good on what they eat, how they breed and their life cycle. Any suggestions would be most welcome. Sandie, St Albans

Dragonflies and damselfly larvae live in water. When it is time for the adults to emerge they climb up emergent vegetation (plants that are partly in the water and partly in the air) such as reeds. To get them in your pond you usually need these types of plants. Paul, Kegworth

Last summer my pond was two years old and I got quite good numbers of azure damselflies and large red damselflies. I also had smaller numbers of the common blue and blue-tailed damselflies. I'm in the same region as you, so you could reasonably expect these species, too. I agree with Paul about emergent vegetation. Having a muddy/silty substrate in your pond will help, too. (Not ordinary garden soil though – use either aquatic soil from a garden centre or, better, some muck from another pond.) If you have fish, keep them at extremely low stocking rates and provide plenty of nooks, crannies and submerged vegetation where the larvae are safe(r) from them. Richard Burkmar, Horwich

The large red damselfly, one of the most likely visitors to your garden.

Fact file

● What's the difference between a dragonfly and damselfly? The former are generally much larger and rest with their wings spread outwards. Damselflies, on the other hand, fold their wings along the backs of their abdomens while at rest. In addition, the eyes of dragonflies tend to meet at the front of the head, while those of the damselfly are on either side of the head. Both dragonflies and damselflies (sometimes called demoiselles) are members of the overall dragonfly order, Odonata.

● There are over 40 species of dragonfly and damselfly that can be found in Britain, including a few migrants that visit this country during the summer by flying across the Channel. One species – the green darner – has even been known to appear on our shores from America!

● Dragonflies are an ancient order of insects, preceding even the dinosaurs. Fossils have been found of specimens with wingspans of over 75cm.

John Ellis, Nottinghamshire Wildlife Trust, advises:

If you have a garden pond it is highly likely that you will have seen various species of dragonfly and damselfly in the garden. You may have been lucky enough to see a pair mating or even egg laying taking place.

What you probably will not have seen is the larval stage or nymph. On emerging from the egg these interesting creatures go through a number of stages known as 'instars' before they become mature nymphs. Depending on species and, to some extent, weather conditions they will spend at least one winter and in some species several winters as nymphs, before emerging when conditions are right.

Nymphs have gills so they do not need to surface for air, which means they have few predators apart from other nymphs. They are themselves predators and are ambush feeders, using vegetation, debris or the bottom mud as camouflage, and they will take any moving prey that swims past their place of concealment. The larger species even take fish.

When the time comes for metamorphosis into the adult insect the nymphs will undergo subtle changes including the change from gill breathing to air breathing, and they will move to the edges of the water ready for emergence. Most metamorphosed larvae will use emergent vegetation and climb to a suitable position before the nymphal skin splits and the adult emerges.

Dragonfly and damselfly nymphs are quite different in appearance as the smaller damselfly nymphs are slimmer than those of the dragonfly species and have three obvious leaf-like appendages (caudal lamellae), which are absent in dragonfly nymphs. That said, identifying down to species level is far more difficult and a good key, a powerful hand lens and patience are required. If you want to find out more then obtain a copy of the *Field Guide to Dragonflies & Damselflies of Great Britain and Ireland* by Steve Brooks and Richard Lewington (published by British Wildlife Publishing).

Emperor dragonfly

DRAGONFLIES: ATTRACTING THEM

You said...

We have built a large pond for our frogs, toads and newts, and they all seem to be thriving well and this year we have found some dragonfly nymphs in the pond. Does anyone know how they would have got there and what do I need to do to help their survival?
Jacky, Cardiff

As you have frogs, toads and newts your dragonfly nymphs will probably be quite happy as they love munching on tadpoles and the like! They need to have some way of climbing out of the water post-nymph stage, and reeds are good pond additions to help with this. You may find the following website interesting:
www.dragonflysoc.org.uk
whitewolf, Cardiff

Eggs were laid by adults – watch for them when it is sunny. Ensure there are plenty of small creatures for them to eat. Get some mud from an established pond – it'll have some to start you off – also some water with plankton in, for example, water fleas.
nature boy, Croydon

Southern Hawker

What size pond?

● The minimum size recommended by the British Dragonfly Society is 4m². A pond is viable below this size but with much less variety of dragonfly and damselfly interest, perhaps only one or two species of damselfly at best.

● This is because, in their aquatic larval stage, dragonflies are voracious carnivores and in too small a volume of water would soon eat themselves out of house and home! You will still get adults visiting a 'puddle', and even egg-laying, but the likelihood of the breeding cycle being completed is much reduced. That said, just create as big a pond as you can in the space available and you may get a pleasant surprise.

● Eggs are laid in summer and quickly hatch into small larvae, which then grow and moult through several stages or 'instars'; they go relatively inactive through winter then speeding up again in spring. Most species you are likely to get in a garden pond live for one to three years as an aquatic larva. The life span as an adult is usually two to four weeks depending on the species.

Common blue damselfly

A female broad-bodied chaser, one of the exciting potential dragonfly visitors to your garden.

 Steve Covey, Wiltshire Wildlife Trust, advises:

How to attract dragonflies and damselflies to your garden? Simply stated: just add water! This is because the longest stage of a dragonfly's life cycle is spent as an aquatic larva.

A pond is the best way of providing this and the bigger you can make it the more species you are likely to attract.

If you want a natural-looking pond then an irregular edge is best. You will need to have the deepest point 60-75cm as a refuge against drying out in summer and freezing in winter. The spoil can be used to create a wind barrier on the north- and east-facing aspects. A shallow area on the southern and western edge covered in gravel to provide basking areas can extend out of the water for the adults to bask on, too. A 23 x 30cm ledge is needed for marginal plants to grow on. Butyl is probably the best liner to use covered with soil containing no or little nutrients. A few recommended plants:

Submerged: Common water starwort, rigid hornwort, water violet, spiked water-milfoil and curled pondweed.
Floating: Water lilies, frogbit, amphibious bistort, crowfoot and broad-leaved pondweed.
Marginals: Lesser reedmace, yellow flag, flowering rush, water forget-me not, water mint, common water plantain and lesser spearwort.

This range of plants will provide hunting and emergence sites for larvae; perching and egg-laying positions for adults.

Maintenance involves clearing excess vegetation in the autumn (leave on the bank a few days for creatures to crawl back in). In summer drought conditions, top up with tap water left to stand in a bucket for a few days.

If you are unable to have a pond then provide plenty of nectar plants to attract lots of small insects upon which adult dragonflies will feed. They will come – even if you don't have water.

HERONS AND FISH

You said...

I have a pond which is at risk from local herons, beautiful that they be. Please can anyone suggest a method of covering with netting that will not sag and disturb the fish pond approximately 10ft x 6ft.
Martin, Christchurch

My understanding is that herons will only walk to and into water (not fly in). Go to your local fishing tackle dealer and buy some 30lb nylon fishing line, colourless, and criss-cross the pond. Put posts 9in high about 1ft from the pond perimeter and circle the pond with the nylon. Best of luck.
kirwious, Wimborne

I believe that an artificial heron will deter the real thing from visiting your pond. Might be worth a try and will save you having to net your pond. malcolm newland, Hemel Hempstead

Herons require approximately 400g worth of fish per day.

Keeping herons at bay

● Use netting with a mesh size of 2.5cm. Much larger, and the heron will be able to put its neck through. Slightly larger, and the heron may get trapped.

● If you want much wider mesh, herons have a reach of 60cm, so arrange your netting higher than that level.

● Keep the net taut so that herons can not weigh it down by standing upon it.

● Try planting tall shrubs around the perimeter of the pond. Herons like to be able to keep an eye out for danger while they're fishing, so denser vegetation might deter them.

● Try not to overstock your pond with fish. The fewer fish you have, the less likely the heron are to notice them and move on to easier feeding waters elsewhere.

 Philip Precey, Derbyshire Wildlife Trust, advises:

The nearest thing to a foolproof way of protecting your fish is to cover the pond with tight netting, fixed well above the water surface. For most people, however, this would prove too unsightly and rather defeat the object of an ornamental pond. Otherwise, to the question 'how can I stop herons from eating the fish in my garden pond?', there is only one simple answer: you can't. Any pond stocked with fish will act as a magnet for those animals for whom fish are on the menu, especially when those fish are bright orange!

The best way of avoiding heron problems is not to stock your pond with fish in the first place. Goldfish are voracious predators of aquatic invertebrates; a fish-free pond will be richer in all other pond life, from pond snails and water beetles to dragonflies and newts.

For those who really want goldfish or carp in the garden, there are ways of making life more difficult for predators.

Herons usually land away from the pond and walk into the shallow water. Tight trip wires set back a little from the water's edge can deter them from doing this. However, where fish are abundant, herons have been seen to plunge dive directly into the water!

Plastic herons simply don't work. Where there is a good food supply, herons are quite happy to feed side by side. If anything, a plastic bird is more likely to advertise the presence of an easy meal!

You may not be able to keep the heron away, but you can help the fish to hide. A pond with plenty of submerged vegetation, emergent reeds and floating lily pads will have plenty of hiding places, whilst dropping a few lengths of clay pipe into the bottom of the pond can also help provide a refuge for the fish. In the end, it may be easier to face up to the fact that the herons will go wherever we provide them with food, and simply to enjoy the heron as a welcome addition to your wildlife garden.

DUCKS

We fixed a 5 litre polythene plant pot to a willow stump that leans over our pond. It faced east and we half filled it with dry grass and leaves. Within 24 hours a mallard duck made her nest in it and we now have a brood of seven ducklings to delight us. As well as the pleasure they give us they are also gobbling down the slugs round and about and for the first time for years, our hostas are free from holes!
Osborne, Alcester

Ducks are not the sort of creature one would associate with gardens but it is surprising how small a body of water will attract the odd pair of mallard.

 John Ellis, Nottinghamshire Wildlife Trust, advises:

Ducks can be split into several categories: dabblers, divers, sea ducks and sawbills. It is unlikely that you will find any of the last three groups in a garden environment but of the dabbling ducks, mallard in particular do turn up in even very urban gardens. They will often use gardens without a pond for nesting and over the years I have received calls from people with mallard nesting in the most unusual places including a hanging basket, a window box on the fifth floor of a tower block and on a ledge of a major road bridge in the middle of the city. Whilst not a species of duck, moorhens can and do turn up on garden ponds and may well be present all year, even nesting and raising their young.

There is little you can do to attract wildfowl to use your garden, but if they appear the best policy is to leave them to their own devices and do not start leaving food for them. They will happily eat all manner of food from insects through to sliced bread, but they really are better off finding their own food supply.

Whilst not strictly related to gardens, one of the most common calls I receive is from people rescuing a family of freshly hatched ducklings. Unlike your usual garden bird, a duckling is mobile and has the capability of swimming and feeding from the moment it hatches. Once the brood has all hatched, Mum will take them to the nearest water, even if it means crossing the road and travelling up to a mile. Whilst the ducklings will not be too wary of humans, Mum will be, and at the first sign of human presence she will be off leaving what appears to be an abandoned family. This is not the case and possibly the worst thing you can do is collect up the ducklings and take them home or to a wildlife sanctuary. The best thing to do is to shepherd them across the road and get away as quickly as possible so Mum can return and continue leading them to water.

ME, MY GARDEN AND WILDLIFE

BILL ODDIE

Gardens are a great place to find wildlife. Just take a moment or two to tune in to nature bustling around you – birds singing, bees and other insects humming and the undergrowth rustling. In my London garden I have myriads of birds flocking to the trees, shrubs and feeders, and I've watched a family of foxes cavorting round the shed. You could say that gardens are our biggest nature reserve – they are certainly an indispensable home for wildlife.

Bill Oddie is a well-known broadcaster and ornithologist.

BOG GARDENS

You said...

I have a small patch of earth at the edge of my pond which I'd like to make the most of. I'm thinking of cultivating some plants there to draw in wildlife, so can anyone offer some good suggestions of what to choose? The soil is very wet, as it's so close to the pond.
Fiveways, Stroud

When I moved into my house a few years ago, the garden contained a large, deep pond that I was a bit worried about as I had small children. I filled in part of it, and converted it into a bog garden, which I planted with various marsh plants such as purple loosestrife and ragged robin, along with some creeping jenny to provide cover for little creatures as they move in and out of the pond. It's a great way to make the most of a marshy bit of your garden, both for yourself and for the wildlife.
James R, Doncaster

Royal Horticultural Society

Helen Bostock, RHS, advises:

A bog garden can be built from scratch, as a conversion from a redundant pond or a naturally waterlogged depression, to give a pond an informal edge or to create a wildlife garden as a standalone soft feature. Larger expanses are difficult to maintain and should include stepping stones for access. Mark out the area with sand or string and calculate approximately how much soil will need to be moved given that you will need to excavate to a minimum depth of 45cm. If the figure arrived at seems excessive, double-check your calculations and perhaps reduce the size of the proposed bog – remember that you will be double-handling all the soil. Line the hole with a plastic or butyl liner. Under-laying or lining with sand is not necessary. Bog plants do not like stagnant anaerobic conditions or drying out so lay a length of leaky hose or porous pipe in the bottom and seal the submerged end. This will help aerate the area.

Female common blue damselfly

Bog gardens are patches of wet ground that make marvellous natural additions to your garden, provide completely new habitats for wildlife, and are safer than ponds if you have young children.

What to plant

Suggested plants for marshy areas include purple loosestrife (tall, good for bees), lady's smock, gipsywort, ragged robin, marsh marigold, water forget-me-not, hemp agrimony (tall, good for insects), water avens, marsh woundwort, creeping Jenny (good for ground cover), bird's-foot trefoil, bogbean, brooklime, great burnet, meadow buttercup, common fleabane and skullcap.

What to look for

Ponds and wetlands, such as bog gardens, combine together to attract more wildlife than either habitat does on its own. Here are just some of the creatures that you may find paying a visit.

Insects: The plants will make great perching places for dragonflies and damselflies; meanwhile, orange-tip butterflies may lay their eggs on lady's smock if you plant it.

Amphibians: With an abundance of small flies to feed on, frogs and toads may take up residence. If your wetland is next to a pond, it will also provide froglets with a means of cover when they take their first dangerous hops away from the water.

Reptiles: If you're particularly lucky, your bog garden might even attract grass snakes. To encourage them in, try to build your garden near a patch of lawn or other open space where they can bask on sunny days.

Peg or weigh down the hose and lining edges before covering the hose with a 2.5cm layer of crocks and coarse grit to prevent soil blocking the pipe. Ensure that the inlet connector is a few inches clear of your final soil level and in an accessible position.

Pierce the liner with a garden fork every metre or so and replace the excavated soil removing all perennial weeds and large stones. Depending on soil condition it may be necessary to incorporate well-rotted but aerated leafmould or garden compost. The soil level will now be substantially above where you started but it will settle back down and will be assisted by regular watering. Any remaining persistent perennial weeds and germinating dormant seeds should be removed during this settling period. Do not tread down or artificially hasten this process as soil structure will be lost and compaction will result.

Once the original level has been regained, a variety of native, ornamental and wildlife-friendly specimens can be planted in late winter or early spring. Plan carefully for differing levels of sun, shade and soil acidity/alkalinity as many bog plants are particular.

Birds are probably the most popular garden visitors. Here, Andrew Halstead of the RHS provides an overview of how to attract them to your garden, and look after them once they're there.

A survey carried out by the British Trust for Ornithology has recorded more than 140 species of bird that will take food in gardens. Some of these, however, are infrequent garden visitors and probably only about 30 species regularly make use of gardens. Birds such as pigeons, bullfinches and house sparrows may cause damage, but most birds are welcome for the added interest they give to gardens. Other birds, including robins, wrens, tits and house martins, help to control insect pests, while song thrushes feed on snails. Seed-eating birds, such as chaffinches, greenfinches, sparrows and goldfinches, reduce the seeding of weeds. It is possible to make a garden more attractive to birds by planting and managing it in a manner that meets their needs.

Water

Birds need a supply of water throughout the year for drinking and bathing. A pond with a gently sloping side can meet this need, but in the winter it is likely to freeze over. At such times the provision of non-frozen water in gardens is particularly important. Ornate bird baths are expensive and no more effective than a shallow-sided container placed on the ground. It should be at least 30cm in diameter and capable of holding up to 5cm depth of water.

Providing natural food

During the summer nesting season, most birds, including those classed as seed eaters, will collect insects and other invertebrate animals to feed to their young. There is not much that gardeners can do to enhance the insect supply, since to do so might jeopardise the health and appearance of the garden plants. It should, however, be borne in mind that insects and other invertebrates are an essential part of many birds' diets, and their presence in gardens should be tolerated if no obvious harm is being caused to plants.

There are many garden plants that provide food in the form of berries or seeds. Much of this food becomes available in the late summer/autumn when birds need to build up their fat reserves for the coming winter. The true bird gardener will not, of course, complain if the berries are stripped off within a few days of becoming ripe! Seed-feeding birds can be catered for by delaying the cutting back of annual and herbaceous plants until late winter. The withered foliage will also provide hiding places for overwintering insects and spiders, and so give insectivorous birds a feeding area. Listed below are some cultivated and native plants that provide either berries or seeds for birds. Some wild plants that occur in gardens as weeds, such as groundsel, chickweed, dandelion, fat hen, thistles and nettles, are good providers of seeds but are too troublesome to be encouraged. Those wildflowers listed below will sometimes seed themselves freely but they have the merit of being sufficiently attractive to earn a place in gardens, especially in semi-natural areas. Some of the native trees and shrubs are also available as named cultivars; these are also likely to be good for birds, especially where the cultivar has been selected for its superior berrying.

(B) = berries, (S) = seeds

CULTIVATED PLANTS *Berberis* spp. (B); *Cotoneaster* spp. (B); crab apples, *Malus* spp. (B); firethorn, *Pyracantha* spp. (B); mountain ash and whitebeams, *Sorbus* spp. (B); holly – female cultivars, *Ilex* spp. (B); privet, *Ligustrum ovalifolium* (B); *Daphne mezereum* (B); honeysuckle, *Lonicera* spp. (B); some single-flowered ornamental cherries, eg *Prunus avium*, *P. cerasus* (B); some

rose species, eg *Rosa rugosa*,
R. moyesii (B); *Viburnum
betulifolium* (B); Oregon grape,
Mahonia spp. (B); *Photinia davidiana*
(B); thorns, *Crataegus* spp. (B);
sunflower, *Helianthus annuus* (S).

NATIVE PLANTS Blackberry, *Rubus
fruticosus* (B); elderberry, *Sambucus
nigra* (B); hawthorn, *Crataegus
monogyna* (B); alder, *Alnus glutinosa*
(S); birch, *Betula pendula* (S); holly –
female plants of *Ilex aquifolium* (B);
ivy, *Hedera helix* (B); yew, *Taxus
baccata* (B); guelder rose, *Viburnum
opulus* (B); wayfaring tree, *Viburnum
lantana* (B); purging buckthorn,
Rhamnus catharticus (B); alder
buckthorn, syn. *Frangula alnus* (B);
wild roses, eg *Rosa canina*, *R.
rubiginosa* (B); mountain ash, *Sorbus
aucuparia* (B); whitebeam, *Sorbus
aria* (B); musk thistle, *Carduus
nutans* (S); field scabious, *Knautia
arvensis* (S); devil's bit scabious,
Succisa pratensis (S); greater
knapweed, *Centaurea scabiosa* (S);
teasel, *Dipsacus fullonum* (S).

Blue tit

Supplementary feeding

This is particularly worthwhile in
the winter and early spring when a
combination of cold weather, short
days and scarcity of natural foods
puts birds under severe pressure. A
variety of foodstuffs, such as
peanuts, seed mixtures and fat
balls are available from most
garden centres and pet-food shops,
as are bird tables and other
containers for dispensing food.
Other types of food readily taken
by birds are half coconuts, scraps of

bread and cake, cooked vegetables,
especially potato, and fruit such as
apple. Avoid very salty or dry foods
such as salted peanuts, crisps and
desiccated coconut. Some food
should be scattered on the ground
to cater for birds such as
blackbirds, thrushes, fieldfares and
redwings which are reluctant to
use bird tables. It is advisable to
change the position of a bird table
from time to time to avoid stale
food and excrement accumulating
around it. If squirrels become a
problem it is possible to purchase
feeders that are surrounded by a

strong mesh that will exclude
squirrels while allowing small birds
access to the food.

Shelter and nest sites

Birds need sheltered places where
they can roost at night or shelter
from inclement weather. While
some garden birds, such as collared
doves and starlings normally roost
in trees, many of the smaller birds
prefer the shelter provided by
shrubs and hedges, especially those
with a dense branch structure.
Conifers and evergreen shrubs will
give protection against cold winds

in the winter. These plants will also provide nest sites for many birds, as will some of the more vigorous climbing plants such as clematis, ivy and honeysuckle. In order to avoid disturbing nesting birds, pruning and hedge cutting should, where feasible, be delayed until late summer when young birds will have fledged. Hedgerows and shrubs bearing berries should not be cut back until late winter or after the berries have been eaten.

Robin

Nest boxes

Some birds can be encouraged to nest in gardens by providing them with nest boxes. Boxes with an entry hole 3cm in diameter will be used by tits, while a larger hole of 5cm will give access to house sparrows and starlings. Open-sided boxes will be used by robins, spotted flycatchers, pied wagtails and wrens.

Great tit

Objects such as old kettles or flowerpots pushed sideways into hedges or dense shrubs may also be used by these birds. Nest boxes should be sited in places where they will be away from disturbance by humans and cats, and away from bird feeders so the nesting birds do not have to defend their territory from other birds seeking food. Avoid sites that expose the box to full sun during the middle of the day. During the winter, remove the nest material from any boxes that have been used. This will evict most of the overwintering fleas and other blood-sucking insects and mites that would otherwise make life miserable for next summer's occupants.

Wren

NEST BOXES

You said...

Now that it's June and the blue tit chicks have fledged, should we clean out the nesting box or simply leave it alone?
kep, Burrough on the Hill

Personally, I would leave it until September and clean it out then. Put in a little dry straw to encourage birds to roost there in the winter. However, it really wouldn't do any harm to clean it out now if you feel you'd rather do that.
Richard Burkmar, Horwich

Here's a good tip: if you're putting up a new nest box for the first time, fit it with a hinged lid. That way you'll be able to clean it out without having to remove it from the tree you've fixed it to in the first place. It's good to clean out boxes, as parasites can breed in there, and be harmful the following spring to the new avian inhabitants.
Larkrise, Totnes

After the end of each breeding season, all nest boxes should be inspected and the old nesting materials removed. The box should be cleaned with boiling water to kill any parasites. Do not use insecticides or flea powders.

Size matters

Many garden and woodland birds nest in holes and may be attracted to a **small-hole nest box**. The particular species attracted will depend on its local distribution and population, and on the size of hole provided in the nest box. An entrance hole of 28mm in diameter will admit blue tit, great tit, coal tit, tree sparrow and pied flycatcher; whereas a slightly larger hole of 32mm in diameter will also attract house sparrow, nuthatch and lesser spotted woodpecker.

On the other hand, a variety of species may be attracted to an **open-fronted nest box** placed in a garden, the commonest of which will be the robin and wren, although it could also be used by pied wagtail, spotted flycatcher and black redstart.

If you are considering building a nest box of your own, here are two pointers to bear in mind:

1. If your nest box has an entrance hole, then the roof should be hinged, for ease of cleaning out, either by a non-ferrous hinge and screws or by a rubber strip. If you have an open-fronted nest box, a hinged roof is not necessary.

2. Small drainage holes should be drilled in the floor.

David North, Norfolk Wildlife Trust, advises:

Blue tit nest

Whatever did birds do before we provided nest boxes! No wildlife garden is complete without at least one nest box and even without a garden, nest boxes attached to buildings may be used by birds such as house sparrows, starlings or blue tits. As both the house sparrow and starling are now on the red list of birds of highest conservation concern, providing safe nesting sites can really make a contribution to helping species in decline.

The easiest birds to attract to nest boxes are the hole-nesting species such as blue and great tits. There are many good designs available but why not try making your own? Here are some tips: use wood at least 15mm thick; thick wood provides better insulation and also helps the box last longer. Make sure your design includes an easy way to clean out the nest box at the end of the year (always a good idea, to help reduce parasite infection) – a hinged lid is the commonest way of doing this. Early winter is the best time to put nest boxes up. Birds like blue tits and wrens may use the box for roosting in cold weather and many species select nest sites early in the year. If a box is not used after two years try moving it to a different location. The range of birds that can be attracted is huge. There are specialist designs suitable for species ranging from tawny owls and barn owls to swifts and tree creepers. To decide which boxes are worth trying in your wildlife garden, assess the habitat and check out what species are present in your local area. There is little point putting up nest boxes unless the local habitat provides good feeding areas for young to be raised successfully.

Be creative! An old kettle in a hedge with the spout facing downwards can make a perfect nest site for robins. However, if you do use unconventional items ensure they are safe and can't, for example, fill with water.

Providing nest boxes is one of the simplest ways of attracting birds to breed in your garden and in return the birds will give you many hours of pleasure watching their activities.

NESTS

You said...

I 'recycle' my animals' fur (one dog, one cat) when they have been combed by lightly pushing the fur in our beech hedge. The birds come for it quickly, and have the last laugh by utilising their sworn enemies' coats! Waste not want not!
Louie, Lincoln

Whenever I clean out the hairs from my hairbrush I always throw them into the garden, as birds use them in making their nests (apparently and hopefully)!
Marita, Nottingham

It's amazing what birds use – and where they nest too. A couple of years ago, I had a pair of robins nesting in the hopper on my outside wall that collects the water from the upstairs bathroom. We very quickly realised that we wouldn't be able to have a bath for a couple of weeks without washing away the nest and nestlings. Fortunately, we have a very accommodating neighbour who just happens to have three bathrooms!
Gardengnome, Newbury

One year, I had a robin nest in the wheel arch of my car! We're a two-car family, however, so we weren't completely stuck for transport. Sadly, it turned out the nest-site was not the wisest place that the adults could have chosen. After only a few days, before the eggs had even hatched, a cat wrecked it.
Lagomorph, Prestatyn

Blackbird on nest

What's in your garden?

According to an RSPB survey in 2005, the top 10 most common garden nesting birds are:

Nesting species	Percentage of gardens
Blackbird	66.2
Blue tit	56.5
House sparrow	46.1
Robin	32.7
Great tit	23.6
Dunnock	18.0
Collared dove	17.2
Greenfinch	13.8
Magpie	11.0
Song thrush	10.6

Birds such as great tits and blue tits use a variety of items to build their nests, like this one made out of feathers.

Mary Porter, Lincolnshire Wildlife Trust, advises:

Birds' nests have to be built somewhere safe, secret and weatherproof. Do not go looking for nests. Once their 'cover is blown' the birds might be put off or even abandon eggs or young.

Early nesting birds, such as blackbirds, need a snug hedge out of cold weather. Leyland cypress hedging is often a magnet for nesting birds as it provides dense and cosy foliage.

However, it is rarely kept thick enough to be safe. As a general rule, if you can put your fist in your hedge, a cat, sparrowhawk or magpie could get in easily, too. A dense, prickly hedge perhaps containing holly, hawthorn and blackthorn, is ideal.

Birds' nests are protected by law. It is an offence to knowingly destroy one that is being used or built. If you really want to look at a nest, wait until the bare branches of winter reveals it.

As a brief guide, finches make a cup of twigs, roots and mosses, lined with feathers, woolly seeds or hair and are 2m or more above ground level. Thrushes and blackbirds make a cup constructed from twigs, leaves and mud and can be near the ground or up to 2m above it.

A small dome-shaped nest made of mosses and lichens with a lining of feathers, from ground level up to about 2m, and with a round side entrance, is the home of the wren. The male makes several to show off to the female and it is only the one that she picks that gets the cosy lining.

Robins like a cavity, such as a hole in a wall and will take readily to boxes, as do, of course, blue tits, house sparrows, tree sparrows and starlings.

BIRDBATHS

You said...

Can anyone advise me how we can encourage birds to use our birdbath? Chiswick gardener, Chiswick

The young blackbirds and robins love a birdbath but they also like some large pebbles in it to stand on so that the water isn't too deep for them. Penny, Oxford

Hi Penny, I made one, too, from an upturned dustbin lid filled with stones. The birds prefer drinking from this out in the open, than the pond or the water tray by some trees and shrubs. Ioulall, Glenrothes

Place the water in an open clearing within easy flight of high branches so they can be safe from predators. Keep the water fresh and in winter, make sure that you keep it unfrozen. Feeding will encourage them to visit the bathing area, too. Put out fruit, seed, ground peanuts, monkey nuts, water-soaked bread crusts and raisins/sultanas on the lawn. Hang out bird feeders with peanuts/ seeds/ fat balls. The latter are cheap from the stall outside Sainsbury's in Chiswick. Feed the same time every day. I did it at about 6am and then again at 5pm. The jungle telegraph will quickly spread and you'll get lots of birds. I got blue tits, coal tits, thrushes, starlings, woodpeckers, blackbirds, magpies and jays. Have some tall trees. Leave roses to form rosehips, plant ivy up walls for the shelter and berries. Also, holly, sunflowers, honeysuckle, etc. Wild woman, Whitton

Ernest Charles provide birdbaths and many other wildlife gardening items. Browse their online catalogue at www.ernest-charles.com.

Fact file

Dust bathing: Not all bathing takes place in water. Some species, like house sparrows, also like to 'wash' themselves in earth or dust, splashing around just as if they were in a bath. The probable reason for this is that the earth helps them to remove old traces of preening oil that has built up in their plumage and that water simply washes over.

Drinking techniques: Most birds drink by scooping up beakfuls of water, tipping back their heads and swallowing. The wood pigeon, however, can drink as mammals do, simply lowering the beak into the water and sucking it up.

Safe place: Birds are not the only creatures drawn to birdbaths: cats soon realise that they can provide easy offerings. Make sure you site yours where birds can see potential danger, and ideally close enough to cover for them to escape to it.

Nick Brown, Derbyshire Wildlife Trust, advises:

There is something very entertaining about watching birds bathe and drink. Bathing especially is fun to watch if not somehow a little prurient! Some birds (wood pigeons come to mind) get so engrossed that they go into an ecstatic state, lying there, wet through and staring skywards!

Bathing is something that birds must do to keep their feathers in good shape, free from dust and parasites. If you provide them with suitable birdbaths, some species will bathe regularly: blackbirds, wood pigeons and robins among many others. Sometimes, often surprisingly during or after rain, birds suddenly feel the desire to bathe and do so one after another, or in the case of starlings, all at the same time! Other species bathe rarely or not at all.

Some, such as the chiffchaff, seem to prefer to take a leaf-bath, rubbing their feathers against wet foliage, presumably reducing their susceptibility to predators. Others, such as sparrows, prefer a dust bath.

Drinking is another essential activity for birds, especially seed-eaters like greenfinches. You might expect to see most of the birds that visit your garden also take a drink although, as with bathing, some species prefer to use puddles or leaves. In dry weather, insects such as wasps will come for a drink, as will small mammals, hedgehogs and foxes.

So, birdbaths are essential to any des res wildlife garden – and the more the merrier.

Here are a few pointers:

● Provide both shallow and deep birdbaths.

● Put some low down, close to cover and others out in the open.

● Of course, if you have a pond with a shallow margin, birds may use it for drinking or bathing, but a decent birdbath usually attracts more species, providing them with a flat substrate and a known depth of water.

● There are many fancy designs available, though I still use an upturned plastic dustbin lid and ceramic planter bases.

● A final reminder. Never use anti-freezing agents. The best plan is to empty baths before nightfall, and then refill them in the morning with tepid water. Hot water either cracks the bath or, by some strange quirk of science, freezes over more quickly than cold!

FEEDING BIRDS

Year-round buffet

● Just because spring has arrived, don't be tempted to reduce the amount of food you put out for the birds, as natural food resources can often be at their lowest at this time of year, while the need for it among birds, now that they have broods to raise, is never greater. Live food in particular, can provide the proteins that young birds need in the early days of their life.

● If you feel uncomfortable about handling live food, such as worms, remind yourself that by providing food for the parents, you'll be helping to ensure that they're fed well enough to search for live food for their young.

● By providing food during the summer months, you will encourage young fledged birds to stay in and around the general area of your garden. This in turn makes it more likely that they will continue to use it as their base once the colder winter months arrive.

If you're lucky, you may entice birds such as this great spotted woodpecker to your garden.

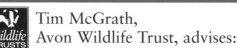

Tim McGrath,
Avon Wildlife Trust, advises:

As a child I was frightened into believing that chicks would choke to death on oversized pieces of food brought to the nest by over-anxious parents. However unbelievable this misconception is, the truth lies in the type of food supplied rather than perhaps the size of the piece.

The traditional feeding of bread has to be done in moderation (as with all diets) and it is critical that when it's offered it is with a plentiful supply of other suitable food. During the peak chick-feeding period (March to July), most young chicks require a balanced diet of high-energy food types usually found in the wild as invertebrates, the favourites being caterpillars or worms.

It is no coincidence that blue tits time the hatching of their one-and-only brood to a bountiful and natural supply of young caterpillars found high in the unfurling tree canopy. By providing waxworms or mealworms at the bird table during this time, the birds will become familiar with a regular site where food is available, allowing the impact of a wet spring to lessen. Even house sparrows and chaffinches, traditional seed-eaters, will feed their young on this available source of protein-rich food, perfect for the growth of young wing muscles.

Between July and March the food selected will vary, but generally food with a high fat or oil content will satisfy most birds. Black sunflowers will attract finches while a high-energy seed mix will help tits, sparrows and thrushes through the winter.

However, as at our own tables, food hygiene is critically important. Populations of harmful bacteria will build up on supplies of food that have not been eaten leading to (at worst) the poisoning of visitors. It is important to keep the table clean, removing rotting food or piles of uneaten scraps. This can be aided by putting out smaller quantities of food and topping up when supplies have nearly gone.

So without doubt, feeding birds is definitely a good thing. Provided with the right type of food at the right time of year, garden birds will thrive on a menu of bird-table delights.

SPARROWS

The house sparrow population has declined by a staggering 62% since 1980.

You said...

We now have managed to get a good community of sparrows after a number of years building nest boxes, one being a multistorey with three holes and various single boxes on the house wall and our garden trees, feeding with a bird table and ground-floor feeders, but not only the birdbath is a must, a sand heap is the added bonus and it seems only the sparrows use this.
Mike, Tewkesbury

Have put up a sparrow terrace for the first time this year. When we weren't looking a great tit moved in. Weird thing is another pair have set up home just the other end of the garden. Their flight paths quite often cross when they are looking for food!
loulall, Glenrothes

Fact file

Nesting: Rarely found nesting in hedges or conifers, house sparrows prefer to nest in holes in buildings or nest boxes. They sometimes take over disused house martin nests. The hole is filled with straw or dry grass then lined with a variety of items from pigeon feathers to hair, and even string or paper.

Breeding: The nesting season is generally from April to August, with most birds laying two or three clutches, and occasionally even four. Each clutch contains up to five eggs, and the chicks hatch after about 12-14 days.

Fledging: Young house sparrows fledge about a fortnight after hatching, and for the first week away from the nest require feeding by their parents, mainly on aphids, caterpillars and weevils.

Winter: During the autumn, sparrows often leave gardens and congregate in large flocks in arable areas, seeking leftover grain from the harvest. By winter, however, they are back at their nesting sites, which they reoccupy throughout the colder months in preparation for next year's spring.

Rachel Shaw, Lincolnshire Wildlife Trust, advises:

The gregarious house sparrow is a joy to have in any garden. They will nest in boxes, take food from bird tables and feeders, and by providing these things you are helping a once-common bird that has vanished from some areas.

House sparrows are one of the great opportunists. They have found a life for themselves in the countryside and in urban environments. But all is not well. Over the last 100 years, sparrow populations have gradually declined and in the 1990s, their population crashed. There has been much speculation about what has caused their spectacular demise: the lack of suitable nest sites; reduction in food supply; increases in predation; and the use of toxic additives in unleaded petrol have all been implicated.

House sparrows haven't declined dramatically everywhere and if you still have them in your garden or local area you can help. They nest in loose colonies, in holes in buildings such as under the eaves or behind the fascias and soffits of roofs. Sparrows will take to boxes if these other sites aren't available. For these colony nesting birds, put a number of boxes in close proximity (20-30cm apart) or use a special terrace box.

One problem is a shortage of food, particularly seeds. In urban areas, development on brownfield sites and makeovers of gardens means fewer overgrown corners, reducing the quantity of 'weed' seeds available. In rural areas, efficiency in cereal harvesting has reduced the amount of grain spillage and tighter hygiene controls have sealed barns and silos against birds. In your garden, try providing food such as sunflower hearts and millet, or allow an area to be wild with annual plants that will provide seeds such as chickweed, fat hen, groundsel, shepherd's purse and vetches.

By providing nest sites and food for house sparrows, gardeners may play an important part in their conservation, perhaps preventing their disappearance from more areas of the country.

SPARROWHAWKS

You said...

I've heard that song birds are down in numbers these days, and that sparrowhawks are up. Is there a connection between these two trends?
LauraT, London

Realistically, sparrowhawks are only just regaining their population levels of a few decades ago, so although they do predate on song bird populations, this is only a natural part of the circle of life. It's far more likely that pesticides and a change in agricultural practices are to blame for the song bird declines.
Larkrise, Totnes

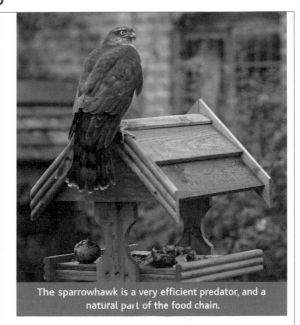

The sparrowhawk is a very efficient predator, and a natural part of the food chain.

Tim McGrath, Avon Wildlife Trust, advises:

It's usually an alarm call and a bluster of feathers that alerts garden-watchers to the presence of a sparrowhawk. Often an observer is rewarded with a glancing view of a fast-moving brown shape hugging the contours of the garden, rapidly passing the bird table, only to disappear over a roof or hedge in a gravity-defying display of ease. Usually the lasting memory is of a staring yellow eye or the absolute silence as this magnificent aerial predator passes by. It is often noted though that after a few moments everything returns to normal and anyone missing the moment may be none the wiser.

Sparrowhawks are the top avian predator that regularly visits the garden. They are a sign of good garden health indicating that there is enough food available for them to survive. They are not the indiscriminate killers that many headlines try and tell us, but natural predators that have evolved over thousands of years. Their predatory habits ensure that only the fittest songbirds survive. They do not hoard their food but only feed on what is needed, often their meals being days apart.

During crisp, sunny mornings in February and March, another side of the sparrowhawk can be observed, for it is during this period when territorial displays are at their peak. Orbiting above the garden both the male and the larger female will complete a heart-stopping rollercoaster flight, fluffing up their downy under-tail feathers, often calling in a high-pitched squeak that secures the pair bond.

So if you are an avid fan of feeding songbirds, you'll have to accept that sparrowhawks will also benefit from your endeavours. But rather than a bad sign, this fabulous bird is a sure indication that you're doing the right thing – so well done (and keep putting out the food)!

OWLS

You said...

Where have all the owls gone in London? They used to hoot every early summer 15 years ago. How can we bring them back? Is it the trees being endlessly lopped at the request of insurance companies?
Cawky, London

Because they're night birds, they're difficult to count, but organisations like the British Trust for Ornithology believe that tawny owls may have dropped in numbers by about a third since 1994. It could well be the reduction of mature trees in many urban places has contributed to this decline, although there's another theory that the constant night-light in towns has made them less effective, too. Keep your old trees, reduce the amount of night-light you transmit, and you may be able to encourage them in.
Larkrise, Totnes

Mike Russell, Sussex Wildlife Trust, advises:

To attract owls to your garden you really do have to have one of a reasonable size, preferably with a number of mature deciduous trees and backing on to woodland for tawny owls, or open farmland for barn and little owls.

Tawny owls, although seldom seen, are the most likely to visit your garden, and can be recorded in quite built-up areas, providing there are enough trees around from where it can roost safely during the day. You are more likely to hear the tawny owl, as it is the one that makes the familiar 'hooo' calls, especially in the autumn. They eat rodents, particularly mice and voles, so can be welcome visitors to your garden. If you have a large garden with a number of mature trees, you could try installing an owl nest box, a long funnel-shaped construction to encourage them to breed.

To attract little owls or barn owls you really need to be in a more rural situation, overlooking open land and surrounded by hedgerows and, particularly for barn owls, rough grassland that contains a healthy population of small rodents. Unlike the tawny owl, both these species can be seen during the daylight hours and will also make their presence known with distinctive calls. Little owls have a rather terrier-like yap, while the barn owl emits a rather terrifying scream.

Nest boxes for barn owls are now commonly used in outhouses and old barns, and they can be quite tolerant of activity carrying on during the breeding season. If you think you have a suitable site for erecting a nest box for barn owls, please contact your local Wildlife Trust for advice on the best location.

Little owls have also been known to use nest boxes, and one placed in a mature tree in or near a hedgerow may well do the trick.

> If a tawny owl box is occupied, it should **NOT** be visited in the breeding season! Apart from the obvious risk that disturbance may cause the parents to desert, there is a real danger of injury, as a tawny owl will attack any intruder and can inflict very serious injuries, especially to the face.

Build a nest box

A tawny owl nest box, *writes the Lincolnshire Wildlife Trust*, is meant to represent a deep cavity and it should be sited high up on the edge of a stand of trees, and fixed at 45 degrees to the horizontal, either on the trunk or a major branch, and facing east. The support batten should be firmly fixed to the box and nailed into position, using 10cm or more galvanised nails; or it may be possible to fit a longer batten across the top of the box and wedge this into a fork between two branches. It may also be possible to attach the box using wire only, but ensure that heavy gauge plastic-covered wire is used and is stapled to the nest box. About a dozen drainage holes (6mm diameter) should be drilled in the base, and a covering of wood shavings put aside.

An ideal size for a tawny owl box is 23 x 23 x 80cm internal dimensions, which requires the following pieces of timber of 2cm thickness:

- two side pieces = 23 x 80cm
- two side pieces = 27 x 81cm
- one floor piece = 23 x 27cm

Glue and screw together, using waterproof glue and about 5cm screws. The fixing batten should be 2.5cm thick, and approximately 71 x 10cm for fixing method 1, or 91 x 10cm for method 2. Thicker timber can be used, but adjust the measurements to give the same internal dimensions. This will be a heavy nest box and will need at least two people to erect it, using ropes and a ladder.

SWALLOWS

According to ancient legend, swallows stole fire from the gods to bring to humans, scorching their middle tail feathers as they did so. Today the swallow's arrival and its promise of warm sunny days ahead is still greeted with pleasure, even if we do caution ourselves in our weather-wary English way: 'one swallow doesn't make a summer'.

You said...

Is there any way that we can encourage swallows that swoop over our pond to nest in our barn? William, Truro

Barn swallows can be encouraged to nest under the eaves or gables of houses and outbuildings by leaving out a tray of wet mud near desired locations for them to build with. Alternatively, artificial nesting cups can be fixed under eaves and gables, preferably 8ft high, sheltered from rain and protected from heat. Please note that nesting cups must be emptied and cleaned between broods due to mites. Do not destroy natural nests, though. Swallows are settled in nests by July or August. SAM, Penryn

 Sarah Bierley, Shropshire Wildlife Trust, advises:

All over the world swallows (of many different kinds) are seen as a sign of good luck and people encourage them to nest around their houses. In China people actually put ledges up inside their homes for them, so powerful is their belief that swallows will bring good fortune.

In past centuries swallows frequently used to nest in chimneys – the warmer the better according to the famous eighteenth-century naturalist Gilbert White – earning them the name of chimney swallow. More recently, barns have been their favourite nesting places, but they will also build their shallow dish-shaped nests in porches, garages and other outbuildings. As more and more farm buildings are converted to residential use, providing swallows with alternative nest sites is increasingly necessary.

Swallows are birds of the open countryside, though they will nest in villages and on the edge of towns, skimming over cricket pitches and other playing fields for insects. If in the spring they appear near your house, leave a window or door open in your garden shed or garage and you could be blessed with a summer of their wonderful, ceaseless twittering and broods of bright-eyed, rusty-throated nestlings.

The loss of diversity in our countryside, a consequence of intensive agriculture, has brought a massive decline in the insect population and consequently the swallow's food supply. You can help give insects somewhere to live by planting native trees and hedging in your garden.

BATS

We have a bat that flies around the house just as dusk is falling, not sure where it 'hangs' out but it must be close... anyone know if there's anything we can put out to make its flight worth while? Got no idea what sort it is as it's too quick!
Pauline, Burrough on the Hill

It's probably a pipistrelle, Pauline – simply because they are the species most often found in these situations. I have pipistrelles in my garden behaving in exactly this way – I don't know where they are hanging out either! A friend of mine came to my garden with his 'bat detector' which can hear the noises made by the bats and make them audible to us humans. It was amazing and he was able to confirm that they were pipistrelles from the frequency of their sounds. You could ask your local Wildlife Trust to put you in touch with your local 'bat group'. Someone would almost certainly be willing to come round and tell you what your bats are.
Richard Burkmar, Horwich

Pipistrelle

Bats often fly around in the locality of their roost just after emerging before going further afield. They feed on insects like moths, so anything you do to attract these will be good for bats, too.

Fact file

● Approximately one in four species of land mammal around the world is a bat – the same ratio as in Britain.

● The best way to identify which species of bat might be flying around your garden is to invest in a bat detector, which you can tune to pick up the frequencies of each species' calls. The common pipistrelle, for example, calls at 45kHz, while the much rarer Nathusius' pipistrelle can be picked up at 37kHz.

● Britain has 17 species of bat, one of which – the soprano pipistrelle – was only identified in recent years by the frequency at which it calls.

● There are over 90 bat groups up and down the country that you can join.

Long-eared bat

Steve Ashton, Tees Valley Wildlife Trust, advises:

Bats are highly active, visiting many gardens throughout the evening and night during the summer. A garden that is good for insects is good for bats, as British bats eat only insects, such as midges, moths, mosquitoes and beetles. Since bats fly they use a lot of energy, so they have huge appetites. For example, a tiny common pipistrelle can eat around 3,000 insects in a single night.

If you want to attract and enjoy bats, you must look for ways to make your garden insect-rich by providing lots of pollen and nectar plants (particularly the evening scented plants). A pond is also another good way of attracting insects. You could try planting a 'bat border' specialising in evening scents to attract night-flying insects. Choose a sunny spot with reasonable soil, backed by a fence, wall or hedge. Mount three bat boxes on a nearby mature tree or fix at least one on the wall or fence behind a piece of trellis. Bat boxes should be mounted between 2m and 10m in height. You could try growing the following plants in a 3m x 1m bed:

Climbing plants
2 x ivy – *Hedera helix*
2 x honeysuckle – *Lonicera periclymenum*
1 x white jasmine – *Jasminum officinale*

Evening scented flowers
7 x tobacco plant – *Nicotiana alata* (white)
7 x night-scented stock – *Matthiola longipetala subsp. bicornis* (white-purple)
5 x bladder campion – *Silene vulgaris* (white)
5 x night scented catchfly – *Silene noctiflora* (white)
5 x evening primrose – *Oenothera biennis* (yellow)
3 x sweet rocket – *Hesperis matronalis* (white-purple)

Plant these roughly 25cm apart, feed and water them in. Sit back in late summer and enjoy the show!

For more information about bats contact your local Wildlife Trust or try the Bat Conservation Trust on 0845 1300 228 or www.bats.org.uk.

BAT BOXES

You said...

We have a bat box halfway up a lime tree but no bats although they are around – any ideas?
KathyMolan, Kineton

 ## Geoff Birrell, Wiltshire Wildlife Trust, advises:

People often ask: 'Is it worth putting up a bat box in our garden?' The trigger for this question is they see bats hunting insects around their garden and like the idea of bats using 'their' box.

A number of county bat groups have their own box schemes in woods and country parks with varying degrees of success, however bats are a law unto themselves and there is no guarantee that the bats using the garden will use the perfectly good box you have provided. The surrounding houses may offer a more attractive roost site.

Buying and siting a bat box is not complicated but you are likely to need a ladder. Quality boxes can be bought from the RSPB, and wildlife magazines advertise other sources. Wooden boxes are lighter and less expensive, concrete ones cost more but will last a lifetime. Both boxes may be used by birds.

Boxes should be at least 3m from the ground and inaccessible to cats. Bats are inquisitive and are likely to look the box over; if it suits them they could move in, if only for a short time. Pipistrelle and long-eared bats use boxes and pipistrelle bats regularly use gardens. Bats are likely to use boxes between April and October, so keep a lookout for droppings underneath the box – often a first sign of their presence. Patience is required as the bats will come and go and a short visit by them may be missed.

It is an offence to deliberately disturb and handle bats so checking your box

Try to site your bat box so that it faces south.

will be limited to watching them emerge at dusk. Counting bats and noting when they use the box is interesting and making a box available can be a worthy conservation exercise.

Bats and their roosts are protected by the law. It is illegal to kill, injure or take a wild bat, as it is to damage, destroy or obstruct access to bat roosts. In fact, as bats often return to the same roosts every year, this protection applies irrespective of whether or not the bats are currently roosting.

If you do find that you have bats roosting in part of your property that is genuinely causing significant problems (and such an occurrence is rare), you can obtain free advice from your local Statutory Nature Conservation Organisation (such as English Nature, or the Countryside Council for Wales), or simply contact your local Widllife Trust.

SQUIRRELS

You said...

A number of companies sell squirrel deterrents. We use a combination of plastic baffles above our hanging feeders and feeder guardians around the feeders. This works to some extent but our latest attempt (and seemingly the most successful) has been to provide the squirrels with their own peanut feeder sited elsewhere in the garden. They seem to prefer the easy meal it offers.
M Toms, Thetford

A bird feeding set from Lakeland seems to have fooled my squirrels. You use an old soft-drink bottle and invert it with a special feeding tray lid, and pierce the base on each side to click in a hanging handle. I screwed a cup hook into the trunk of a tree and hung it up. So far the squirrels have not found a way to knock it off.
Bunty, Ilford

In my view squirrels are still wildlife albeit not as welcome as other wildlife. I put out bird food that gets taken by squirrels but also by the 'thugs' of the bird world, eg rooks, crows and wood pigeon, because these creatures need to survive. I get tremendous pleasure watching squirrels' antics, playing and chasing, and so do the children. Occasionally a sparrowhawk has taken a small bird and once took a blackbird, which is a horrible sight, but it would not stop me encouraging any wildlife into the garden.
Troodles, Holt

Delightful creature or destructive tree rat? Opinions are sharply divided when it comes to the grey squirrel.

Penthouse suites

● Squirrels aren't just potential problems in the garden, they can also cause damage in loft spaces. If they get in, they can chew through loft insulation, timbers, electrical wiring and even pipework. To keep them out, check to see if there are any holes leading through to your loft space. If you find one, the RSPCA advises using strong wire netting with a mesh size no larger than 25mm to block it until the proper repairs can be made.

● If squirrels have already entered, and even nested in your loft, wait until the young have left the nest before you block it up. Not only is it cruel to cage them in, but once they die, their bodies will decompose and encourage insect infestation.

● One further piece of advice: many people have found that leaving crushed mothballs around the loft can act as a good smell deterrent to squirrels seeking a pleasantly aromatic new home.

Graham Game, Essex Wildlife Trust, advises:

Although we have two types of squirrel in the UK, it is the grey that we are most likely to see in our gardens, rather than the native red that is scarce and now confined to a few areas of forest.

It is true to say that the grey has been incredibly successful since it was first released in 1876 in Cheshire, and has taken over to become very widespread across the UK. Bigger and more robust than the red, the grey squirrel is seen by nature conservationists as a major pest; as an invasive non-native or 'alien' mammal it gets off to a bad start, but its reputation is further damaged as it is undoubtedly a destroyer of native trees and even bird eggs on occasions. They have no natural predators, can have up to two litters of young each year, and can live for eight to nine years.

Although the government encouraged shooting in the 1940s and 1950s, they are now far too well-established to be culled

effectively. But of course it's not that simple. In our gardens, its liking for chestnuts, hazelnuts and acorns sees our 'tree rats' burying these in the autumn in the faint hope that it will remember where they are hidden to see them through a harsh winter. Of course many are forgotten, and in the spring, young hazel and oak saplings burst forth, but hopefully not in the middle of your pristine lawn!

Whatever the conservationists may think, many people love to see grey squirrels in their gardens, and I personally do not blame them. They are of course incredibly mobile, quite cute and a delight to watch especially for the young, the elderly, sick or people otherwise confined indoors.

Be careful though when putting out bird feeders – ensure that they really are squirrel-proof as the little blighters are nuts about nuts, and can easily nibble through the wire mesh to destroy a nut feeder.

RED SQUIRRELS

Red squirrels have disappeared from many parts of the country, but your best chance of discovering one in your garden is if you live in Scotland, north England, the Isle of Wight or scattered parts of Wales.

You said...

I'm fortunate enough to live in one of the few places in the country where red squirrels still have a foothold. Is there any way I can encourage them into my garden, or are they too timid to move into such places?
GordonL, Isle of Wight

Lucky you. I have to drive dozens of miles if I want to have a chance of seeing a red. To answer your question, red squirrels will indeed visit the garden, and even come to your feeder, but you need to live alongside a habitat which supports them, as they do not stray far from their breeding grounds. If you have grey squirrels in your garden, however, it's best not to encourage reds, as there's a potential risk of infection. Gardengnome, Newbury

 Louise Bessant, Red Squirrel Conservation Officer, Northumberland Wildlife Trust, advises:

In some parts of the country people are still lucky enough to see red squirrels, and enjoy feeding them in their gardens. There are a number of guidelines that must be followed if your red squirrels are to remain healthy.

The feeders must be cleaned regularly, as old food and droppings can harbour diseases. Do not provide food in areas where both red and grey squirrels are seen, as this will also increase the risk of disease transmission between animals.

Squirrels need a varied diet; they particularly like hazelnuts. Do not feed sweet, dried food such as raisins as this can lead to calcium deficiency.

Take care when locating feeders. A good location is at head height, against a wall or group of trees, so the squirrel doesn't have to cross open ground and can make a quick escape from cats and other predators. Unfortunately red squirrels do not have good road sense, and many are killed on roads every year. Do not encourage red squirrels to cross roads to reach feeders by ensuring that feeders are placed on the same side of the road as their woodland.

Northumberland Wildlife Trust has an information sheet on the supplementary feeding of red squirrels. Please email mail@northwt.org.uk, or send a self-addressed envelope to Garden House, St Nicholas Park, Gosforth, Newcastle upon Tyne, NE3 3XT.

MOLES

Moles do not eat plants and their diet consists mainly of worms but also includes soil pests such as slugs, cutworms and leatherjackets.

Did you know?

● Living underground insulates moles from cold weather and they remain active throughout the year.

● Their day is divided into alternating periods of activity, lasting about four hours, in which they feed and dig or repair tunnels, and periods of rest.

● When feeding, they do not dig through the soil looking for food, but run along their tunnels and eat any animals which have fallen into the tunnel.

● The mating season is February to March and the young are born in April to May.

● The average litter size is four and the young are reared in a nest made of hay or dry leaves in an underground nest chamber.

● The lifespan of a mole is about three or four years.

Neil Beamsley, Northumberland Wildlife Trust, advises:

Whether you love them or hate them, the European mole is certainly a unique feature of Britain's natural history. Most people will more readily recognise the mole's 'hills' rather than the creature itself, because the only individuals you're likely to see are the young as they make their way from the nest in early summer.

The mole is capable of some truly industrious feats, despite its diminutive size. It is usually found in areas of established grasslands such as parks, gardens, golf courses or agricultural pasture. It will spend almost its entire existence in a subterranean network of tunnels, designed to entrap its staple diet, the earthworm. One mole can have a network of tunnels that extend over an area as large as 1,000m², and can tunnel up to 20m of new tunnel per day. The molehills commonly seen in parks and gardens, are created as the mole repairs and extends its tunnel systems.

To some, these garden residents provide a source of freshly aerated soil, with each molehill containing up to 5L of earth. To most however, the mole is a constant source of frustration. From the domestic garden, where up to 15 fresh hills a day can ruin manicured lawns, to agricultural areas, where molehills can contaminate silage fields and damage machinery.

Methods of mole control vary from the lethal to the mildly suggestive. Traditionally, moles have been controlled with the use of earthworms laced with strychnine hydrochloride. This method can, however, kill other creatures which feed on earthworms, so it has been banned.

Humane traps for capturing moles alive for release elsewhere are sometimes available from garden shops. It is advisable to check live traps at least twice a day as active small mammals can die of stress or starvation if held in traps for too long. Captured moles should be released as soon as possible at least a mile away into deciduous woodland or other suitable uncultivated areas.

On an agricultural scale, harrowing then rolling fields may persuade the mole to dig elsewhere. In domestic gardens sonic deterrents are available, which emit vibrations that discourage moles. Children's windmills or glass bottles pushed into the tunnels will produce similar sounds when the wind blows.

BADGERS

You said...

I have recently moved to a new home and was told by the previous owners that there is a badger sett at the bottom of the garden. I wondered if there is anything I should be doing (or not doing) to make sure I do not discourage or disturb them. If anyone has any suggestions I'd love to hear them!
Jenny, Linslade

I have a badger digging craters in my lawn. I tried to discourage its visits by using a product that they dislike the smell of but to no avail. So I bought a CCTV camera and now I film it. I've even begun to like it now I can see it.
Connie, Bristol

Until recently we had a holiday home on the Devon coast and had a badger sett practically in front of our window. Every night we put treats out and were visited by the family who didn't seem to mind us all hanging out of the window above them just as long as we kept very quiet. They loved sponge cake!
Mary, Stratford-upon-Avon

Badgers are increasingly having to adapt to urban life, as pressures on their natural countryside habitat increase.

Fact file

Although it's best not to encourage wild mammals such as badgers to become over-dependent on artificial feeding, they will still benefit from food in times of need, such as in winter and spring. Feeding them during these times may also help deter them from damaging your garden. If you do occasionally feed them, remember that you are trying to replicate their natural earthworm-based diet, with high protein and moisture content. Suggestions for badger food include:

● Wet and sloppy cat or dog food. If you provide dry pet food, then make sure you provide a bowl of water, too, to help them avoid dehydration.

● Fruit such as apples, plums or pears.

● Nuts such as unsalted peanuts or brazils.

Adrian Coward, Somerset Wildlife Trust, and the Somerset Badger Group, advises:

Badgers are creatures of habit, and they live in a social group (or family) in a particular territory. This territory may include your garden, many neighbouring gardens, parks, other sites, and surrounding fields and woods if you live in the country.

Almost invariably badgers will enter gardens in search of food. Often new developments or other major land use changes will reduce the foraging areas available to badgers and cause them to search in gardens that may not have been entered before. Badgers are normally nocturnal so garden visits are generally unseen during the night, unless the badgers have a sett nearby when the animals may visit early in the evening. They tend to follow well-used routes when moving around their territory, so the entry point into your garden should be easy to find.

Being omnivorous, badgers will eat many things, but most of the time they search for earthworms and insect larvae. When chafer grubs are taken, badgers can dig holes in lawns to get to them. Quite often badger-foraging in gardens can be seasonal so that visits fluctuate depending on the time of year. Feeding badgers is not recommended as they may become dependent on it. A few food scraps or some peanuts will attract them, but it is more important to provide water when it is very dry or frosty.

Badgers have been voted the best-liked British mammal. Watching them in your garden foraging for food, perhaps causing acceptable disruption (although an electric fence can help exclude them from vegetable plots), can give great pleasure and be educational for younger members of the family. The badgers will also remove some harmful creatures which may otherwise damage your crops, fruits and flowers.

If having badgers in your garden does cause you concern, then help and advice is at hand by contacting your local Wildlife Trust and local Defra office.

FOXES

You said...

My regular fox diner gets an assortment of food and I usually assess what the first choice is – have I just 'educated' her badly or do all foxes have a sweet tooth? The first choice is always doughnuts/scones over the more sensible eggs or meat. Perhaps I should leave out some dental floss for her, too...
Kelmscott, Farnham

I guess the foxes are like us – they have an innate fondness for sweet things because in nature sweet foods (fruit, etc) provide a quick energy fix. Processed foods contain refined sugar in unnaturally high quantities and this is not good for us or the foxes. Processed foods containing a lot of sugar are so new that neither we nor the foxes have had time to evolve a dislike for them – even though they are not particularly good for us.
Richard Burkmar, Horwich

I saw a fox sitting on top of our compost bin in broad daylight recently – the first time I've seen one in our built-up area during the day.
Sue, Bishops Stortford

Foxes are omnivores, eating virtually anything they come across.

Safety point

Many foxes are injured by forcing their snouts into tin cans in search of food, and cutting themselves on attached lids, so if you leave out old cans near where foxes might be rooting around, make sure you take the lids off first.

Did you know?

● In the wild, foxes rarely live for longer than about seven years, and many don't even make it beyond two years.

● A fox's territory may be anything from a few hectares (in urban areas) to 20,234ha (in the Highlands).

● The fox only has one natural predator (other than dogs and man) in the UK – the golden eagle.

Rosemary Atkins, Avon Wildlife Trust volunteer, advises:

An urban garden may provide a better opportunity for observing foxes than the countryside, particularly if there are a few shrubs from behind which they can survey the surroundings, or a shed with a 12cm gap underneath where cubs could be reared. Attracting foxes to the garden is not difficult, indeed one or more may be passing through already in a search for food and their keen noses quickly tell them whether or not it is worth stopping. Surrounding a garden with 2m-high walls or fences is no barrier as foxes are agile climbers and the only deterrent is not to feed them. Daytime is spent underground, although in summer they enjoy basking in the sun.

Foxes are beautiful, opportunistic animals, eating anything from mice or beetles to the contents of plastic sacks and discarded takeaways. Meat bones, poultry leftovers, peanuts, apple cores or tinned dog food put out at dusk will encourage foxes and may also attract badgers and woodmice. When natural food is plentiful, foxes and badgers will tolerate each other, but if scarce, the badger will chase the fox away. Foxes are unlikely to attack cats because of their claws.

How do you know if a fox has visited the garden?
● You may hear fox cubs yikkering when playing hide and seek around the bushes and flowerbeds (so you need to protect precious plants).
● Look out for their faeces, twisted like thin rope showing the remains of beetle wing cases or small fruit stones and a wisp of hair in the pointed end.
● The pungent, acrid smell of fox urine is very noticeable in the early morning or after a shower of rain.

Watching foxes in the garden is fun and informative. To watch them at night, switch on an upstairs light to illuminate the garden; but they may disappear at the slightest movement or noise.

HEDGEHOGS

We have had a hedgehog visit our garden which has proven to be fascinating for parents and children alike. We have been told that they are great for keeping down the slugs. Is this true and how can we encourage the hedgehogs to return and stay with us?
Teresa, Lampeter

Hedgehogs will eat slugs but they don't really like them much and they only form a small part of their diet.
JJ, Bristol

Creating some hedgehog-friendly habitats around your garden could help – a pile of leaves, some long grass, overgrown corners of the garden are useful. A log pile will also provide homes for beetles and a host of other creatures that the hedgehog may like to munch on. Or you could go the whole hog (ha! terrible joke!) and make a hedgehog box!
whitewolf, Cardiff

Contrary to popular belief, it is not a good idea to feed cows' milk to hedgehogs. It can make them ill. Cat or dog food, with a dish of water, is much better.

Homes for hedgehogs

● Hedgehogs will often stop visiting a garden as winter approaches if there is no suitable hibernation site available to them.

● Piles of logs or leaves are great potential sites for hedgehogs to build a winter nest (hibernacula). Be careful around bonfire night for this reason: hedgehogs may be sheltering in the log pile you plan to burn, so make sure you move the wood to a new site shortly before lighting it.

● If you haven't got any suitable nesting sites, you might tempt hedgehogs to stay in a purpose-built hedgehog house. You can buy one from many garden centres or build one yourself (making sure you follow an approved design to allow sufficient ventilation).

● For a free leaflet on how to build a hedgehog house contact the British Hedgehog Preservation Society on 01584 890 801 or see their website www.britishhedgehogs.org.uk.

Caroline Langham, Herefordshire Nature Trust, advises:

Hedgehogs are nature's own pest control system! They munch their way through a myriad of garden pests, eating around 100 slugs, beetles, caterpillars and insect larvae and other invertebrates each night. A resident slug-eater is a welcome visitor to any wildlife garden. Make your garden as hedgehog-friendly as possible by following these tips:

Food: Hedgehogs love creepy-crawlies, so make sure you avoid using insecticides. Let plants form clumps, leave dead seed heads on plants during winter and set up wood piles in the garden to provide homes to the creepy-crawlies that hedgehogs eat. They are particularly fond of slugs, so be careful with your slug control (see page 63 for information on slug pellets). If you want to watch hedgehogs feeding you can supplement their natural diet by putting extra food out at dusk. Cat or dog food made from white meat is a good option. You can even find special hedgehog food at many garden centres.

Water: A water supply that hedgehogs can reach is very important, particularly during the summer. Place shallow bowls of fresh water at several sites. If you have a pond, make sure that it is safe for hedgehogs. Although hedgehogs can swim, they can drown in ponds that they cannot get out of easily. If yours has slippery or steep sides, make sure you create a ramp so they can escape. A ramp can be as simple as a piece of chicken wire firmly fixed and draped into the pond. It is also important to keep pond levels topped up so the sides aren't too high.

Shelter: In daytime, hedgehogs will look for somewhere to rest. This may be in a nest they have built, or simply under some leaves, among tussocks of grass or in the thick grass at the bottom of a hedge. Make sure you are not too tidy so that there are lots of places that a hedgehog can rest. It is important to be careful when you are cutting back these areas as Strimmers® and mowers can inflict serious injuries on hedgehogs.

British Hedgehog Preservation Society (BHPS) is a small national charity dedicated to safe guarding the future of the European hedgehog.

BHPS has been involved in much hedgehog research since its formation in 1982. In recent times it has been right at the heart of the Uist debate – and key players in the rescue and relocation of hundreds of hedgehogs that would have otherwise faced an unnecessary death. Details of this and other campaigns can be found on our website www.britishhedgehogs.org.uk

For 2006 we have launched a new leaflet 'Gardening With Hedgehogs' to help gardeners reduce some of the problems that hedgehogs may encounter in the garden.

BHPS needs your support – Individual membership is just £7.50 per year.

Please see our website or contact us for details of membership, leaflets, our Hogalogue gift catalogue and much more.

British Hedgehog Preservation Society
Hedgehog House, Dhustone
Ludlow, Shropshire SY8 3PL
Tel 01584 890 801

Email bhps@dhustone.fsbusiness.co.uk
www.britishhedgehogs.org.uk

ME, MY GARDEN AND WILDLIFE
IOLO WILLIAMS

I'm not a gardener. For years, in fact, I've managed to escape gardening by claiming to be a wildlife gardener and therefore allowing my lawns and hedges to run riot. This was successful, to a degree, as the brambles were full of warblers and small mammals, the hedges alive with thrushes and my lawns were a haven for frogs and toads. Now, however, we have moved to a new house and this has given me a golden opportunity to create a wildlife garden from new. So far, I have a hedgerow in place, made from six different species of native trees, including hazel, holly and lime, and I have erected boxes for birds, bats and insects around the garden and surrounding fields. Last month, my eldest son and I created several woodpiles and hedgehog hibernation sites around the periphery of the garden and we will be making more of these over the next few days. This winter, I shall be planting more native shrubs such as guelder rose, plants such as teasel, and creating a small wildflower meadow.

Next winter, I am hoping to create a pond so that some of the toads, palmate and great crested newts from next door's impressive pool can wander into my far less impressive puddle. As a non-gardener, I am trying to maximise my output for minimum input so easy maintenance is the key. One of the wonderful things about all this work has been watching new wildlife colonise what was previously a barren field. We

Iolo Williams is a wildlife broadcaster and author, who has made many nature programmes for BBC Wales and S4C.

now have nesting redstarts and great tits, toads and newts hibernate beneath our garden shed and every night, a tawny owl calls from the garden fence. As time passes, the garden can only get better and better and one day soon, I may finally be able to lay claim to being a true wildlife gardener.

'One of the wonderful things about all this work has been watching new wildlife colonise what was previously a barren field.'

MICE

Wood mice are mainly nocturnal creatures, but can sometimes be seen during the day, particularly when food is scarcer to come by.

You said...

We have lots of wood mice living just outside our kitchen window that we often see during the day, normally on our bird feeders. I thought these mice were usually nocturnal, so is daytime activity normal for them? Katevet, Hereford

We have wood mice living between the tiles and the felt of our garage roof which delight us by visiting the nearby bird table for their food. There is a nest area in the roof of the bird table and the mice have a shuttle relay to quickly move food into the nest area, then to carry it bit by bit up the pyracantha and into the roof of the garage. On entering the garage we hear the 'patter of tiny feet' along the roof felt and know that after four years they are still alive and thriving. wildlife gardener, Danbury

 Sue Tatman, Cheshire Wildlife Trust, explains:

Mice are far more common in gardens than most people realise. They are mostly nocturnal and very shy, so they are rarely seen, although they can appear at dawn or dusk. Quite often, people only see mice when the cat brings one home!

The most common garden mouse is the wood mouse. It is easily identifiable by its dark brown coat, huge ears and long, thin tail. The wood mouse is found across Britain. Its natural habitat is woodlands and hedgerows, but it finds conditions much to its liking in many gardens. It has a varied diet, feeding on seeds, nuts, fruits and insects, and it can find abundant food supplies in most gardens.

They are great climbers, and will sometimes climb up bird tables to dine on the food we put out for the birds.

Wood mice are not generally a nuisance to gardeners, although a row of freshly sown peas or beans can be an irresistible temptation, and they are quite capable of digging up and consuming the lot! Wood mice are great hoarders, they like to collect spare food, especially in autumn to see them through the winter. These food caches are usually underground. However, if you find a pile of seeds or cherry stones at the back of the greenhouse or shed, or even in an unused bird box, a wood mouse is the most likely culprit.

There are two other mice that sometimes appear in gardens. In the south of England the wood mouse's larger cousin, the yellow-necked mouse, is sometimes seen. The yellow-necked mouse usually lives in woodland, so is more likely to appear in mature gardens with plenty of seed-producing trees and shrubs.

The house mouse is the same size as a wood mouse, but is a uniform grey-brown colour. This species has a long association with mankind: it has been living in and around our homes and farm buildings since prehistoric times.

Indoors it can be a pest, eating and fouling stores of grain. Nowadays it generally lives out in hedgerows and scrub during the summer, only attempting to come inside during the cold hungry winter months.

Fact file

Winter: Wood mice enter a state of torpor during very cold months, a state similar to hibernation, so as to conserve energy.

Breeding: This species has a very long breeding season, starting in March and lasting through to autumn, or even winter if the weather is mild. Between two and four litters per year is the average.

Predation: Wood mice have many enemies. Foxes, stoats, weasels, badgers and cats all hunt it down, and it is the commonest prey of the tawny owl.

Food: When 'vegetarian' food, such as nuts and seeds, is scarce, wood mice will turn carnivorous, hunting down snails, insects and earthworms.

Territory: A male will spend the night searching for food across an area about half the size of a football pitch.

Hazel dormice are rare but occasional and delightful garden visitors.

RATS

You said...

We have had a compost heap for over 25 years without problem until this winter when it was colonised by a rat or rats. Environmental health appear to have got rid of the rat(s) but they advised we get rid of the compost heap. Any suggestions as to how we might replace it safely?
mik, Bolsover

I have three black compost bins which I bought through the council. They make good compost and there is no place through which rats could crawl to build a nest.
Paul, Leeds

You could try covering any veg/kitchen waste you add to the compost heap with a layer of soil, mature compost, leaves or other less attractive material.
whitewolf, Cardiff

If only cats would catch rats instead of birds!
brown, Derby

Brown rats are among the commonest British mammals, found virtually everywhere on the mainland except some mountain regions.

Did you know?

● There are two types of rat in Britain, although it is the brown rat that you are most likely to see in your garden.

● Britain's original black rat, the creature behind the seventeenth-century plague, has largely been displaced by the brown rat, which came to this country aboard ships in the eighteenth century.

● Before human transport gave them their current worldwide populations, brown rats were originally only native to east Asia and Japan.

● Brown rats live for up to about 18 months in the wild.

● Rapid breeders, they can produce up to five litters per year, each containing as many as eight young.

● Rat territories are approximately 50m in diameter.

Philip Precey, Derbyshire Wildlife Trust, advises:

Rats are probably the least popular visitor to the wildlife garden, associated as they are with plague and pestilence. Whilst their bad reputation is not entirely deserved, they can spread some very nasty diseases and most people would agree that rats should be discouraged from taking up residence in your garden.

It is almost inevitable that rats will turn up in your garden every now and again, but the occasional visit by a rat should not be cause to worry. Indeed, their antics can be just as entertaining as any of the other visitors to the garden. However, if they find a good source of food and sufficient shelter, rats may do more than just occasionally pass through, and this is when problems may occur.

Rats can be usually be discouraged by taking away their sources of food and shelter. The most obvious source of food in a wildlife garden will be your bird table. Only put bird food on the bird table or in hanging feeders: avoid scattering food on the floor, if you find it is encouraging rats. Make sure that any food that does fall from the feeders is cleared up regularly. Rats are excellent climbers and can also jump surprisingly high; once they have taken up residence, it won't be long before they are sat on the bird table or even hanging from the peanut feeders. By this point, it will probably be necessary to stop feeding the birds altogether until the rats have gone.

Another source of food may be the compost heap. Avoid putting meat, dairy products, eggs or cooked foodstuffs on the compost heap. If rats have become a problem, it would also be wise to avoid composting root vegetables or fruit, all of which will prove a tempting snack for resident rats.

Tidying up overgrown areas of the garden can help to reduce the availability of suitable homes for the rats, but to really succeed at this you will have to work together with your neighbours; you will never get rid of the rats if there is an old mattress stuck in the brambles next door!

Sometimes, no matter what you do, the rats will remain and it may be that you just have to grit your teeth and call in the professionals.

COMMON LIZARDS

You said...

How do you encourage lizards? We have had one or two in the past 10 years, but numbers don't seem to be increasing or decreasing. Robin, Monymusk

Try to give them plenty of nooks and crannies to hang out in. Trouble is they tend to like the kind of places which don't look very pretty. A pile of rubble overgrown with vegetation for example. Or a piece of corrugated tin left in a wild corner. They do like to be able to soak up the sun, too – an old tyre in a rough patch would be great! Quite a challenge in a garden! Richard Burkmar, Horwich

Two years ago we found a common lizard had made a home in our rockery. To encourage it to stay we built a small wood pile at the back of the rockery and the lizard started to make use of it. The next year in March it appeared again and sunbathed regularly throughout last summer. This year, however, no sight of it. Any idea how long they live? Meander, Whittlesey

 Beverley Heath, Wiltshire Wildlife Trust, advises:

The two lizards which frequently live in gardens are the slow-worms (which are dealt with page 200) and viviparous or common lizards. Both give birth to young enclosed in just a membrane from which they emerge almost immediately.

In gardens they need a food supply, protection from predators, shelter and places to warm themselves. Viviparous lizards are very active above ground, hunting in low vegetation for insects, spiders, slugs, snails and worms.

Domestic cats are by far the worst predators in gardens. Others are hedgehogs, blackbirds and grass snakes, about which we would not wish to do anything except provide refuges: piles of logs and stones and plenty of low plants. When attacked, both lizards can break off their tails to escape. These regrow later.

Reptiles are not really 'cold-blooded' but, while active, maintain their body temperature mostly from external sources. Viviparous lizards keep it at about 30°C by basking in direct sun, particularly in early morning and late evening, on stones, logs and so on. These should face east, south and west for use at different times of day. From late October lizards need frost-free places to hibernate, from which viviparous lizards begin to appear around February. This species uses existing deep refuges such as disused animal burrows or partly buried piles of small boulders.

Common, or viviparous, lizards are welcome garden visitors. They can live for up to eight years.

SLOW-WORMS

You said...

When we took on our allotment last year it was very overgrown. We dug most of it over, left part of it covered with black fabric to suppress weeds. Last weekend I pulled the fabric back to reveal at least 20 slow-worms underneath. I moved them to another covered area and am hoping this won't affect them too much. There were also lots of woodlice under the fabric which I believe are a favourite meal for slow-worms.
Bex, Torpoint

Oh, what a joy to behold. We have a healthy slow-worm population, too. They predate heavily on slugs so are the gardener's friend. They don't seem to mind being disturbed too much as long as they have somewhere to shelter and bask. Old carpet and log piles and compost bins are best.
AllotmentBod, Bristol

We get slow-worms here in Oxfordshire due to being surrounded by heathland. I try to leave undisturbed long grass areas for them but I'm afraid the mower has had at least one victim.
HB, Abingdon

The UK breeding population of slow-worms has been estimated at 660,000 – and falling.

Did you know?

● Because they are lizards, slow-worms, unlike snakes, have eyelids.

● Slow worms are one of Europe's most commonly distributed reptiles, found virtually everywhere except the far north, southern Spain and Ireland.

● They can be found as far afield as north-west Asia.

● During hibernation, they sometimes bury themselves under soft substrates, such as wood chips or leaf litter, so just their head is visible.

● During the mating season, female slow-worms may pair themselves with several males. Males sometimes fight each other for the right to mate.

● Young slow-worms spend much of their time in ant nests, feeding on larvae, while their interlocking scales protect them from ant bites.

● Slow worms are protected by the Wildlife and Countryside Act 1981 from being sold, injured or killed.

Sarah Rowlatt, Gloucestershire Wildlife Trust, advises:

Help the helpful slow-worm!

Do slow-worms live in your garden? Although frequently mistaken for snakes, slow-worms are in fact legless lizards, totally harmless to humans and helpful to the gardener. Like all British reptiles, slow-worms are under threat and legally protected, and will gain from your help in the garden. In return, at dusk or after rain, they will emerge from hiding places to feed on slugs, snails, beetles and woodlice.

Unlike snakes, slow-worms are small, slender and glossy, with small mouths and tiny eyes. Females are bronze-brown, males light-brown or silver, and they range in length from 30cm to 50cm. Like all reptiles, slow-worms are cold-blooded and need the sun to become active. They hibernate from October to March, mate in April, and the young are born live around September, 7cm long and around six to twelve in number. As they grow they shed their skins (and if caught will also shed tails!)

Slow-worms naturally inhabit rough grassland, heathland and moorland throughout most of the British Isles. Although very common in southern and western England, they are now scarce in regions of intensive arable farming. Fortunately they thrive in many man-made habitats – town and country gardens, rough areas around farm and industrial buildings, roadside verges and disused railways – providing they are not over-tidied with use of pesticides.

If slow-worms still inhabit your region, do encourage them! Give them piles of rock, rubble or logs to hide under, patches of long grass for hunting, and a sunny compost heap for breeding. Put out corrugated iron, black plastic or a piece of old carpet and on sunny days they will bask beneath it (and can be gently viewed). Remember that they are vulnerable to low-set lawnmowers, disturbance of breeding heaps and occasional predators like stoats and cats.

GRASS SNAKES

At my school we have a large, well-used compost box which has been in use since last year. We're hoping that grass snakes will start using it.
Longshanks, Farnborough

Well, you are in a good part of the country for them I think, but you can only really wait and hope. To be of most benefit for wildlife though, compost heaps shouldn't be disturbed (ie turned) too much. The best times are mid-April to mid-May (after hibernation and before breeding) and October (after breeding but before hibernation). Good luck and... be patient!
Richard Burkmar, Horwich

It's that time of the year again and the 'love/hate' relationship with grass snakes begins. I know they are rare but why do they have to always choose my compost bins to curl up in? They always give me such a fright when I see them curled up on top of the heap or nearly step on them in the vegetable patch! Maybe it relates back to our distant ancestors, but they give me the CREEPS!
orpheus, Tunbridge Wells

Our pond is quite small, but the birds enjoy bathing in it and there's a healthy newt population. Last summer I was surprised to find a grass snake in it. It must have been one metre long. Was it after the newts?
Hilary, Ashford

Paul Newman, Somerset Wildlife Trust, and the Reptile and Amphibian Group for Somerset, advises:

Grass snakes are the most commonly encountered snake, as they are basically a lowland species, with a liking for ponds and other water bodies. Their most favoured diet consists of frogs and newts, as well as small mammals, invertebrates and ground-nesting birds and their eggs, and fish.

Garden ponds with a population of frogs are therefore a prime target for a visit by grass snakes, and they have been known to frequent the same pond for several weeks, gradually depleting the frogs, and any goldfish or koi as well!

As with all native reptiles, grass snakes spend the cold months from late October to March in hibernation, although they may emerge to hunt on mild days, even in mid-winter. They respond to the temperature of their environment, rather than sinking into a deep torpor. Upon emerging from hibernation in late March or April, adults will seek out a mate, and after successful mating, females will brood the eggs internally for a few weeks, and will lay them in early summer.

Preferred sites for laying usually involve decomposing vegetation, such as compost or manure heaps. This again brings them into contact with people, who find the clumps of eggs when removing the material for their gardens. Sadly, often the eggs are crushed, deliberately or accidentally, or left exposed to

The grass snake is Britain's longest snake, reaching over1.2m in length.

fail through cold. Incubation can take from six to ten weeks, depending upon the actual temperature of the site, and the baby snakes break free of the leathery eggshells to make their way in the world. They are entirely self-sufficient from day one, feeding on small invertebrates, often growing fast enough to need to slough their skins several times before autumnal hibernation. They are of course extremely vulnerable at this stage, and a high proportion are preyed upon by predatory animals and birds.

All British snakes are protected by law, and harming or killing them is a criminal offence. Smooth snakes and their habitat are given total protection. It is an offence to disturb or even handle them without a licence.

Although grass snakes are not venomous, they can and do bite, with the risk of an infection, as with any wild animal.

Further information on grass snakes, and other reptiles, can be obtained from local Reptile and Amphibian Groups, which are usually affiliated to county Wildlife Trusts.

Fact file

● The grass snake is Britain's biggest and longest snake, often reaching over 1.2m in length. A long-lived one can grow to almost 1.8m, although this is quite rare. Adult adders and smooth snakes rarely grow more than 61cm to 76cm in length respectively.

● Grass snakes almost invariably have a cream or yellow 'collar' with a black edge, just behind the head, and as most people will look at the head when seeing a snake, this is the easiest feature to identify.

● The ground colour of their skin is usually a greenish-beige or greenish-grey, and can be almost any shade in this range. Black vertical bars are found along the flanks, and small black spots along the back.

● Occasionally a melanistic form is found, which is very dark brown to black all over; the yellow collar in these cases is very hard to see.

UNUSUAL CREATURES

The golden oriole is a magnificent but occasional visitor to Britain's gardens in the summer. One of the great joys of having a wildlife garden is that you never know what might unexpectedly drop in.

You said...

The most spectacular bird I have seen in my garden is a curlew that landed on the lawn last Saturday. They do nest in the more inaccessible parts of this area, but to have such a magnificent bird land in the garden close to the house was a real treat.
Peter Murray, Hamsterley

Pheasant

Mary Porter, Lincolnshire Wildlife Trust, comments:

Among the occupants of the wildlife garden there often lurk unusual creatures. Some are small and are around a lot of the time but go unnoticed. Some are bigger and can cause great excitement when they appear.

Among the latter category are migrant birds. Gardens that are on a migrant route, by the coast or perhaps near a river valley can be lucky to play host to waxwings or even a hoopoe. Large gardens, perhaps with a few trees at the bottom, may hide a woodcock. Gardens can also attract other migrants like the hummingbird hawk moth, which can be seen looking every bit like a miniature hummingbird, hovering from flower to flower, perhaps on buddleja flowers or honeysuckle in the summer.

Less obvious are the invertebrates, which hide in long grass, meadows or 'habitat piles' of logs or stones.

The 'devil's coach-horse' is a rove beetle, which rears up its back end when threatened. It looks alarming, but is quite harmless. Scorpion flies can also look a bit worrying, but are, again, perfectly harmless. They are quite large insects, with mottled wings. The male has a curved abdomen which looks like the sting of a scorpion.

The leopard slug is a large, grey/brown slug with black dots and dashes for markings. Its food can include other slugs! Slugs are mainly vegetarians, but there is another carnivore, the shelled slug, which has the remnants of a shell on its back. It lives mostly underground, often in well-manured soil or compost, looking for its prey, earthworms.

If you have long grass or a meadow, you may have grasshoppers and crickets. After heavy rain in early summer, look out for something about 40cm long that looks like a hair, waving around in the air. It is the thunderworm, a nematode parasite of caterpillars or grasshoppers.

CATS

You said...

My garden is like the M56 for cats to enter and leave their calling cards, although we do not have a cat. Can anyone suggest how I can stop them from depositing their mess, and needlessly killing small birds? cocker, Chester

Fiona Dennis, RHS, advises:

Much-loved pets can be the bane of nearby gardeners, whose plots they use as toilet areas. Holes are scraped in flower and vegetable beds, particularly where the soil is newly cultivated and vulnerable young seedlings can be destroyed. Gravel paths also prove attractive sites for defecation. The local tomcats will also scent-mark their territories by spraying urine on plants, which can scorch foliage. Damage to the bark of trees and shrubs, caused by cats sharpening their claws, is another form of territorial marking. Cats also have a habit of sunbathing on their favourite plant, *Nepeta faassenii*, or ornamental catnip, crushing plants in the process. Problems are most severe in high-density housing areas, where cats are numerous and gardens small.

Repellents: These include products containing pepper powder (Bio Pepper Dust, Secto Pepper Dust) and essential oils (Growing Success Cat Repellent). Such repellents give only short-term protection and need frequent reapplication. Remove any cat excrement before use. A physical repellent is Catscat, which is a mat

Cats are responsible for many millions of bird deaths every year in Britain's gardens. If you have a cat, you can help protect birds by making sure your cat wears a collar with a bell, and by feeding it when birds are at their most active in the garden – around dawn and dusk.

made from a web of soft bendy spikes.

A cat repellent plant, sold under the names of Scardy Cat or *Coleus canina*, is available from Thomson & Morgan, Poplar Lane, Ipswich IP8 3BU, Tel: 01473 680199. The foliage produces an unpleasant smell when touched. This plant can be grown out of doors in the summer but needs frost protection in the winter, and overwintering in a cool greenhouse.

Another kind of repellent which is motion activated is a water jet (such as Scarecrow, sold by

Rockwell products). In both instances, they need to be moved around in order to catch the cats, who will otherwise learn a 'safe' route past the repellent.

Electronic devices: These are mainly sold by mail order so look for advertisements in the RHS magazine *The Garden* and other gardening magazines. Most produce ultrasonic sound (barely audible to human ears) when triggered by a motion sensor. Some cats flee when they come within range, while others, perhaps the more dominant local cats, hold their ground and carry on regardless. The best results are in open gardens where the ultrasound is not baffled by shrubs or fences. Place the speaker at one end of the garden as sound travels away from the device in the direction it is facing.

Deterring cats

Cats roam freely through their territories and are too agile to be excluded by fencing or netting. However:

● Netting may help keep cats away from small areas within the garden.

● Flower borders densely planted with perennials are less appealing as toilet areas – no bare soil to scratch.

● Keep seed rows well watered as cats dislike wet soil, preferring loose, dry earth and mulch.

● Use one or more of the cat deterrents on the market. They fall into two groups: repellents that offend the cat's sense of smell or taste, such as cocoa shell mulch, and electronic scaring devices. Neither type causes harm.

FOCUS ON... TREES

Trees are a vital part of the habitat of Britain's gardens, providing nesting materials and places, food sources, and cover for a great variety of creatures. Sarah Durrant of the RHS provides an overview of the leafy attributes of your garden.

It's great to have trees and hedges in your garden, both for you and the wildlife, but before you leap out there and get planting, there are a number of points you need to consider. First of all, it is important to choose species suited to local conditions, such as soil type and exposure, and those that will not outgrow the space available. Select good quality, healthy trees with a well-balanced branch system. If grafted, the union should be well-healed. Check for obvious signs of damage to the trunk.

not like root disturbance, establish better from container-grown stock. The container should be appropriate to the size of tree. A tall tree growing in a small container will almost certainly be pot-bound. Avoid container-grown specimens that have moss or liverworts on the compost surface as these indicate old stock. Ensure container-grown trees are not pot-bound, taking them out of the container to inspect the root system. Also avoid trees with long circling roots or where thick roots protrude through the drainage holes.

BARE-ROOTED: Young bare-rooted trees one to three years old establish well but are increasingly difficult to obtain compared with container-grown stock. Pre-ordered bare-rooted stock is usually available from about November and should arrive wrapped in polythene to prevent drying out of the fibrous roots. The tree should have a well-developed root system spreading evenly in all directions. Do not buy trees with 'hockey stick' roots, where all the growth is on one side. Early planting will allow some root growth before temperatures rise in the spring.

ROOT-BALLED: Larger semi-mature trees and some evergreens, especially conifers, are available root-balled. This is where the root system has been held in place with fabric and, sometimes, wire mesh. Root-balled trees have usually been

'undercut' (root-pruned) or transplanted several times to encourage the development of a fibrous root system. They often establish better than container-grown trees as they have been grown in soil in the open ground rather than a peat-based commercial compost. Although these trees are relatively expensive, the fibrous root system remains more intact. Buy and plant root-balled trees when dormant, in autumn or early spring, following the same criteria as for bare-root and container-grown trees.

How to plant trees

TIMING: The ideal time to plant a deciduous tree, whether bare-rooted, root-balled or container-grown, is from autumn to early winter. Evergreens also establish well if planted in autumn or early spring. Do not plant in frozen or waterlogged soil and avoid the summer months when trees are likely to dry out. It is often necessary or opportune to buy a container-grown tree or shrub in leaf or blossom when conditions for planting are not ideal. Rather than plant, it is better to place the container in a sheltered position. Water as necessary and occasionally feed with a liquid fertiliser until the best planting time. This will ensure the plant gets off to a good start.

PLANTING PREPARATION: Make the planting hole at least three times

SIZE: Occasionally, large, semi-mature trees are required for screening or other purposes. However, trees less than 1.2m tall, called 'whips' or 'maidens', are much cheaper and establish more quickly, often catching up with larger specimens planted at the same time. The larger the tree, the greater the risk of it failing to establish. Check the supplier's warranty and replacement policy if buying a large, expensive tree.

CONTAINER: Some trees, such as magnolias and eucalyptus, that do

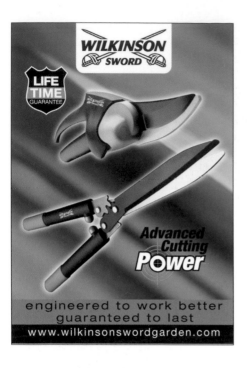

the diameter of the root spread of bare-rooted plants, or three times the diameter of the pot if container-grown. Excavate to about the depth of one spade blade. The diameter of the hole is more important than the depth as the majority of root activity takes place in the top 30cm of the soil. Fork over the base and sides of the hole to break through smeared surfaces and aid drainage, but do not dig over the base because the disturbed soil will settle, resulting in the tree being too deep once planted. In grassed areas, round planting holes are easier to mow around, but square planting holes aid root penetration at the corners on heavy soils. A square hole within a mowing circle combines the two.

PLANTING DEPTH: Planting too deeply prevents essential air movement to the root system and makes the lower trunk vulnerable to disease. The point where the roots flare out from the trunk should be level with the surrounding soil. This point will be very clear on bare-rooted trees but on container-grown stock scrape away the compost from the top of the root ball to reveal this point.

Place a few spadefuls of the soil back in the centre of the planting hole and use your heel to form a low cone. Sit the tree on this cone and ensure the roots are evenly spread out. Do not add organic matter to the planting hole as it decomposes causing the tree to sink. Check whether the tree is sitting too low by placing a cane

A hosepipe with holes in, planted under a new tree, will help aeration.

across the hole. Add more soil under the root ball to raise it.

On fertile soils it is not necessary to add additional organic matter and may be counterproductive as it discourages the roots from growing out into the surrounding soil.

It is not beneficial to apply fertiliser until the following growing season. However, an inoculant of mycorrhizal fungi (increasingly available from good garden centres) is often considered to help trees establish in poor soils. It may form a symbiotic relationship with the feeder roots until natural soil organisms can take over.

Replace the backfill in the hole and work it around the roots, gently shaking the stem to settle the soil but ensuring the planting depth is not altered. Firm gently from the outside of the hole, working towards the tree to remove any air pockets, taking care not to damage the roots. Do not firm too heavily on clay soils as this may compact the ground and impede drainage. Avoid forming an inward sloping saucer as the accumulation of excess water and debris may, over time, result in stem or collar rot. When completed, fork the surface over lightly and water well.

A pruning saw is good for coppicing trees. You should, however, wear gloves!

You said...

I want to remove a silver birch tree suffering from dieback. Can a new birch tree be planted in the same place if the old roots are removed? What is the best time for planting?
ed, Royston

I have recently discovered that an unknown plant which grew from a stray seed in one of my pots is a silver birch tree. It is now three years old and 6ft tall. I can't accommodate a tree which could eventually reach 70ft or more in my tiny garden so I want it to go to a good home. I have a message out to my local preservation society but does anyone have any other ideas who might be able to give this beautiful tree the space it deserves?
Georgie, Enfield

If you would like to keep the tree, you could coppice it. Every few years (when it gets too big), cut it right down to a foot or so. New shoots will regenerate from the 'stool'. Individual coppice stools can last for many hundreds of years in this way – much longer than individual trees. It's a management technique for broad-leaved trees that's been used for millennia.
Richard Burkmar, Horwich

Stumps, suckers and coppicing

Many species of trees have the ability to regenerate from stumps left after coppicing (the art of cutting of trees and shrubs to ground level allowing vigorous regrowth and a sustainable supply of timber for future generations), producing shoot growth from the stump itself or suckers from the roots. Several months may elapse between cutting back and the first signs of regeneration.

Many living trees and shrubs may produce sucker growths from their roots. Some trees are naturally shallow-rooting, but tree roots may develop nearer the surface where there are difficult growing conditions, such as a high water table or an impervious subsoil, deterring deeper root development. Near-surface roots are more likely to produce sucker growths. In grassed areas where roots are surfacing, it is possible to raise the soil level slightly by up to 5-7.5cm. Between October and February, strip off the turf, raise the soil level and replace the turf. Do not be tempted to raise the soil too much as this may lead to the progressive deterioration and eventual loss of the tree.

Often suckers may appear following root damage resulting from incautious digging or forking around trees or shrubs, or following lawn spiking. They can also appear where roots are severed during excavations, or where roots break the surface of a lawn as they increase in girth and suffer mower damage. Sucker growths are often a nuisance in lawns or appear between paving stones, and they may often force their way through bituminous paths. If they develop in out-of-the-way situations and remain unnoticed they will in time grow to tree size. Trees that most often fall into this category are poplars, flowering cherries, ornamental and fruiting plums, sumach, lilacs and false acacias.

Sarah Durrant, RHS, advises:

Any tree or shrub will suffer some degree of stress when uprooted, resulting in a check in growth. However, the shock of transplanting will be lessened and the plant given the best chance of survival if the suggestions set out below are followed. It must be borne in mind that attempting to move any established tree or shrub is taking a risk, however carefully the transplanting is undertaken and that there are some plants in particular (eg *Rosa*, *Magnolia*, *Rosmarinus*) that do not, as a rule, establish well, or even survive, after transplanting.

The best time
Deciduous plants such as *Forsythia* and *Philadelphus* can be moved at any time from late October to mid-March. Evergreens, such as camellias and rhododendrons, are best moved during October when the soil still holds some warmth, or late March to April when it is beginning to warm up after the winter. This allows the roots to re-establish themselves quickly, essential with evergreens that carry their leaves throughout the year and can be badly damaged by desiccation (drying out) if the roots are not active. This is particularly likely in periods of drying winds in spring.

Preparing the plant
The most successful way of moving trees and shrubs is to start preparations a year in advance. At some time during the dormant season (November to February), dig a trench one spade blade wide, following the guidelines under the section 'Lifting and moving' (right), but severing only the side roots. Fill the trench with sharp sand. This

operation encourages trees and shrubs to repair damaged roots and to grow new fibrous feeding roots into the sharp sand. On completion of the transplanting one year later, these fibrous roots will be vital in helping the plants to re-establish quickly and minimising the shock of root loss.

Whether or not you delay transplanting for a year, tidy up the plant by pruning out any old, worn-out wood but do not prune hard. Nutrients are stored over winter in young branches and stems, and hard pruning will deprive the shrubs or trees of the nourishment essential for early growth and good recovery. Where necessary, further pruning or shaping can be done once the plant is well re-established.

Make an exploratory excavation on one side of the plant to determine the extent of root spread. The main area covered by feeding roots is usually along, and extending beyond,

Our native wildlife hedge-mix mimics the species invasion of a typical country hedge over the centuries and will host a wide range of insects, animals and birds to bring added colour & life to your garden.

Pace out the length of your intended hedge and let us quote you for sufficient plants to create your own corner of the country in your back garden.

Alternatively, send £2.00 (2005-06) for our detailed, highly readable, illustrated and unputdownable catalogue listing the hundreds of native & ornamental trees & shrubs that we grow at our Cumbrian nurseries in the Howgill Fells...........

the spread of the branches. Larger specimens may have root masses of 90-120cm or more in diameter and 40-45cm or more in depth. Loosely tie in any spreading branches before lifting. Some thicker, deeply penetrating roots may need to be severed cleanly with a sharp knife or secateurs. Ideally, the tree or shrub should be lifted as a large root mass or ball of fine fibrous roots with soil adhering to them. If a shrub lifts with few or no fibrous roots then it may not re-establish satisfactorily.

Lift the plant carefully, causing as little damage to roots as possible and minimum disturbance to the soil ball. Place on a piece of damp sacking or similar material for transporting and keep the roots covered to avoid drying out by wind or sun. Where possible, lift and replant in one operation.

Particular care is needed in moving established specimens of plants liable to sucker, such as flowering cherries, since, if the thicker roots are damaged, suckers may be produced at the damaged point.

If plants are to be moved to another garden or cannot be replanted for some time, first spread leaf litter, well rotted compost or processed shredded bark on the sacking. Set the plant on this, then work more of the material over and around the roots before drawing the sacking around the stem and tying it firmly (but not so tightly that the bark is damaged). If it cannot be replanted for some time, place the plant in a cool situation out of direct sun or in dappled shade, pile leaf litter around and over the wrapped roots, untie the branches, and keep it well watered. In hot spells, evergreens and conifers will benefit from light overhead spraying in the evening or early morning. This treatment is particularly useful if you are planning a move in late spring and wish to take valued plants with you. They can be lifted in advance when still dormant and with care, can remain preserved in this way until the following

autumn when weather and soil conditions are suitable for planting.

Replanting

Check the size of the prepared hole, making sure that roots can be spread out to their full extent and to the same depth as before. To check depth, place the tree or shrub in the hole, then lie a cane across, matching it to the soil level mark on the plant. If necessary, take out the plant and add or remove soil as required. Then place the plant in the hole, carefully arranging it to achieve the best effect. Large plants and those being moved to windy sites may require staking at this point. Begin working the soil in between the roots, which should be well spread out. Firm carefully to eliminate air pockets as you fill in the planting hole and also break down the sides of the hole so that as the roots grow, they are not checked by a wall of firmer soil. Aim not to plant your tree into the same soil in which any previous tree of that species became diseased. The disease may get passed on to your new tree.

Aftercare

All plants should be watered in well immediately after planting to settle soil and fill large air pockets. It may be necessary, in a dry spring, to continue watering transplanted trees and shrubs once or twice a week if the weather remains dry. Spray with water occasionally if buds are slow in breaking, particularly during a period of cold, drying easterly winds. Cover the planting area 5cm deep with a mulch of wood chippings or other organic material to reduce the surface evaporation of soil moisture.

Evergreens need particular attention after planting to prevent them drying out and should be sprayed overhead during warm or dry weather until well established. They can suffer from drought even in the winter months when newly planted.

DANGEROUS TREES

You said...

I have an ash tree under threat from an insurance company. It has been there for more years than the house it is supposedly threatening. I have offered to have it crown- and root-pruned but the insurance company is still not accepting. Has anyone any experience how to proceed? I do live in a densely populated area which is becoming denser by the minute with the new Arsenal Stadium, thus losing more trees and more open space – and I feel very strongly the need to maintain (responsibly) as many trees as possible in the area. Can anyone give me some advice?
Cawky, London

Perhaps you could contact the Arboricultural Association for advice? Wild Woman, Whitton

Contact your local tree section at the council who should be able to advise you. We also have an ash at the bottom of our garden and many would like it felled. Luckily, it has a conservation order on it!
janet, London

USEFUL CONTACTS

THE TREE ADVICE TRUST: Alice Holt Lodge, Wrecclesham, Farnham, Surrey GU10 4LH; Tel: 09065 161147 (£1.50/min); www.treehelp.info.

THE ARBORICULTURAL ASSOCIATION'S DIRECTORY OF CONSULTANTS AND CONTRACTORS: The Secretariat, Arboricultural Association, Ampfield House, Romsey, Hants SO51 9PA; Tel: 01794 368717; www.trees.org.uk.

BUILDING RESEARCH ESTABLISHMENT: Bucknells Lane, Garston, Watford, Herts WD25 9XX; Tel: 01923 664000; www.bre.co.uk.

ROYAL INSTITUTION OF CHARTERED SURVEYORS: 12 Great George Street, Parliament Square, London SW1P 3AD; Tel: 0870 333 1600; www.rics.org.

Trees and the Law

● A tree (shrub or climber) normally belongs to the land on which it is growing, regardless of how it got there and is the property and responsibility of the owner of the land. The owner may be liable should the tree cause any damage to neighbouring property.

● Before taking steps to remove or reduce in size any tree thought to pose a risk to property, it is advisable to make sure it is not protected by a Tree Preservation Order (TPO). Trees that make a significant contribution to the amenities of the area may be covered by a TPO served by the Local Planning Authority whose permission must be obtained before any protected tree is pruned or felled. Similar constraints apply in a conservation area.

● Where there is any doubt regarding trees near property, professional advice should be sought. Some aspects of tree assessment, such as identity, condition, age, potential size and growth rate may require the specialised knowledge of a qualified arboriculturist.

● A structural engineer should be able to advise on soil characteristics, building construction and on any structural damage encountered. Chartered building surveyors can advise on structural damage, potential damage or the construction of new buildings and extensions near to existing trees.

It would be wrong to assume automatically that all trees growing close to buildings are potentially hazardous. Where structural damage occurs it would be equally wrong to blame the close presence of trees without careful assessment of the site. Other factors may be responsible for damage to the structure.

William Denne,
RHS, advises:

Trees growing in close proximity to houses can pose problems in several ways. On clay soils during periods of drought they may further dry out the soil to the extent that it shrinks, resulting in the foundations becoming displaced due to lack of support, leading to structural cracking, particularly around windows and doorways. Conversely, the removal of large trees that have previously kept the soil in a permanently drier condition may cause swelling or soil heave (the reverse of shrinkage).

Roots may penetrate and block cracked and damaged drains, resulting eventually in the bursting of the drain. The subsequent flow of water into the soil may wash soil particles away causing a cavity. Where there are large cavities in the soil there is no support for the foundations, which may then fail to adequately support the building at that point. Modern systems are normally well sealed and have flexible joints installed where root growth or soil movement is likely.

The spread of branches impedes light and in time may cause damage to roofs and guttering. Physical damage may also occur where a tree is growing very close to a building or boundary wall, and as the root or stem increases in girth there is actual contact with the structure. In these circumstances light buildings such as garages and porches are most likely to be at risk. Root penetration of brickwork is only likely to occur where the brickwork is old and crumbling due to breakdown of mortar or poor quality bricks. Roots, particularly of shallow rooting trees such as *Prunus* may also disturb paving and other hard surfaces.

Damage to foundations due to subsidence and heave

Damage to the foundations of dwelling houses and similar buildings or structures where the foundations are relatively shallow can occur as a result of the root action of nearby vigorous-growing trees, both evergreen and deciduous.

Damage of this type appears to be confined to shrinkable clay soils, and some shrinkable peat soils, particularly in areas where seasonal rainfall is low and summer temperatures high, such as with the London and Essex clays.

During periods of summer drought, clay soils naturally lose moisture, shrink and crack. This is greatly increased where a large, fast-growing tree is nearby, taking up moisture from the clay and transpiring it through its leaves.

If a tree causes shrinkage of the soil near a house, this will occur at the side where the tree is growing. The weight of the building may then push the foundations on that side downwards and outwards. Where repeated year after year the foundations, increasingly lacking the support of the soil on the tree-facing side, subside and collapse outwards. This will cause distortion and outward movement of the walls at that point, with structural cracking and the loss of alignment of doors and windows. Winter rains will swell the clay and close the soil cracks to a greater or lesser extent each winter, but the weight of the building means there is a slow outward movement of the clay.

Root spread

Soil type, situation, soil moisture levels and relationship to other trees nearby are all variable factors that can influence root spread and development. There are also variable factors of tree habit with the extremes of tall and fastigiate, and low and weeping. In view of such variables, it would seem unwise to equate the root spread of a tree with its height.

Only a limited amount of information has been published on the subject, but it seems that roots can often extend for a radius wider

than the height of the tree. In any case, unless the conditions around a tree are uniform, (unusual in a garden), the extent of the root system is likely to follow an irregular pattern and be very difficult to predict.

Assessing the risks

In attempting to assess potential risks to a property, the type, age and construction materials of buildings must be considered. There appears to be more risk with buildings up to four storeys constructed before the 1950s, as they will frequently have foundations only about 50cm deep, whereas, the foundations of later buildings will usually be 1m or more.

The type of soil and its degree of moistness may vary considerably; clays with a high plasticity level appear to pose the greatest risk. The nature of the surrounding area, what other trees and shrubs are planted there, whether the soil is subject to drying out or the presence of a ground water flow helping to keep it constantly moist, are all factors that must be considered. The type, age and health of the trees in the immediate vicinity are also

Removing limbs from trees

Tree limbs may need removing or shortening for aesthetic considerations or they may pose a hazard to people, buildings, vehicles or the tree itself. Prior to undertaking any work it is essential to ascertain if a Tree Preservation Order (TPO) is in place or if the tree is in a Conservation Area. If either is the case then permission must be sought from your local council before any work can begin. Potentially dangerous limbs can in theory be removed without permission but the penalties for breaching the legislations, inadvertently or not, can be severe.

SAFETY is of prime importance when working with trees, so make an honest appraisal of your capabilities, assess the area in which any branches may fall and erect warning signs or barricades if necessary before beginning. If in any doubt engage a professionally qualified tree surgeon or aboriculturist. Branches should not be cut back flush to the main trunk or left with a large snag as these will result in excessive dieback or poor callusing and healing. The ideal point is immediately outside the 'collar', which is normally visible as a distinct bulge – occasionally continuing all the way around the branch. The 'collar' may extend some way out but should not be cut into even if a 'snag' appears to remain.

LARGER BRANCHES should be cut back in stages to reduce the risk of damage to the main stem and collar. Begin with an undercut, cutting upwards halfway through the limb following with a downwards severing cut between 2.5-5cm further out. Additional pairs of cuts may be required before a clean final cut can be made resulting in a stub with an intact collar.

MOST TREES ARE BEST PRUNED IN LATE WINTER but some, such as hornbeans, pears and cheries, should have limbs removed in mid- to late summer.

WOUND SEALANTS and dressings are not generally used except where the short-term protection afforded may be some defence against fresh wound parasites such as silver leaf fungus. Many trees (eg birches and maples) exude fluid or 'bleed' prodigiously following pruning in late winter or early spring. This is unlikely to have any deleterious effect and may even be of benefit by preventing the entry of harmful parasites.

variable factors. The greatest risk is from young, vigorously growing trees. As they reach maturity their moisture demands decrease and, therefore, so do the risks.

The distance from tree to property is also significant. A high proportion of recorded instances of damage relate to trees positioned some 10m or less from a property, but only a few recorded instances result from trees standing 20m or more from a property. (See the publication *Tree Roots and Buildings* listed on page 279.) Included are details of root spread, and maximum tree-to-damage distance recorded for commonly planted trees, during the Kew Tree Root Survey (1971 to 1979).

Poplars account for much of the recorded damage, but reports indicate that various other fast-growing trees, such as lime, willow, oak and elm, can also cause such problems. Even ornamental conifers, vigorous-growing shrubs and climbers planted close to buildings may contribute towards such damage. Maximum tree-to-damage distance recorded for willows (*Salix* spp.), for instance, is 40m.

TREES IN CONTAINERS

By introducing potted trees and shrubs into areas of your garden that won't support earthbound trees, you increase the amount of habitat available for wildlife.

Tree seed in containers

The easiest way of sowing tree seed is to do so in containers.

● Choose a free-draining soil-less compost for seed quick to germinate and a loam-based compost for seed slow to germinate.

● Cover the seed with fine grit or perlite to a depth of 6mm.

● Place the seed where it will receive the appropriate minimum temperature, eg a cold frame or greenhouse.

● Transplant the seedlings as soon as they are large enough to handle and harden off. It is best to use rootrainers or deep pots, and plant out the seedlings as soon as possible. This will avoid too much root disturbance and prevent the roots from becoming pot-bound, which will hinder establishment.

Sarah Durrant, RHS, advises:

Trees in containers can be used to frame doorways, provide a focal point and are ideally suited to small gardens, courtyard gardens or patios. Problems associated with tree roots or suckering from plants such as sumach can be avoided by growing trees in containers. Ideal subjects for containers include trees suitable for topiary, such as yew, holly and box, and fruit trees on dwarfing rootstocks such as M26 or M9. They are useful for cultivating tender plants such as citrus or olives, which can be moved to frost-free conditions in winter.

In most cases growing a tree in a container will restrict its ultimate size. It is best to avoid larger, fast-growing trees except for shorter-term planting, as they may become too large and prone to toppling over. Trees tolerant of coppicing are another possibility including tulip trees, eucalyptus and willows.

Containers: Terracotta pots provide weight for stability but should be frost resistant. Lighter plastic pots are better if plants require moving around. Pot plants up in

stages, aiming for a minimum final pot size of 45cm if the plant is to be moved around. Larger pots can be used where trees are to remain *in situ* all year round.

Compost: A loam-based compost such as John Innes No 3 is best in most cases and provides weight for better stability. For plants requiring ericaceous soils, use ericaceous John Innes composts or an ericaceous multipurpose compost. Place 5cm of crocks or gravel over drainage holes and raise pots on feet in winter to avoid waterlogging.

Care: Container-grown trees are more prone to drying out and need regular and thorough watering. Several waterings may be needed to wet the full depth of compost. Use rainwater for ericaceous plants, although tap water is better than none if you run out. Apply a controlled-release fertiliser at the start of the growing season or use a liquid feed at regular intervals.

Refresh the compost in spring by removing 5cm of dry, loose compost near the surface and replacing it with some fresh compost mixed with some controlled-release fertiliser. If trees are tolerant of root disturbance, every three to five years remove the tree from its pot and tease out the roots, loosening the old compost. After trimming the larger roots, repot in fresh compost.

HEDGE PLANTING

You said...

Having just planted 200 blueberry bushes, we are struggling with very strong winds. As we want to attract birds and insects (yes we will net the berries) we have planted native hedgerows but these will take a while – any ideas?
susanp, Redruth

At Duchy College they plant non-native species as they grow fast, then when the native species have grown, they cut the non-native species down. So the non-native species protect the native species!
Shirley, Camborne

In order to establish a hornbeam hedge I put up baffles of green netting – sold as windbreak netting. The hedge took off and I was able to lose the windbreaks after a year and a half. swifty, Hurcott

Tony Dickerson, RHS, advises:

Hedges are wonderful ways of delineating borders in your garden, or between you and your neighbour's garden, and they provide a wealth of opportunity for wildlife, too.

The RHS provides a very useful advisory leaflet on hedge preparation and planting, which for reasons of space is reproduced here. We publish many such leaflets on all types of subjects: you can find them by visiting www.rhs.org.uk.

The ideal time to plant a deciduous shrub, whether bare-rooted, root-balled or container-grown, is from autumn to early winter. Evergreens also establish well if planted in autumn or early spring. Do not plant in frozen or waterlogged soil and avoid the summer months when plants are likely to dry out.

Ground preparation

Dig over an area 60-90cm wide and one spit (or one spade blade) deep. Do not double-dig because the disturbed soil will resettle, resulting in the hedging being too deep once planted. Instead, lightly fork over the base and sides of the trench to break through smeared surfaces and aid drainage. Remove all weeds. For long runs of hedging it may be necessary to use a rotovator to prepare the soil. This should be done while the soil is relatively dry in early autumn, especially on heavy clay soils, otherwise the rotors are likely to smear the soil beneath the level of cultivation, impeding winter drainage.

Do not add organic matter to the bottom of the trench as it decomposes causing the shrub to sink. On fertile soils it is usually unnecessary to add additional organic matter at all and may be counterproductive as it discourages the roots from growing out into the surrounding soil. However, on sandy or heavy clay soils, organic material such as garden compost, or a proprietary tree and shrub planting mix, can be incorporated into the backfill (the soil dug out from the hole) to improve soil structure or spread over the soil surface and lightly forked or rotovated in. It is not beneficial to apply any fertiliser until the following growing season.

On poorly drained soils, fork into the bottom of the trench horticultural grit and composted bark and form a ridge about 15cm high to plant into. Do not add organic matter or grit to the bottom of a trench, as this merely creates a sump. Soils that become waterlogged in winter may require a permanent drainage system.

Planting

Planting too deeply prevents essential air movement to the root system and makes the lower stem vulnerable to disease. The point where the roots flare out from the stem should be level with the surrounding soil. This point will be very clear on bare-rooted stock, but, on container-grown plants scrape away the compost from the top of the root ball to reveal this point.

Use secateurs to remove any badly split or torn roots. Soak bare-rooted hedging for about 30 minutes prior to planting. If planting is delayed, plant the transplants in a temporary hole in a piece of spare ground and keep watered as necessary.

Replace the backfill in the hole and work it around the roots, gently shaking the stem to settle the soil but ensuring the planting depth is not altered. Using your heel, firm gently to remove any air pockets but take care not to damage the roots. Do not firm too heavily on clay soils as this may compact the ground and impede drainage. When completed, fork the surface over lightly and water well.

Many pot-raised hedging plants are planted too deeply in their pots, and do best if surplus compost is removed, so that they can be planted with the roots just below soil level. Secondary adventitious roots are common in pot-grown shrubs, originating from the buried part of the trunk. These should be pruned off close to their point of origin.

Thoroughly tease out the roots. Do not be afraid to open up a congested root ball

using a sharpened piece of cane to disentangle the roots if necessary. If this is not done, the roots will frequently fail to grow out into the soil and the shrub will fail to establish. Prune back to the edge of the root ball any circling roots. Damaged roots should also be trimmed back.

When planting it is always advisable to remove the covering from the root ball. Left on, hessian and similar materials may take several years to decay, particularly in light, sandy soils. Establishment failures can occur where root wrappings are left in place after planting. However, some suppliers will not guarantee to replace where wrappings are removed.

Hedge protection

Small hedging plants do not need staking or other support but in exposed sites new hedges benefit from a temporary windbreak for two or three years until they are established. Use a suitable fabric netting or plastic mesh on the windward side attached to strong stakes, firmly driven into the ground. The top of the stake should be at least 15cm above the tops of the plants and the barrier positioned at least 60cm away from the hedge.

In some areas it is necessary to protect young hedging from damage by rabbits or other animals. If this is necessary use wire netting secured to stakes with the bottom of the netting sunk 15cm below ground.

HEDGE LAYING AND MAINTENANCE

You said...

I planted some small saplings as a hedge just over a year ago – a mix of hazel, dogwood and other natives – but I don't want it to grow more than about 3ft high. How do I ensure that it remains short but bushy and how long will it take to establish into a proper thick hedge? Can anyone recommend some good flowers that will grow in the base? Carolynn, Devizes – 11 Apr 2005

Cut your hedge back now to about six inches lower than you want it to be. It will look a bit bare for a week or two, but will soon shoot. Then clip – the more often you do it the bushier it will become. But it will shade out plants at the roots, so it is best to plant perennials a short distance away. richard, Bristol – 23 Apr 2005

When cutting your hedge cut it at a very slight angle so it narrows the higher you go. This will allow light to reach the lower parts of the hedge. Noel, Okehampton – 12 May 2005

Hedge laying is a skilled activity. It is also potentially dangerous requiring appropriate equipment and safety wear. Many agricultural colleges and the BTCV run courses (Tel: 01491 821600). The National Hedge Laying Society lists training courses and publishes a list of hedgelaying contractors (Tel: 01926 814196) http://members.lycos.co.uk/hedgelaying/nhls7.htm.

Royal Horticultural Society

Tony Dickerson, RHS, advises:

Over time hedges deteriorate, especially if they are neglected. With a very poor hedge it may be necessary to coppice the stems or grub it out and replant. Where growth is good but thinning near the base, laying will rejuvenate a hedge by encouraging new growth. Hawthorn is the best species for laying but most of the common deciduous hedge shrubs such as ash, blackthorn, elm, field maple and hazel are also suitable.

There are several regional styles but the general principles are similar. Hedge laying is undertaken in winter. The hedge should be allowed to grow to about 2.5-5m in height with main stems 5-10cm thick at the base. Stems larger than about 20cm, awkwardly shaped or out of line should be removed. Work usually takes place on the ditch side of the hedge.

Renovating your hedge

Type and time: Many hedges respond well to renovation (eg beech, hawthorn, holly, hornbeam). Most conifer hedges cannot be hard pruned as they do not re-shoot from old wood, so they require regular light trimming (an exception to the rule is yew, which can be cut back hard). Renovate deciduous hedges in mid-winter, evergreens in mid-spring. If possible, feed the hedge well in the season prior to renovation.

How much to take off: Hedges which respond well to hard pruning can be reduced by 50% in height and width. Because hard pruning removes many growth buds it is best carried out in stages. If reducing both the height and width of the hedge, cut back the top and one side in the first year, and cut the other side the following year. If recovery is poor, delay the second cut for another 12 months. Conifer hedge renovation is limited to tying-in branches to cover holes.

Side growth is cut away from the lower stems and debris cleared from the bottom of the hedge. Elder should be removed and the stump dug out as it will not lay. The main upright stems (known as pleachers) are cut almost through near the ground on the opposite side of the face to the direction of lay and pushed over at an angle of approximately 35 degrees in the direction of the rising slope. Stakes of hazel or ash are driven into the hedge line every 40cm and the pleachers woven between. Binders or heathers of coppiced hazel, sweet chestnut or willow are then twisted around the top of the stakes to secure the pleachers. The cut stubs of the pleachers are trimmed to keep the stools from rotting. The gap at the end of a laid hedge is usually filled with unwanted pleachers cut from the hedge. Properly trimmed, a well-laid hedge may last 50 years or more before it starts to thin at the base.

Maintaining a good shape: Use garden lines tightly stretched between stakes as a template. Ensure the hedge tapers slightly towards the top, so that optimum light reaches the lower parts of the hedge.

Aftercare: It is essential to mulch and feed hedges after renovation. Spread a nutrient-rich mulch, such as garden compost or well-rotted manure around the hedge after pruning. Alternatively apply a general fertiliser, such as Growmore, over the root zone at the first signs of new growth. Water the hedge thoroughly during dry spells in the first growing season following renovation.

You said...

Does anyone have any tips about making living willow fences?
Denman, Aboyne

Relatively simple – cut your willow diagonally (1.5metres-ish), leave to stand in water at least a week (2 or 3 if possible) and then insert firmly in ground 10cm+ depth. Tie together so there is little wind disturbance... it's probably best to do it between March and May but I have seen willow take from almost any time of year – just make sure you want it where you put it, because once it gets going there's no stopping it.
Robin, Monymusk

COURSES AND WORKSHOPS ON WORKING WITH WILLOW ARE RUN BY:

THE BASKETMAKERS' ASSOCIATION
Isobel Edge (Hon. Sec.), Highlanes Farm, Brockton, Eccleshall, Staffordshire ST21 6LY; email: isobeledge@hotmail.com.

THE CENTRE FOR ALTERNATIVE TECHNOLOGY
Machynlleth, Powys, Wales SY20 9AZ; Tel: 01654 705 950; www.cat.org.uk.

THE HENRY DOUBLEDAY RESEARCH ASSOCIATION
Ryton Organic Gardens, Coventry CV8 3LG; Tel: 02476 303 517; www.hdra.org.uk.

LIVING WILLOW
25 Chalk Road, Walpole St Peter, Wisbech, Cambridgeshire PE14 7PN; Tel: 01945 584 774; www.livingwillow.com.

THE ROYAL HORTICULTURAL SOCIETY
Wisley, Woking, Surrey GU23 6QB; Tel: 01483 224 234; www.rhs.org.uk.

WILLOW POOL DESIGNS
9 Weston Houses, Dove Nest Lane, Endmoor, Nr. Kendal, Cumbria LA8 0HA; Tel: 01539 567 056; www.geocities.com/willowpool.

Living garden structures – such as arbours and tunnels – using willow are easy and fun to create.

Royal
Horticultural
Society

Helen Bostock, RHS, advises:

Willow stem harvesting begins in autumn and may continue through to early spring; projects are carried out during these months. Some specialist growers supply instructions along with suitable plant material. Store live stems with the bases immersed in water until needed.

Choose a part of the garden that is naturally moist and sunny, avoiding areas with open drains. Ideally clear grass away from the base of the structure before planting. The staves (willow stems) can be pushed 30cm or more into the ground making a hole first for thicker stems. Arbours, tunnels, wigwams and living fences can be created, incorporating simple or complicated weaving designs.

Any point where stems cross may pressure graft together. Encourage this by tying joins together with garden string or thin pieces of willow. Shoots will sprout from the staves inserted into the ground. Trimming can be carried out in the summer or left until winter. New growth can also be woven in to fill gaps in the design or strengthen the structure. Use a basic weave to take the new shoots under and over the framework branches. Weaving is best left to the winter, as the shoots are very brittle in the summer and liable to snap.

To keep down weeds apply a deep mulch of bark chippings or composted bark around the staves, or plant through a weed-control membrane. Water the site thoroughly in dry spells. Although willow will grow in most soils, a moisture-retentive soil and sunny site will encourage more vigorous growth.

If woven willow baskets are intended to hold soil, line the weaving on the inside with plastic or fabric before filling with soil to make the woven stems last longer.

Alternatives to willow for living bowers and arches include lime (*Tilia* spp.), whitebeam (*Sorbus aria*) and laburnum. These are best planted as young trees and initially trained over a framework. New shoots are tied in as they grow and, if a clear stem is required, lower laterals are progressively removed.

Once the plants are established, any training supports can be removed. The leading shoot can be woven back and outward-growing shoots trimmed on an annual basis.

WHERE TO GET YOUR WILLOW CUTTINGS

R GOODWIN & SON
Ashman's Farm, Kelvedon, Colchester, Essex CO5 9BT;
Tel: 01376 573 236; Email: ashmansfarm@aol.com.

AF HILL & SONS
Dunstall Court, Astwood Lane, Feckenham, Nr. Redditch,
Worcestershire B96 6QH; Tel: 01527 892 472;
www.willow1.fsbusiness.co.uk.

EDGAR WATTS LTD
Willow Works, Bungay, Suffolk NR35 1BW;
Tel: 01986 892 751; Email: edgarwatts@talk21.com.

WEST WALES WILLOWS
Martinique Farm, Wolfscastle, Haverfordwest,
Pembrokeshire SA62 5DY; Tel: 01437 741 714;
www.westwaleswillows.co.uk.

WILDLIFE CORRIDORS

Try and find out where local populations of species occur near your garden. By adapting your own garden to their needs, you can help provide them with a 'stepping stone' from one habitat to the next, increasing their chance of survival and diversity.

Rupert Higgins, Avon Wildlife Trust, advises:

Both towns and countryside can be inhospitable for wildlife in modern Britain. Many species survive in isolated pockets of habitat, separated by kilometres of farmland or development.

Some species are naturally adapted to this situation, for example the pond skaters and water boatmen that appear in new ponds almost immediately. Other species, however, are not adapted to cross even narrow barriers of unsuitable habitat, and for these wildlife corridors are vital.

The best wildlife corridors have long, unbroken belts of high-quality habitat – for example a wooded stream providing wetland and woodland corridors, or a dense hedge connecting two woodlands. Sadly, few such corridors survive in our crowded island, but many species can utilise discontinuous or scattered pockets of habitat – wildlife stepping stones rather than wildlife corridors.

How does this affect the wildlife gardener? If we wish to attract animals to our garden, we have to be aware of wildlife networks in our area and tailor our aspirations accordingly. Even a perfectly crafted wildflower meadow, for example, will not attract marbled white butterfly if the nearest herb-rich grassland is kilometres away. A more subtle effect is that if you succeed in establishing a population of a species in your garden, in the long term it will suffer if isolated from any other population through the lack of a suitable corridor – some of these effects are felt over decades, rather than months.

Thinking in a wider context, your garden can have beneficial effects well beyond its own boundaries. For example, your patch of meadow may allow butterflies to move between two nature reserves, or the nearest railway cutting and your local allotments. Make your garden a wildlife stepping stone – it will benefit you, your neighbours and wildlife.

ME, MY GARDEN AND WILDLIFE

SIR JOHN BURNETT

Twenty years into retirement, the area is smaller and vegetables are out. Labour-saving has become important so that trees, shrubs and perennials are the order of the day, hoeing is rare, committed weeding is low on the priorities and lawn-mowing is higher and less frequent. This still maintains enough colour and seasonal change to please us and provide a visually enjoyable, reasonably tidy backdrop for tea in the garden or parties.

But there is a huge bonus: it gives a great boost to wildlife – itinerant foxes visit more often, there are more nesting sites and berries for birds, insects seem to be on the increase and there's plenty of woody litter, especially since I just heap up woody prunings and amputations and a larger range of self-introduced weeds. Following the life cycle of the weeds is fascinating and it has been a special pleasure, for example, to find that, as in Scandinavia, red dead nettle does exist as two distinct races – a spring flowering and an autumn flowering kind. Then we've doubled the range and number of garden birds. There are now four pairs of nesting blue tits, two of blackbirds and two of thrushes and one of hedge sparrow, or dunnock, to add to the robin and wren that we had before. The number of queen wasps seeking a site for their nests in the spring seems to have increased as have the numbers and kinds of bumblebees. Kinds and number of ants have multiplied generously in the less-frequently-cut lawn and these attract foraging green-spotted woodpeckers – which we never saw before.

The diversity of toadstools, too, is more apparent and having been a professional mycologist I find I have greatly increased the number of fungi, slime moulds and the insects that feed upon them, many of them pretty small. So, an especial personal pleasure is to search the garden for wildlife at the level of a strong lens or simple microscope, say 30x or 40x magnification. The beauty and diversity of the microfungi that develop on the bark of a discarded cutting or the unbelievably rich world that is revealed when dead inflorescences or discarded bark are kept for a few hours in a

Now retired, Sir John Burnett was chairman of the National Biodiversity Network Trust, and vice-president of The Wildlife Trusts.

moist, enclosed container takes some believing and leaves one astounded – wonderfully coloured sporangia of slime moulds or their creeping, macroamoeboid plasmodia; an incredible diversity of sporangial types of microfungi, and veritable armies of mites of all sizes and colours.

Far from being incompatible, gardening and wildlife can enhance one's life enormously and for less effort than pursuing either alone.

'There are now four pairs of nesting blue tits... and one of dunnock, to add to the robin and wren that we had before.'

SHRUBS

You said...

I have a small garden which, because of time constraints, needs to be very low maintenance. Ideally I would like to stock it with ground-covering shrubs which look nice all year round but which are friendly, if not positively advantageous, to wildlife. My soil is very heavy yellowy clay. What would be the best shrubs for my purpose?
Julian Brown, Nailsworth

My own preference would be for native shrubs Julian – they are normally far better for wildlife because they have coevolved for millennia. For rapid ground-cover, you could do a lot worse than ivy (a fantastic wildlife plant) which although often thought of as a climber, is equally adept at scrambling over the ground – Chris Beardshaw used them like this in his garden at the 2005 Chelsea Flower Show (The Trailfinders Recycled Garden).

Hawthorn is cheap, fast-growing, beautiful and brilliant for wildlife: what more could you ask for? It will do very well in your soil. Hawthorn, like many other native shrubs (and unlike many conifers) will stand heavy pruning and shaping (although it will set less fruit when pruned). What about guelder rose – another beautiful native shrub?
Richard Burkmar, Horwich

The butterfly bush

Buddleja, also known as the 'butterfly bush', is one of the best-cultivated shrubs for attracting butterflies into your garden. At least 10 garden species love feeding from it, and its late flowering enables the species that overwinter as adults to stock up in preparation for their hibernation.

● The plant grows to up to 7m in height, and is best grown against a wall that receives plenty of sun.

● Try mixing various species of the shrub: *Buddleja davidii, B. crispa, B. globosa* and *B.* x *weyeriana* are all suitable, and by flowering at various times provide nectar for butterflies through the summer from May to October.

Essex skipper

 Lynette Whitehouse, Northumberland
Wildlife Trust, advises:

Evergreens, in particular species like Leyland cypress, have become so overused in conventional gardens that wildlife gardeners often overlook their value. Many blackbirds, however, owe their existence to the excellent screen the Leyland provide during the vulnerable nesting period. Selections of evergreen trees and shrubs not only provide a structural component to the garden but also benefit wildlife in many ways. The yew, Scots pine and holly are all native and well worth growing if space allows, while ornamental shrubs like mahonias, viburnums and evergreen varieties of cotoneasters bear flowers and berries adding to the food supply available to wildlife.

EVERGREEN VALUE FOR WILDLIFE

Cotoneaster (*Cotoneaster dammeri*)	Flowers attract bees followed by abundant berries
Firethorn (*Pyracantha* species)	Winter berries and spring flowers
Holly (*Ilex aquifolium*)	Secure nesting sites and berries (Berries grow on female specimens only, so grow at least one male nearby to ensure cross-pollination)
Oregon grape (*Mahonia aquifolium*)	Early flowers for nectar, autumn fruits loved by blackbirds
Scots pine (*Pinus sylvestris*)	Pine cones attract crossbills
Viburnum (*Viburnum tinus*)	Early flowers for nectar
Yew (*Taxus baccata*)	An excellent nesting hedge

233

SHADED GARDENS

You said...

Advice please. We have a 7m² piece of back garden, which is shaded by a sycamore tree and a beech tree. Would like to grow anything that would grow and which would be good for birds and wildlife. Any suggestions very welcome. Thanks.
zurrieq, Littleover

A good plant for a shaded garden would be ivy – fantastic wildlife plant.
Richard Burkmar, Horwich

Shade-tolerant plants are not always very colourful, but can provide delightful foliage, like this variegated box, and make excellent habitats for wildlife.

Planting and aftercare

● The nature of the soil, position and density of branch and leaf canopy, are varying factors, which may considerably affect results.

● In all situations thorough site preparation is advisable, with well-decayed organic matter (compost or leafmould) plus a dressing of a general or organic-based fertiliser, worked well into the soil.

● Autumn planting will allow plants time to become established before the leaf canopy develops in spring.

● Provision of a deep mulch, thorough watering-in and careful attention to watering for at least the first full growing season are important factors in successful establishment.

Royal Horticultural Society

Leigh Hunt, RHS, advises:

Under the leaf canopy of larger trees, growing conditions are often poor as there is a lack of moisture and nutrients because of strong competition from the trees. In addition, the reduced light levels are unsuitable for many plants and attempts to grow many of the more floriferous sun-loving plants will be unsuccessful. At best, the growth will be drawn and elongated and the flowering poor. Unfortunately, shade-tolerant plants are in many cases not very colourful in flower, but often there is consolation in attractive or interesting foliage.

Where branches are held high, as with oak, it may be possible to grow various plants well beneath the canopy. If plenty of humus and moisture are present in the soil, or can be added, it may be possible to grow spring-flowering bulbs and similar plants, such as snowdrops, anemones,

from the south-west. In consequence, there is a greater chance of successful planting on the south-west side of trees where rain is more frequently driven under the canopy and there is more light, than to the north-east where conditions under the branched canopy will usually be drier and more shaded.

Grass under trees: To establish grass under trees, a proprietary 'shade' grass seed mixture, which includes shade-tolerant grasses, can usually be obtained from garden centres. However, the shade-tolerant grasses cannot survive regular close mowing, and they will soon deteriorate if cut to a height of less than about 5cm. They cannot be maintained to a 'fine-lawn' standard. In very poor conditions, it may be necessary to re-sow or re-turf annually. In these conditions a better alternative is to mark the limitations of poor growth, then replace the unsatisfactory area of turf with gravel or suitable shade-tolerant ground-covering plants. Ivy is the most reliable choice in deep shade.

bluebells, lily-of-the-valley and hardy cyclamen, clustered around the base of the trunk itself.

Under trees in which the branch canopy is low and spreading, few plants will thrive except along the perimeter of branch spread, and planting may need to be a matter of trial and error, with emphasis placed on ferns and low-growing evergreen shrubs, but not the variegated kinds, which need good light conditions. Common ivy is worth trying in even the gloomiest conditions.

Conifers: Difficult conditions are to be found under conifers, as these areas are dry in summer and winter, often with an accumulation of dead needles or debris creating very acidic conditions where nothing may grow satisfactorily.

Position: This is also an important point, as the prevailing rain-bearing winds are

Gardens in exposed locations are often subjected to strong winds and in these situations this is the major constraint on plant growth. Therefore, it creates difficulty in encouraging wildlife.

You said...

We have a very windy garden, being about 250ft above sea level and about one mile from Penzance. We lose so many plants due to the weather. We have trees and shrubs, to encourage a micro-climate, and the garden is walled with about 2ft of strong trellis to filter the wind. We cannot think of anything else we can do.
Cherry, Penzance

Wind-breaks are really about the only thing you can do, although you might perhaps want to consider planting living ones instead of the trellis. Hawthorn makes a good windbreak, can be planted close together, and will provide extra refuges in your garden for wildlife. Perhaps, too, you could provide homes for insects to give them somewhere protected to stay.
Gardengnome, Newbury

Benefits of living windbreaks and shelterbelts

1. They reduce wind speed and its damage. Damage includes desiccation and scorching of evergreens, windrock of shallow-rooted plants such as *Buddleja* and roses, broken fences, shattered greenhouse glass and scattering of containerised plants.

2. They afford shelter to plants, allowing a wider range of more tender plants to be grown

3. They provide shelter for pollinating insects, which increases fruit set in orchards and the fruit garden

4. They reduce moisture loss from soil and plant foliage

5. They reduce damage from salt-laden winds in coastal areas

6. They provide protection from drifting snow

7. They screen unsightly views and increase privacy

8. They reduce heating costs to greenhouses and dwellings

9. They can make a good habitat for wildlife, especially if using mixed species

Sarah Durrant, RHS, advises:

Royal Horticultural Society

Windbreaks are any type of barrier that reduces wind speed. They are usually a single line of defence (although the planting row can be single or double) and can either be man-made, or made of living plants. They include hedges and fences and can be adapted to any size of garden.

Shelterbelts are also designed to reduce wind speed but are formed of trees and shrubs usually over 4.5m in height. Three or four lines of defence arranged in a staggered manner are the most effective. Shelterbelts are not usually clipped, as would be expected for a hedge. They are useful for the larger garden where hedges are insufficient.

Siting: Windbreaks are normally best sited to face the prevailing winds. These usually come from the south-west in the UK. Wind coming up over a hill can be complicated by gusts coming around the hill and may require shelter on several sides. Air can also be funnelled along valleys, between lines of trees or between tall buildings, making planting in these areas particularly difficult for plants to establish.

Porosity: A screen filtering 50-60% of the wind is ideal to reduce its strength. Unlike impermeable structures, such as solid walls or fences, semi-permeable screens do not suffer from the problem of damaging wind eddies produced on both the leeward and windward sides.

Size: Wind slips around the sides of the windbreak leaving a triangular rather than a rectangular-shaped area of protection on the leeward side of the screen. Consequently, the windbreak should be wider than the area

needing protection or should be extended down the sides to reduce strong winds wrapping around the ends. A windbreak can reduce wind on its leeward side a distance of 10 times its height.

Living windbreaks: Young plants (less than 90cm in height) will establish best. Planting can be fairly close with 60-90cm between most plants within the row. Large trees such as *Pinus radiata* should be spaced 3-4m, while smaller growing hedging plants, such as hawthorn, can be planted as close as 45cm. In deep shelterbelts plant the tallest trees at the centre, with shorter trees or shrubs at the front and back. Keep well mulched, watered and weed-free until established.

Shrubs may be planted between the lines of trees in shelterbelts to ensure wind is being slowed at the base of the belt where branch loss on trees can cause gaps. Poplars, which become bare at the base over time, can regularly be cut back hard to promote shoot density low down. Windbreaks can be maintained by trimming to keep within bounds. Bear in mind that conifers (with the exception of yew) will not regrow if pruned hard back into old wood. Within a shelterbelt, individual trees or shrubs can be removed entirely to thin out established plantings.

Man-made windbreaks: These have the advantage of giving immediate protection from the wind. They can be used alone, or in conjunction with a living windbreak. In the latter, they are usually designed to be removed once the trees and shrubs making up the living windbreak have reached an effective size.

All artificial screens will require fixing to a supportive structure such as wooden posts or iron stakes. As a general guide, posts for screens under 1.5m should be 9cm in

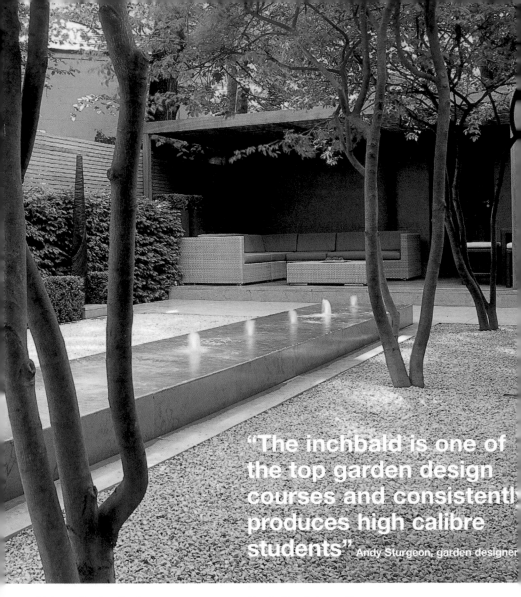

"The inchbald is one of the top garden design courses and consistentl produces high calibre students" Andy Sturgeon, garden designer

Diploma Garden Design
MA Postgraduate Diploma Garden Design
MA Garden Design Dissertation
Part-Time Garden Design (12 weeks)
Garden Design on Saturdays (five days)

For further information please contact:
Inchbald School of Design
32 Eccleston Square
London SW1V 1PB
Telephone 020 7630 9011

www.inchbald.co.uk
www.wales.ac.uk/validation

PRIFYSGOL CYMRU UNIVERSITY OF WALES

London garden by Luciano Giubbilei
Photography © Steve Wooster

inchbald

diameter, spaced at twice the screen height. Posts for screens between 1.5-4m should be 10-15cm in diameter, spaced at intervals equal to the height of the screen. Fix the cladding to the windward side of the posts. Flexible cladding should be pulled as taut as possible between supports.

PLASTIC SCREENS: Woven or extruded plastic netting is available to the amateur gardener. Black is the least intrusive colour for this netting, but it may still be considered too unsightly for highly visible areas of the garden.

For taller screens (larger than 1.5m), where wind reduction is paramount, heavy-duty plastic strapping is very effective. One such product on the market is Paraweb. This is more often used in nurseries than in the garden, but can be invaluable for giving protection in large, windswept gardens. The mail order supplier LBS Horticulture (Tel: 01282 873333) offers a range of windbreak materials.

FENCES: Solid fences are unsuitable for slowing wind due to the eddying effects described above. However, any fence meeting the desired 50-60% porosity will make a good windbreak. Woven hurdles made from willow, hazel, heather or bamboo can make attractive alternatives to the traditional wooden fence.

SUITABLE PLANTS FOR WINDBREAKS AND SHELTERBELTS:

A dense line of evergreens or conifers can cause some problems with wind turbulence in the same way as a solid barrier. It is preferable when planting several lines of plants, such as in a shelterbelt, to alternate rows between evergreens and deciduous.

What to plant

PLANTS FOR COLD AREAS

CONIFEROUS TREES: *Calocedrus decurrens, Juniperus scopulorum, J. virginiana, Picea abies, P. pungens, Pinus contorta, P. nigra, P. sylvestris, Pseudotsuga menziesii, Thuja plicata, Tsuga canadensis.*

DECIDUOUS TREES: *Acer campestre, A. negundo, A. platanoides, A. saccharinum, A. pseudoplatanus, Alnus glutinosa, A. incana, Celtis occidentalis, Fraxinus excelsior, F. pennsylvanica, Liquidambar styraciflua, Platanus occidentalis, Populus alba* f. *pyramidalis, P. deltoides, P. nigra* 'Italica', *P. tremula, Salix alba, Tilia americana, Ulmus pumila.*

SHRUBBY CONIFERS AND EVERGREENS: *Juniperus communis, Pinus mugo, Taxus baccata, Thuja occidentalis.*

DECIDUOUS SHRUBS: *Amelanchier canadensis, Caragana arborescens, Cornus mas, Corylus avellana, Crataegus laevigata, C. monogyna, Elaeagnus angustifolia, Lonicera tatarica, Prunus spinosa, Syringa vulgaris, Tamarix.*

PLANTS FOR MILD AREAS

(asterisk* indicates plants requiring minimum 5°C)

CONIFEROUS AND EVERGREEN TREES: *Acacia dealbata*, A. melanoxylon*, Cedrus deodara, Cinnamomum camphora*, Cryptomeria japonica, Cupressus macrocarpa, Eucalyptus amygdalina*, E. obliqua*, Grevillea robusta*, Magnolia grandiflora, Metrosideros excelsa*, Pinus halepensis.*

DECIDUOUS TREES: *Albizia julibrissin*, Maclura pomifera, Morus alba, Quercus suber.*

SHRUBBY CONIFERS AND EVERGREENS: *Carissa macrocarpa*, Chusquea culeou, Hakea salicifolia*, Phyllostachys flexuosa, P. nigra* f. *henonis, P. viridiglaucescens, Pittosporum tobira, Pleioblastus gramineus, P. hindsii, P. simonii, Pseudosasa japonica*

Deciduous shrubs: *Ligustrum vulgare, Pyracantha angustifolia.*

PLANTS FOR COASTAL AREAS

CONIFEROUS AND EVERGREEN TREES: *Picea sitchensis, Pinus contorta* var. *latifolia, P. nigra* subsp. *nigra, Quercus ilex.*

DECIDUOUS TREES: *Acer pseudoplatanus, Alnus, Carpinus betulus, Crataegus monogyna, Populus alba, Salix alba, S. caprea, Sorbus aria, S. aucuparia.*

SHRUBBY CONIFERS AND EVERGREENS: *Bupleurum fruticosum, Elaeagnus x ebbingei, Fargesia, Hippophae rhamnoides, Lonicera nitida, Pinus mugo, Pyracantha, Rhamnus alaternus, Sasa palmata, Semiarundinaria fastuosa, Ulex europaeus.*

DECIDUOUS SHRUBS: *Baccharis patagonica, Berberis, Prunus spinosa, Rosa rubiginosa.*

DRY GARDENS

You said...

I would like to buy some new plants for my garden that would attract bees and butterflies however my garden is very dry as I have several fir trees running down either side. Can anyone suggest some drought-loving plants that would survive in fairly dry conditions and still attract a variety of insects? Bunty, Ilford

If I were you, Bunty, I would wait until the fir trees have run down the garden and then shut the gate! Seriously, though, maybe some of the shinglebank or heathland plants might help as they tend to grow in dry conditions.
Troodles, Holt

Lavender, particularly the variety Dwarf 'Munstead' is attractive to bees and butterflies. Sea holly and *Sedum spectabile* are also good butterfly plants which survive quite happily in dry conditions. malcolm newland, Hemel Hempstead

Ways of reducing the need for water

● Keep the soil free of weeds.

● Conserve moisture in the root zone of woody plants by applying and maintaining a 5-7cm mulch of organic matter (composted bark; rotted manure; leaf litter) or with gravel or black polythene.

● When preparing for sowing or planting on free-draining soils, dig in well-rotted organic matter to improve moisture retention.

● If watering is essential, irrigate in the evening; there can be considerable moisture loss to the atmosphere, particularly in warm, sunny conditions, following daytime watering.

● Frequent light watering encourages shallow rooting and there is more atmospheric loss. Water thoroughly; during extended summer drought periods at about seven-day intervals; in spring or autumn at 14-day intervals.

● Water around plants, not over them, to reduce evaporation loss.

● Plant closely, not widely spaced (unless well mulched). This keeps the soil shaded and root areas cooler, reducing evaporation loss and discouraging weeds.

● Consider reducing areas of lawn. Turf grasses will usually survive a period of drought but without irrigation, will look dry and dead. Drought weakens turf, favouring invasion by moss and weeds.

● Plant trees, shrubs, climbers and perennials in autumn when less watering will be needed and they can establish from early in the spring before any risk of summer drought.

● In windy situations use windbreak materials to give wind protection after planting. Plant windbreaks for permanent wind protection.

● Save and store rainwater by installing water butts.

Leigh Hunt, RHS, advises:

Climatic variation has brought more frequent hot, dry summers, combined with dry winters, resulting in falling water tables and depleted reservoirs in some regions. Conserving water use in gardens is of increasing importance with less reliance being placed on mains supplies, which can be subjected to extended periods of restriction during the summer months.

Many drought-tolerant plants suitable for planting in the UK come from the Mediterranean or similar regions where hot, dry summers and cool winters with little or no frost are the norm. For overwintering in open situations, take care to choose only plants that are fully winter hardy. Slightly tender plants can often be grown successfully in mild coastal gardens, close to, or trained to, a warm, sunny south- or west-facing wall, or in a very sheltered border, such as the Mediterranean borders at Wisley.

The following is a list of herbaceous plants and annuals suitable for UK planting, good for wildlife, and which usually show good drought tolerance when established, although in severe conditions some signs of stress may be encountered. All will, however, need attention to watering for one or two years until well established.

Where a genus only is given, all species within the genus can be considered; where a single species or several species are mentioned, these are among the preferred or most suitable species for consideration. Within larger genera, tolerance of drought conditions may vary considerably.

HERBACEOUS PERENNIALS: *Achillea filipendulina, A. millefolium, A. ptarmica, A. tomentosa, Alchemilla mollis, Anaphalis margaritacea, A. triplinervis, Asphodeline lutea, Baptisia australis, Carlina acaulis, Catananche caerulea, Centaurea cineraria, Centranthus ruber, Cerastium tomentosum, Crambe cordifolia, Crepis incana, Cynara cardunculus, Dianthus* (border carnations; pinks), *Echinops, Erodium, Eryngium, Euphorbia, Geranium endressii, G. macrorrhizum; G. oxonianum; G. riversleaianum; G. sanguineum, Gypsophila paniculata, Heuchera, Linum perenne, Liriope muscari, L. spicata*, Marrubium vulgare, Melissa officinalis, Nepeta* (x *faassenii; nervosa;* 'Six Hills Giant'), *Oenothera fruticosa, O. macrocarpa, Origanum laevigatum, O. vulgare, Papaver orientale, Phuopsis stylosa, Sedum spectabile, S. spurium, S. telephium), Stachys byzantina, Symphytum ibericum* ('Hidcote Blue'), *Tanacetum parthenium, Verbascum, Veronica prostrata.*

ANNUALS: *Alcea rosea* (biennial), *Alyssum, Amaranthus, Brachyscombe, Calendula, Cosmos, Eschscholzia, Felicia, Gazania, Lunaria annua,* Mesembryanthemum, *Papaver somniferum, Portulaca, Salvia farinacea*

GROUND COVER: *Brachyglottis* (Dunedin Group) 'Sunshine'*, *Cotoneaster conspicuus* ('Decorus'), *C. dammeri)*, Cytisus decumbens, Duchesnea indica, Genista hispanica, G. pilosa, Hedera colchica, H. helix, H. hibernica)*, Hypericum calycinum*, Juniperus rigida* subsp. *conferta, J. horizontalis* (incl. 'Wiltonii')*, *Liriope muscari, L. spicata)*, Melissa officinalis, Nepeta faassenii, N. nervosa), Origanum vulgare* (incl. 'Aureum'), *Osteospermum ecklonis*, Pachysandra terminalis*, Santolina chamaecyparissus*, Stachys byzantina, Teucrium* x *lucidrys*, Vinca minor*.*

Key * – denotes evergreen or semi-evergreen.

WET SOILS

Willow trees grow well in gardens with a high water table.

Trees for wet soils

There are many trees that will grow successfully in permanently moist soils, but few will survive long spells of flooding or waterlogged conditions. Air and water need to be available for plant roots. Saturated soils will have insufficient oxygen for healthy root function and may lead to root decay. A high water table will encourage roots to be produced near the soil surface, making them more vulnerable to drought in dry weather.

Preparation: Before planting trees in wet conditions, drainage may need to be improved. On soils prone to wet conditions in winter and drought in summer, such as heavy clays, improve the soil by incorporating bulky organic matter or inorganic material such as coarse grit or pea shingle. This should be done over as large an area as possible – around 1sq.m. If severe waterlogging or flooding is a problem artificial drainage will be necessary.

Planting: Improve drainage at the base of the planting hole by forking through any compacted soil. Fork through the sides of the planting hole or break down the sides into the planting hole when backfilling. This avoids creating a planting 'bucket' or sump, which fills with water. On heavy soils prone to winter wet, protect the finer surface feeding roots by planting trees on a slightly raised mound to improve drainage around the root system.

Trees suited to wet soils: Alders (*Alnus*), willows (*Salix*), swamp cypress (*Taxodium distichum*), dawn redwood (*Metasequoia glyptostroboides*), poplars (*Populus*) and sweet gum (*Liquidambar styraciflua*).

Guy Barter, RHS, advises:

Few plants will tolerate and survive extended periods of waterlogged or flooded conditions, but quite a number of plants may be grown successfully in soils that are permanently moist if there is some oxygen in the wet soil. Below we suggest some shrubs and herbaceous perennials that will have a better-than-average chance of survival in poorly drained sites where it is impractical or impossible to drain adequately. Where only a genus is mentioned, such as *Populus*, all the species in the genus can be considered. Cultivars of the species listed, such as *Hydrangea macrophylla* 'Altona', are also suitable.

SHRUBS: *Andromeda polifolia* * ‡, *Aronia arbutifolia*, *Arctostaphylos uva-ursi* * ‡, *Arundinaria* *, *Berberis* x *stenophylla* *, *Calycanthus floridus*, *C. occidentalis*, *Clethra alnifolia*†, *Cornus alba*, *C. florida*, *C. sericea*, *Diervilla*, *Enkianthus campanulatus*, *E. cernuus* f. *rubens*‡, *Erica tetralix* * ‡, *Gaultheria hookeri*, *G. procumbens*, *G. shallon* * ‡, *Hippophae rhamnoides*, *Hydrangea macrophylla*, *H. paniculata*, *Hypericum beanii*, *Ilex verticillata* * ‡, *Kalmia angustifolia*, *K. polifolia* * ‡, *Kerria japonica*, *Ledum* * ‡, *Leycesteria formosa*, *Lindera benzoin*‡, *Magnolia grandiflora* *, *M. virginiana*, *Mespilus germanica*, *Myrica cerifera* *, *M. gale*‡, *Neillia thibetica*, *Photinia villosa*, *Phyllostachys* *, *Physocarpus opulifolius*, *Prunus spinosa*, *Rhododendron hippophaeoides* *, *R. periclymenoides*, *R. viscosum*, *Rubus arcticus*, *Salix repens*, *Sambucus*, *Sasa* *, *Sorbaria*, *Spiraea*, *Symphoricarpus*, *Vaccinium corymbosum*, *V. myrtillus*, *V. vitis-idaea* * ‡, *Viburnum opulus*, *Weigela*, *Wisteria floribunda*, *W. sinensis*, *Zenobia pulverulenta*‡.

HERBACEOUS PERENNIALS: *Acorus gramineus*, *Astilbe*, *Caltha palustris*, *Cardiocrinum cordatum*, *C. giganteum*, *Cimicifuga*, *Darmera peltata* (syn. *Peltiphyllum peltatum*), *Dodecatheon meadia*, *D. hendersonii*, *Euphorbia griffithii*, *E. sikkimensis*, *Filipendula ulmaria*, *Gunnera manicata*, *Hosta*, *Iris ensata*, *I. laevigata*, *I. pseudacorus*, *I. sibirica*, *Ligularia przewalskii*, *Lilium pardalinum*, *L. superbum*, *Lobelia cardinalis*†, *Lysimachia nummularia*, *L. punctata*, *Lythrum salicaria*, *Mimulus cupreus*, *M. luteus*, *M. primuloides*, *M. ringens*, *Monarda didyma*, *Primula denticulata*, *P. japonica*, *Schizostylis coccinea*, *Trollius*, *Zantedeschia aethiopica*†.

Key:
† tender
‡ plants that require an acid soil/do not thrive on chalk soils
* evergreen

CLAY SOILS

You said...

I'd like to plant a wildflower meadow in my garden but the area concerned is around fruit trees and large oaks/chestnuts. Would I be able to grow anything in this sort of area. The patch is not in shadow by the trees but the soil is clay. catandsplat, Heathfield

I live in West London and my garden is also on clay. I don't know anything about meadows but my garden seemed too small for a meadow so what I did was plant up native plant borders. I'd say 50% of the plugs I planted survived but the others I think the slugs got to before the effects of the clay. Oxeye daisy grew to 4ft and is in the process of taking over, viper's bugloss always does well, marjoram, tansy, hemp agrimony, scabious, campions, knapweeds, St John's wort, and too many others to list here have all done well. Not a meadow, but still wonderful to look at in suburbia. UB4 gardenener, Hayes

Depending on how the areas under the trees have been treated before determines your next move. Under the dense shade of oaks and chestnuts, I suggest you just go for spring bulbs and wildflowers. Nothing much will thrive once the leaf canopy closes up – copy what you see in any local woods. Fruit trees are much easier – you may be able to incorporate them into a larger meadow or just allow the grass to grow long around the base of trees and plug plant with suitable wildflowers. I have stripped off the turf and sown a wildflower/grass mix from scratch in my own garden but never thought it was a great success (also on clay). Jeff Davis, Leatherhead

Kniphofia rooperi

Preparation for planting

● When planting on heavy clay soil, it is always advisable to attempt some improvement of the planting soil, by working in coarse gritty material and organic matter, such as well-rotted farmyard manure, finer grades of composted bark, leafmould, leaf litter, garden compost or mushroom compost. This will help the roots of young plants to establish more quickly and will also improve drainage around the plants.

● The bottom of the planting hole should be broken up before planting and the sides of the hole broken down during planting using a garden fork (not a spade), otherwise there is danger of a sump being formed in which water could collect, resulting in probable death of plants through waterlogging.

Sarah Durrant, RHS, advises:

It is particularly important that some site preparation is given to shrubs. Cultivars of the species and hybrids listed below are suitable for clay soils.

Shrubs: *Abelia chinensis*, *A.* x *grandiflora*, *A. schumanii*, *Aesculus parviflora*, *Aralia elata*, *Arundinaria**, *Aucuba japonica**, *Berberis* (evergreen and deciduous)*, *Buddleja alternifolia*, *B. davidii*, *B.* x *weyeriana*, *Chaenomeles speciosa*, *C. superba*, *Choisya ternata**, *Cornus alba*, *C. sanguinea*, *C. servicea*, *Corylus avellana*, *C. maxima*, *Cotoneaster bullatus*, *C. dammeri**, *C. divaricatus*, *C. lacteus**, *C. microphyllus**, *C. salicifolius**, *C. simonsii*, *C.* x *watereri**, *Deutzia* x *rosea*, *D. scabra*, *Dipelta floribunda*, *Escallonia**, *Euonymus alatus*, *E. europaeus*, *E. fortunei**, *E. japonicus**, *Fargesia**, *Forsythia*, *Hibiscus syriacus*, *Hypericum androsaemum*, *H. forrestii*, *H.* x *inodorum*, *Kerria japonica*, *Laurus nobilis**, *Lonicera*, *Osmanthus delavayi**, *O. heterophyllus*, *Philadelphus*, *Phyllostachys**, *Potentilla fruticosa*, *Prunus laurocerasus**, *Pyracantha**, *Rhamnus alaternus**, *frangula alnus*, *Ribes odoratum*, *R. sanguineum*, *R. speciosum*, *Rosa*, *Rubus* 'Benenden', *R. cockburnianus*, *Sasa**, *Spiraea* 'Arguta', *S. japonica*, *S. nipponica*, *S.* x *vanhouttei*, *Symphoricarpos albus*, *S.* x *doorenbosii*, *S. orbiculatus*, *Syringa pubescens* subsp. *microphylla*, *S.* x *prestoniae*, *Viburnum* x *bodnantense*, *V. carlesii*, *V. farreri*, *V.* x *juddii*, *V. lantana*, *V. tinus**, *Weigela*.

Shrubs for heavier clay-type soils:

Acer japonicum, *A. palmatum‡*, *Arbutus* x *andrachnoides**, *A. unedo*, *Brachyglottis (Senecio) monroi**, *B.* (Dunedin Group) 'Sunshine', *Camellia japonica**, *C.* x *williamsii*, *Colutea arborescens*, *Fuchsia*, *Genista aetnensis*, *G. hispanica*, *G. lydia*, *Hamamelis‡*, *Hydrangea*, *Magnolia liliiflora‡*, *M.* x *soulangeana‡*, *M. stellata*, *Mahonia* x *aquifolium**, *M. japonica*, *M.* x *media*, *Olearia* x *haastii**, *O. macrodonta*, *Phlomis fruticosa** *Photinia davidiana**, *Rhododendron* (many species and hybrids including deciduous and evergreen azaleas)* ‡, *Rhus typhina*, *Spartium junceum*.

Ground-covering plants: *Berberis candidula**, *Bergenia** HP, *Campanula portenschlagiana* HP, *C. poscharskyana*, *Cerastium tomentosum* HP, *Convallaria majalis* HP, *Cotoneaster dammeri**, *C.* x *salicifolius* 'Repens', *C. suecicus* 'Coral Beauty', *C.* x *suecicus* 'Skogholm', *Euonymus fortunei**, *Forsythia* 'Arnold Dwarf', *Gaultheria procumbens** ‡, *G. shallon*, *G.* x *wisleyensis*, *Genista lydia*, *G. pilosa*, *Geranium* HP, *Hedera colchica**, *H. helix*, *H. hibernica*, *Hemerocallis* HP, *Hosta* HP, *Hypericum androsaemum*, *H. calycinum**, *Juniperus communis**, *J rigidus* subsp. *conferta*, *J. horizontalis*, *J. sabina*, *Lamium galeobdolon* HP, *Leucothoe fontanesian**‡, *Lonicera pileata*, *Pachysandra terminalis**, *Potentilla fruticosa* 'Longacre Variety', *P. fruticosa* 'Manchu', *Prunus laurocerasus* 'Otto Luyken'*, *P. laurocerasus* 'Zabeliana', *Rubus rolfei**, *R. tricolor*, *Sedum album* 'Coral Carpet' HP, *S.* 'Ruby Glow', *Symphoricarpos chenaultii* 'Hancock', *Thymus serpyllum**, *Vinca major**, *V. minor*.

Key: * evergreen
‡ needs acid soil
HP herbaceous perennial

for garden lovers

Veranda
Living

tel 0870 922 0160   www.veranda-living.co.uk

veranda living limited

parchment house gaia lane lichfield ws13 7ls

SANDY SOILS

You said...

I am changing some of my borders from perennials to shrubs. We have a dry, sandy soil. Can anyone advise which shrubs would be better for wildlife?
SallyK, Newent

Arbutus unedo,
Arctostaphylos uva-ursi
Berberis (incl. deciduous species)
Brachyglottis (Dunedin Group) 'Sunshine'
Calluna vulgaris ‡
Chamaerops humilis †
Choisya ternata
Cistus
Convolvulus cneorum
Cotoneaster (low-growing species)
Elaeagnus
Escallonia
Euonymus
Erica ‡
Fargesia nitida
Griselinia littoralis †

x *Halimiocistus sahucii*
Halimium lasianthum
Halimium ocymoides
Hebe
Helianthemum
Ilex
Lavandula
Mahonia
Olearia
Osmanthus x *burkwoodii*
Phlomis fruticosa
Photinia serratifolia
Pittosporum
Pseudosasa japonica
Rosmarinus
Ruta graveolens
Santolina
Vinca
Yucca

Key † tender ‡ denotes lime-hating plants
Where a genus is listed without mention of a particular species or cultivar, all species will be suitable.

Sarah Durrant, RHS, advises:

Evergreen shrubs give cover to wildlife during the harsher winter months. The following species usually show good tolerance of sandy, drier and poorer soils when established. It is essential, however, to prepare planting sites thoroughly, incorporating good quantities of moisture-retentive, well-rotted organic matter, such as farmyard manure, garden compost, leafmould or processed tree bark as the first year or two of establishment are critical to long-term survival. When planting in spring, incorporate a slow-release fertiliser such as Vitax Q4 or Osmocote. John Innes Base Fertiliser is also suitable. Follow with a mulch of bark or similar material. Apply a surface dressing of fertiliser in spring around autumn-planted plants before mulching. Water thoroughly and regularly during dry periods throughout the first growing season. With autumn-planted evergreens, irrigation may be needed on occasion even during the winter months.

You said...

I have a small lawn and would like to put a small tree in the centre to give me something to look at but maybe something that would also attract birds, etc. It cannot be too big because of local restrictions.
Lynne, Guiseley

Try *Sorbus vilmorinii*, which is a Chinese rowan. Mine is 20 years old, about 12ft high with a trunk about 15cm in diameter. Its berries are pinkish white and are normally left till last before birds eat them. A crab apple on a dwarfing rootstock is another possibility. There are many rootstocks available producing different sizes of tree. The variety I have is golden hornet which is very prolific, but I am told John Downie is better for wildlife.
DEREK, St Andrews

A nice tree which the birds love is a hawthorn. We have one in our small back garden and it attracts quite a bird population. We do have fat balls hanging from them which no doubt helps but birds not interested in fat balls use the tree regularly.
cpm, Huddersfield

As with the majority of London residents I have a very small garden, however I have included a mixture of plants to encourage wildlife and lots of vegetables to enjoy the benefits of growing my own produce. As a result I am able to enjoy great-tasting herbs and veg (strawberries, beetroot, chilli, rosemary, leeks, beans and a grape vine) among the beautiful lavender, daisies, dahlias, roses and forsythia.
Bianca, Islington

Rowan trees are particular favourites with birds, and they don't take up too much space, either.

Kim Paterson, the Wildlife Trust for Lancashire, Manchester and North Merseyside, advises:

A small garden is no barrier to wildlife gardening. The fundamental differences are of scale and expectation. I have seen large gardens that are managed and controlled to areas of wildlife deprivation and I have seen tiny backyards in an inner-city environment teeming with unexpected visitors. As they say, size doesn't matter!

The first and most important consideration in designing a wildlife garden in a small area is what you need to use the space for. There is no point having a backyard jungle if you need a place for children to play or a place to sit out. One of the beauties of wildlife gardening is that it isn't all or nothing; you can make small, thoughtful, innovative changes which can have a real effect on attracting wildlife.

The all-important provision of water doesn't need to be a massive water feature. Old sinks and buckets can teem with newts or frogs at spawning time, just by being thoughtfully placed and adapted. Scaling things down may limit the potential somewhat, but we tend to forget that space is three-dimensional. In countries where growing conditions can be limited, there is a centuries-old tradition of vertical gardening, making use of walls, roofs and other structures. In nature, just think of the rainforest or ancient woodland and how these are layered vertically to take advantage of both time and space.

Another key consideration is making use of the wider environment around your garden. A key principle of garden design is to see beyond the boundaries and make your space complimentary. Is there a river or canal nearby, a park or allotments? All these and more can influence the success of any features you decide to put in your garden.

This year in a backyard in Bolton, dragonflies were emerging from an old bath tub to the wonderment of the family living there. Sometimes nature chooses the strangest of opportunities to take advantage of and maybe we should spend more time looking at possibilities rather than restrictions.

Suggested trees for small gardens

Acer palmatum 'Sango-kaku' – 6m

Amelanchier lamarckii – 10m

Cercis siliquastrum – 10m

Cornus kousa var. *chinensis* – 7.5m

Crataegus laevigata 'Paul's Scarlet' – 8m

Malus 'Evereste' – 7m

Malus tschonoskii – 12m

Prunus 'Pandora' – 10m

Sorbus hupehensis – 8m

Small can be beautiful

Gardens attached to urban houses are generally small. Narrow gardens are best subdivided to give the illusion of greater space. Simplicity is the key to getting the most from a small space, particularly courtyards.

You need to consider what uses you plan for your garden. Is it needed for play, entertaining, gardening or relaxing? Draw up an accurate plan to show existing features such as services, boundaries, trees, changes in level or views. Make a special note of aspect and which parts receive the most sun at different times of day or year, whether part of the garden is exposed to wind or is frosty in winter. You often need to live in the property for some time to assess these points. Photocopy the plan and then use the copies to try out different ideas and plans.

A well-designed garden will get the most from a small space and add value to the property. Designs can be by garden designers, professional landscapers or yourself. Many colleges offer part-time courses in garden design for the home gardener.

Climbers on trellis can soften boundaries and provide year-round interest. Larger shrubs or features such as arbours may provide a focal feature and privacy. Any feature plants should have more than one season of interest and successive planting, such as spring bulbs under summer-flowering shrubs, will give a succession of interest in a small space.

If your chosen tree becomes too large, removal or expensive tree surgery may become necessary, and growing plants in the garden may become difficult due to the competition for moisture, food and light.

Trees up to 8-10m in height are usually reasonable for most small gardens, although in some cases a taller tree with a narrow habit may be considered. If even these are too large, big shrubs, container trees or coppiced trees make good alternatives. A narrow tree may give a more formal appearance, with spreading trees providing welcome shade. If you only have space for one tree, ideally look for one with more than one season of interest, such as fruit or autumn colour following flowers. To avoid planting a tree too large for the site it may help to draw a scale plan of your garden and plot the size of your tree at maturity. If planting in the corner of your garden, be aware that most of the canopy will shade neighbouring gardens.

ROOF GARDENS

The black redstart is not a common British bird, with fewer than 100 breeding pairs. One of its favourite nesting sites, however, is urban rooftop gardens.

You said...

I've got a roof terrace the size of a postage stamp but I was amazed to see a fox on it the other morning, staring at me through the kitchen window! It must have jumped about 8ft to get up there. I'm near Battersea Park so it may have come from there where I've seen a few foxes. It gave me a shock, but it was a lovely sight.
Poppy, London

Foxes seem to be everywhere. I've seen one jump over my high garden gate on being disturbed. I also had one that came up onto my balcony (via steps) and eyeballed me. Cawky, London

I love roof gardens. Just think how much extra wildlife-friendly land there'd be in this country if every building with a flat roof had it turned into a garden.
Fiveways, Stroud

Royal Horticultural Society

Helen Bostock, RHS, advises:

If you live in a building without its own garden, establishing a roof or balcony garden is the ideal way to create your own mini horticultural haven, and encouraging wildlife (although foxes are admittedly rarely found on a roof or balcony).

Before designing any roof garden, it is essential to check with an architect or structural engineer how much weight the roof can take, whether planning permission is needed and also to check whether or not the roof is waterproof. Ideally, place heavy containers near load-bearing walls, or over a load-bearing beam or joist.

The main drawbacks of roof gardens and balconies are the strong winds and sunshine they are generally subjected to. Take advantage of any existing protection, such as walls or fences. If erecting trellis or screens ensure that any fixings are well supported. Balconies also often have the additional problem of an overhang, which prevents rainfall from reaching the containerised plants. Hosepipe access on balconies is also usually limited.

Because containers will dry out rapidly in the excess heat and wind, attempt to provide quite a deep container. If using small containers, use ones made of non-porous materials such as plastic, metal or fibreglass to reduce potential moisture loss. The container should also be lightweight, and drainage should be optimum. Peat-based or peat-substitute composts are more lightweight than loam-based materials, and can be lightened further still if required by adding material such as perlite. Bear in mind, however, that adding additional drainage materials will increase the water demands of many plants. Large plants should be well anchored to stop them from blowing over.

Containerised plants will need watering all year round, except in freezing conditions. In summer, plants may need watering twice a day if not more. Run-off of excess irrigation water or rainfall requires an outlet to a drainpipe. This must be easily accessible for cleaning purposes. An automated irrigation system saves labour, but may only be cost-effective for larger areas. It is essential to check planters periodically to ensure plant roots remain contained. Standing pots on pot feet deters root escape.

Windbreak plants such as *Pinus mugo* and phormiums tolerate both sun and wind and can act as a shield for less robust plants. Dense evergreens such as *Viburnum tinus* and junipers will create shelter if the existing structure does not. Low-growing plants (including most alpines) can avoid the worst of the winds, or are sturdy enough to withstand them. Dwarf spring-flowering bulbs can also withstand exposed sites.

WANT TO KNOW MORE?

The following books and articles should help you on your way:

Balconies & Roof Gardens by Jenny Hendy (New Holland Publishers (UK) Limited, 1997, ISBN 1 85368 680 8).

Roof Gardens, Balconies & Terraces by Jerry Harpur and David Stevens, (Mitchell Beazley, 2000, ISBN 1 84000 273 5).

'Refuge in the Sky' by Louisa Jones, *The Garden*, January 1999, pp 34-37.

Building Green – A Guide to Using Plants on Roofs, Walls and Pavements by Jacklyn Johnston and John Newton, (The London Ecology Unit, 1992, ISBN 1 871045 18 5).

'Roofing Veldt' by Noel Kingsbury, *The Garden*, June 2001, pp 446-449.

'Up on the Roof' by Nigel Dunnett, *The Garden*, May 2002, pp 380-383.

FRONT DRIVES

A garden designer should be able to help you create a front garden with a parking space and will advise on materials and plantings. Designers can be found through the following organisation: Society of Garden Designers, Tel: 01989 566695; www.sgd.org.uk.

You said...

Parking is at a premium in my street, and I've had to convert my (small) front garden into a drive. Although there's a car sitting there now, is there any way I can still do my best to make it of value to wildlife, too? Gardengnome, Newbury

There are plenty of low-growing plants that you can place around the edges of your parking space. Herbs, for example, such as thyme, will give bees plenty to keep them occupied. And if you leave your car long enough, there's always the possibility that some interesting lichens will grow at the base of the windows! LauraT, London

Choosing the right paving materials

When correctly laid, most modern paving materials shed water off their surface, resulting in excess water running away into sewers and drains rather than soaking into the land. While a driveway's design can help reduce this, the choice of material is also very important. There is now a choice of porous paving with small gaps that allow the water to run through, whether in the surface or by built-in drainage channels. The following list is not exhaustive, but explains three different options. It's worth checking with local suppliers and builders for new and local materials.

Matrix paver trays: Made from recycled plastic, the many hexagonal cells hold a resin-bonded aggregate of your choice. The plastic trays' standard colour is green, but any shade can be requested if the order is large enough. To ensure the water can drain away, they must be laid as the manufacturer recommends. Matrix paver trays are made by Addastone. Prices range from around £60/sq.m (for DIY) to £100/sq.m (installed). Tel: 01825 761333; www.addagrip.co.uk.

Aquaflow block pavers: These look like normal block pavers, but have channels cut in the ends to allow water to penetrate through the surface. Again, they must be laid as the manufacturer recommends to ensure the water can drain away. This product (and other Aquaflow paving) is available from Formpave. Prices vary from £35-£60/sq.m (installed), depending on labour costs. For product details, log on at www.formpave.co.uk. For stockists and availability, call 01594 836999.

Gravel: This traditional product is available in a wide range of colours and sizes. By its nature, it has drainage gaps between each stone and is not ruined by oil stains. Contact your local builders' merchant to order the material by the tonne (the cheapest way at around £45 a tonne, which is equivalent to £2.25/sq.m). Specialist building suppliers will offer a wider range of bagged products (more expensive at around £4-10/sq.m).

Royal Horticultural Society

Leigh Hunt, RHS, advises:

Traditionally, the idealised front garden contained a stripy lawn and neatly clipped hedge. But now many homeowners are having to make driveways for Britain's 34 million cars and vans instead. Yet the loss of front gardens is not just a case of horticulture versus the car. Many homeowners are being forced to make the decision because they live in streets without drives and, consequently struggle to park, with the nearest space some distance away. Although each front garden is only a tiny patch of land, multiplied by the number of houses in a city or town, they total a vast area. For example, take an average street and turn all the front gardens into driveways and the result is the equivalent of tripling the width of the road. And the reduction of green space gives less area for rain that falls on roads to run off into, potentially causing flooding.

While there is a need for car parking, there are still opportunities to maintain plants and encourage wildlife even into paved front gardens. All too often, front gardens disappear under a wall-to-wall driveway. However, this isn't usually needed. A rectangle the size of a car-park space may be all that's needed, with 75cm either side to allow room to manoeuvre.

Alternatively, two parallel rows of paving to take the car wheels may be all that's required and, if surrounding hard standing is needed, gravel can be used. Look for 'dead' space that you can't park on. This includes along the edges of walls and corners. House walls and fences will also provide perfect support for climbers. If two parallel rows of paving are used, there's a chance to plant low-growing thymes, bugle, alyssum and creeping jenny, too. These will survive car shade for a few days and the occasional running over. Containers can also be used in places where borders cannot be dug.

Start by considering where the rain will drain to. This needs to be away from the house, but can it be into a border or onto a lawn? Choosing the right paving material will also help (see left). Wildlife, including birds and insects, can rely on our gardens for food and shelter, particularly in towns and cities. Try to include shrubs for birds to nest in and plants that bear berries or flowers.

There are wider issues to be aware of, too. Local governments are aiming to ensure a good quality of life for everyone, based on social, economic and environmental values. Although this doesn't give councils power to improve matters, such as denying planning permission for driveways, it does mean that we will all be encouraged to do our bit, whether by taking part in greenspace projects or recycling.

To find out more about local strategies and events in your area, contact your council.

FUNDING FOR WILDLIFE GARDENS

Community wildlife gardens are a wonderful way of working together with other local community members who have the same goal – to develop or enhance a green space for the benefit of wildlife and people.

You said...

Our group runs a wildlife garden in central London and is looking for funding to make improvements – a new pond, improved pathways, wildflower planting trials and bird-feeding equipment. Any suggestions?
Jane Campbell, London

Hello, Jane. Looks Like Mayor Ken has some commitments in this area. It might be worth getting in touch. See www.london.gov.uk/mayor/strategies/biodiversity/docs/final_sum.rtf. Georgie, Enfield

Try going to your local CVS council for volantary services; they have a reference book called *The Funder Finder* I think or try your local library.
enviro man, Mansfield

 Lynette Whitehouse, Northumberland Wildlife Trust comments:

Whether it is the creation of a wildlife pond on an existing site, or a complete wildlife garden development on disused land, how the project is going to be funded both initially and in the long term, needs to be given lots of consideration. So how can you raise these funds?

Organise your own fundraising event: These can be a great deal of fun and can range from sponsored walks to jumble sales. Importantly, they also help to raise awareness of the intended project among people in the local area. This can prove advantageous, as it may lead to people offering volunteer support with other aspects of the project.

Contact local businesses; sponsorships from local businesses are often valuable inputs to projects. In addition, if the companies are approached with a specific request for materials or tools to facilitate your community project, you may receive gifts in kind or at cost price. Your local garden centre may be able to provide you with shrubs or a local tree surgeon may be able to drop off some woodchippings.

Apply for a grant: The key is to research who may be suitable to contact at an early stage, while other project details are being researched. This will speed up your process of gaining application forms, etc, from the relevant organisations once you are in a position to do so.

The availability of funding will determine the scale of the project. Large-scale projects can be broken down into phases and developed over several years. Grant-giving organisations receive thousands of applications a year, so you need to make sure yours stands out – tailor your application to the interests of the grant-giving body. Be aware that most grant-giving bodies will strictly not fund a project if work begins before the offer of a grant has been made.

Whichever method(s) you choose to gain funds for your project, it is worthwhile setting out the following;

● Establish a name and maybe a logo for the project

● Include an outline of the project:
  ● Aims/objectives
  ● Final design proposal
  ● Sketches, artwork, photos
  ● Press cuttings

● Outline of estimated costs:
  ● Materials/equipment
  ● Labour costs
  ● Insurance
  ● Training

To gain cost estimates of materials, tools and installations, use trade magazines or contact relevant contractors to obtain quotes. Keep records of all successful grant-giving bodies and donations made so you can thank them at a later stage.

Who to turn to

It's Your Space is primarily a website resource to inspire local people to apply for funding to transform a community space including parks or gardens on their doorstep. It gives links to a variety of funding sources and advice on applying, and gives many examples of local people who have already taken things into their own hands. It encourages people and organisations to sign up to the Manifesto for Better Public Spaces and explains the essential 10 ingredients that make a great public space. For more inspiration and information visit www.itsyourspace.org.uk or Tel: 0161 872 0901.

Awards For All is a UK-wide Lottery grants scheme aimed at local communities. The scheme awards grants of between £500 and £5,000, in a process that is intended to be simple and straightforward.

A variety of projects are eligible, including those which enable people to get involved in community activities or which promote heritage or the environment. The aims of the Awards for All scheme are to extend access and participation, increase skill and creativity, and improve the quality of life. Applications must be for a specific project or activity, and the grant must be usable within one year. A project to plan and create a community wildlife garden is one of the examples of possible projects

given in the guidance booklet. For further information, simply visit the Awards for All website at www.awardsforall.co.uk.

Changing Spaces is a Big Lottery Fund programme to help communities in England improve their environment. There are three priority areas: Community Spaces, Local Community Enterprise, and Access to the Natural Environment. The programme is worth £243 million in total, and there will be two types of schemes available: open grant schemes, and portfolio schemes.

Open grant schemes will be managed by a number of award partners, appointed in August 2006, and launching their grant schemes soon afterwards. The kinds of projects sought are those that, for example: encourage people to use community spaces by improving access to them and developing local awareness of them; improve biodiversity and wildlife habitats; and educate people about the natural environment.

Portfolio schemes will be made up of a number of pre-identified projects which complement one another in delivering the desired outcomes identified by the Changing Spaces programme.

For more information, visit the Changing Spaces website by going to www.biglotteryfund.org.uk and looking under Funding Programmes.

GreenSpace (formerly Urban Parks Forum) is a not-for-profit organisation set up to help those committed to the planning, design, management and use of public parks and open spaces. GreenSpace is a membership organisation dedicated to promoting the importance of public spaces while increasing awareness of related issues. It promotes the regeneration of public parks and open spaces in towns and cities throughout the UK and supports the investment being made in these important social and cultural assets.

It organises a number of events, produces publications and good practice information, and its website has invaluable information on how to find the right fund for your project or enterprise, and how to make an application for funding.

For more general information visit www.green-space.org.uk or Tel: 0118 946 9060.

Environmental Action Fund is a Defra funding scheme that awards grants for voluntary groups from £25,000 up to £250,000 per year. In order to qualify for a grant the project must fit in with the government's sustainable development objectives and have a clear work plan. To find out if you are eligible for a grant, how to apply and guidance notes for applicants visit www.defra.gov.uk/environment/eaf/index.htm or Tel: 020 7082 8680.

URBAN GARDENING

You said...

We live near Newcastle airport, a fairly built up area on the edge of greenbelt. Our quarter acre plot is made up of a lawn edged with flower beds, an abundance of shrubs, deciduous trees and fir trees, rose bushes, including the Alnwick Castle rose, a bird table, nesting pouches, a beech hedge and a laurel hedge, home to many birds. We enjoy seeing and listening to blackbirds. robins, blue tits, wood pigeons, an occasional wood pecker, bull finches, thrushes and sparrows. We have lots of visiting butterflies on the buddleias in summer. We have hedgehog visitors who enjoy some dog food and we lie in bed listening to hooting owls. We have glimpsed a large fox passing through the garden and we regularly have red squirrels in the garden. We love our garden and spend as much time as possible outdoors all the year round, delighted by the wild life attracted to our quarter acre plot.
pontac, Ponteland

I live in a small commuter blob near Preston, which was expanded by new town build in the 80's. Thanks to some nifty planning design it's criss-crossed with footpaths and green spaces which means if you make a bit of an effort for wildlife you get some fantastic things. So far, in my garden, I've had frogs and toads (the pond helps), vast variety of small birds, several spps of spider inc. the obvious araneidae, salticidae and pisauridae; bumble bees (which I'm trying to persuade to nest), long-tailed field mice and most excitingly some jays and a sparrowhawk which got a takeout from the bird table and sat on a log in the garden eating it. Considering the garden's your regular new development postage stamp it's amazing how much you can find and it's a real treat to be able to watch it all.
K, Preston

Plenty can be done with even the smallest of spaces.

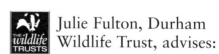
Julie Fulton, Durham Wildlife Trust, advises:

Urbanisation is occurring at a rapid rate throughout the world and is widely regarded as being detrimental to biodiversity. At present there are an estimated 15 million gardens in the UK, covering an area five times the size of Greater London and larger than all of the designated National Nature Reserves combined. In urban areas, residential zones account for more than 60% of the area and typically a quarter of British cities are private gardens. Therefore domestic gardens have the potential

to play a crucial role in supporting urban biodiversity.

Although urban gardens will never act as substitutes for many semi natural habitats, they are certainly not 'wildlife deserts'. Gardens can offer a rich variety of resources and habitats, such as ponds, that may be increasingly rare elsewhere. The common frog has benefited from the construction of thousands of garden ponds across the UK. Indeed urban gardens contain arguably some of the richest wildlife habitats in Britain, home to hundreds of species including some of the rarer ones. The juniper pug is a scarce moth whose natural food plant is rare, but which successfully exploits ornamental junipers in domestic gardens.

An average sized garden is capable of supporting up to 3,000 different species. Butterflies and insects benefit from nectar-giving plants such as primrose, sweet rocket and aubretia or even areas of long grass. Birds have a better chance of surviving thanks to food and shelter provided for them by householders. Even in the smallest of backyards many flowers, vegetables and even fruit can be grown in pots and containers.

With the problems being experienced by wildlife in the wider countryside, where many species are in severe decline, gardens can offer staggeringly rich habitats if gardeners put a little more thought into how they garden.

COMMUNITY GARDENS

A community garden works by getting the people around it to recognise the existence and significance of the wildlife on their doorstep and to celebrate it.

You said...

Our local community is starting to do some community gardening, with small areas of previously scrap ground, wooden plant boxes and window boxes. This is an area of back-to-back housing, in the floor of the Burnley Valley in Todmorden, the Harley Bank area. The area is now being improved by the local council, it is presently a polluted, overcrowded area of factories mixed in with victorian back-to-back housing, where nearly all wildlife has been wiped out for a hundred years or so.

The area is between a wonderful park with wildlife on the other side of the main road, and beautiful semi-wild countryside on the other side of the railway track. It would be good if the community gardening here could form a link between these two areas of wildlife, and help to heal up pollution and damage still here from the industrial revolution with its mining, etc.
towngarden, Todmorden

A teacher at my daughter's school in Ilford has created a wildlife haven from a previously abandoned piece of garden about 12ft square with overhanging trees. He has encouraged the children by planting wildlife shrubs and nectar plants. They have put up bird feeders and have increased the visiting songbird population so much that the children are now bird-spotting in their own gardens and telling their parents what type of bird it is! Unfortunately the nesting boxes are still uninhabited but a local birder has given them advice about perches and cover for the fledglings when they leave the nest. The children are growing sunflowers and sweet peas as well as night-scented plants to encourage night-flying insects and hence bats. I think it so satisfying to share your outdoor space with local wildlife.
Tree, Ilford

Kim Paterson, the Wildlife Trust for Lancashire, Manchester and North Merseyside, advises:

The idea of community gardens feels like a rather modern concept, one that aims to use the garden as a way of bringing people together in a positive way in joint action for a common purpose. Community gardens are very much about social inclusion and regeneration, whether rural or urban.

In a way community wildlife gardens are new. For thousands of years the garden has been about the taming of nature. Sometimes this was in the context of a community such as a monastery garden, but more often than not it revolved around the individual or the family. Originally the aesthetic value of a garden was generally subservient to the utilitarian or productive value. Gardens were our way of conditioning the landscape or of holding back wild nature for something more practical and secure.

As generations have passed, fashions and social mores have changed leaving their mark on the development of gardening. Paradoxically this has led to a situation where, particularly in urban areas, we seek to hold back the threat of the concrete jungle by welcoming back the wildness of nature.

Fortunately nature is singularly adept at taking advantage of the slightest of opportunities and with our encouragement, or sometimes through our non-intervention, remarkable things happen in the most unlikely of places.

On a practical level the basic components of wildlife gardening are essentially the same whether it is your own garden or in a community garden. Food, shelter, water and ecological variety appropriate to the surrounding area.

The things that are different in a community garden may seem small, but they are fundamental. It requires an active and enthusiastic group of people with a common aim of taking a piece of land they probably do not own and making it a haven for wildlife. While their aim might be in common, their motivations almost certainly will be very varied, so the project must be flexible, responsive to individual needs and recognise the dynamics, both good and bad, of the ways communities work.

For further advice

The Federation of City Farms and Community Gardens (FCFCG) is the representative body for city farms, community gardens and similar community-led organisations in the UK.

● There are 59 city farms, nearly 1,000 community gardens, 75 school farms and a number of community-managed allotments in the UK.

● An estimated 500,000 people volunteer on them and they attract over three million visitors each year.

● FCFCG promotes and represents its members at a national, regional and local level.

● It also provides a wide range of services, advice and support for city farms and community gardens, whether they are well-established or just getting off the ground.

● You can contact the FCFCG at www.farmgarden.org.uk, or by calling 0117 923 1800.

ALLOTMENTS

You said...

I've just taken on a fabulous but badly neglected allotment near where I live. It's been organic for quite a long time and I'm keen to keep it that way. But now that I've managed to clear it out, and I've dug it over, and now started to plant, I'm concerned as to how to defeat the slugs, whitefly and greenfly which seem to love my plot. I'm wondering if anybody has any tried and tested organic solutions that they can suggest to help me out?
Thank you.
Kate, London

Slugs – put some plastic cups full of beer into the ground and the slugs will drown (ahh). I use derris dust on my broad beans – not sure if this counts as organic or not. Some other things like cabbage and fruit bushes you just have to net over to protect from wildlife. Ladybirds are nature's pest eaters but even they can't cope with all the bugs on my broad beans, unfortunately.
cdrewett, Croydon

I took on my allotment last year so I reckon I'm in pretty much the same sort of situation. My plan is to plant lots and lots of flowers (marigolds and the like) to combat the flying ones that like to invade my patch, and put out some plastic milk bottle collars in order to make it a bit more difficult for the slugs that want to make their home there! Best of luck!
cricket, London

Allotments provide the perfect opportunity to grow fresh produce while experimenting with organic approaches to cultivation.

Planning

Once you've got your allotment you need to decide what you want to grow. Make a list of what fruit and vegetables you like to eat, and consider areas such as a fruit cage, herb garden, cut flower border, wildlife patch and green manures. Ask your allotment neighbours about local pests such as rabbits and deer and think about incorporating suitable defences if none are already present.

Larger structures can be costly, so consider how much use they will get before installing them. A greenhouse is a luxury whereas windowsills are normally sufficient to raise transplants: besides, many sites prohibit greenhouses, so check before renting. Compost bins and rainwater butts also need careful placement in the early planning stages.

Consider how much time you will be able to spend at the site. If time is limited, then incorporate low-maintenance ideas such as planting through plastic mulches to reduce weeding time. Allotment crops will rely on regular watering if they are started off using over-exuberant irrigation. Some crops, such as runner beans, need regular harvesting to ensure continual yield, so if you're off on holiday, offer a pitcy-your-own beans scheme to your neighbours.

Guy Barter, RHS, advises:

There are many reasons for renting an allotment – not least of which is to grow fresh produce. There are the health benefits of a place you can escape to unwind in peace and quiet, with some gentle exercise away from everyday pressures. Conversely, allotment sites are sociable places, great for meeting like-minded people. There is a growing trend towards a wider mix of cultures and ages alongside the traditional plot holders. Tips on growing and cultivating abound, making this an ideal environment for the novice gardener.

Start by contacting your local authority for information on available allotment sites; local authorities have a duty to provide allotments. These plots may be statutory, temporary or there may be privately owned sites available to rent. Information about a local horticultural society or allotment association may appear in the local papers or at the library.

A full plot is 10 rods (approximately 250m²), but half plots are usually available if this is too much to manage. Ground rent is normally very reasonable. Most but not all sites have water, but check what other facilities are available such as a storage shed, compost and toilets. Check also if there are any limitations in the lease which, for instance, prevents fruit-tree planting or the erection of structures such as greenhouses, polytunnels or sheds, and if there are problems such as theft and vandalism. Popular sites may have a waiting list.

You may wish to join a local or national society for guidance and benefits.

For more information

● The National Society for Allotment and Leisure Gardeners (NSALG) offers advice to its members on allotment matters and a low-cost quality seed scheme. Visit the society at www.nsalg.org.uk, or Tel: 01536 266576.

● Many allotment gardeners grow organically and the Henry Doubleday Research Association (HDRA) advises its members on organic gardening and runs the Heritage Seed Library. The HDRA is at www.gardenorganic.org.uk or Tel: 024 7630 3517.

● To help with growing and planning there are some useful reference books. Try *The New Vegetable and Herb Expert* by Dr DG Hessayon or *RHS Fruit and Vegetable Gardening*, Editor-in-Chief Michael Pollock. *The Half-hour Allotment* by Lia Leendertz is full of excellent advice, too.

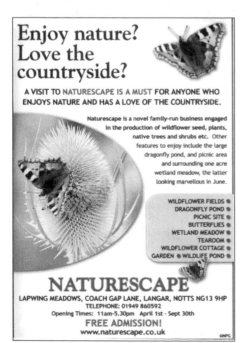

NURTURE YOUR GARDEN, NURTURE YOURSELF

Graham Game of The Wildlife Trusts explains the
therapeutic benefits of gardening for wildlife

Gardening has become almost a 'national institution' in Britain, but why do so many of us seek the thrill of growing and nurturing living things?

The simple answer is that the elemental forces of nature touch us at a very profound level indeed, and we need this connection because we know in our hearts that it's good for us. Furthermore, we are hardwired to go outside and connect with nature in some way – gardening at home is just the easiest and most satisfying point of contact for many of us.

Of course some brave souls will go further and stride out into the wilderness with their packs and Swiss army knives, and, consumed with missionary zeal, they will conquer the hills and mountains they encounter, but for the rest of us, there's just no place like home.

If our homes are our castles, then our gardens are where we really reign supreme, but how many of us realise that by nourishing our plants we are also nourishing ourselves?

There are many scientists and academics who claim that nature is good for us: Stephen Kaplan believes that interaction with nature is a restorative therapy that can positively relieve stress and fatigue, while biologist EO Wilson went still further by suggesting that we humans have a genetically encoded affinity with nature, and that this relationship increases our wellbeing, and in turn our capacity to care for our environment – he called this Biophilia.

Even the Victorians understood the value of gardening as therapy, and today there is an abundance of evidence to prove that it is simply good for us – indeed horticultural therapy is a rapidly developing discipline thanks to the work of people like Jenny Grut and her work in gardens and on allotments with traumatised victims of torture, and organisations such as Thrive with its horticultural therapy projects. The gardener is in a unique position to be able to gain a deeper understanding of nature's infinitely wondrous workings, and is able to draw on that healing power to restore balance and harmony in themselves.

So why is gardening so good for us?
These days, stress and mental ill-health issues are becoming more common; the

---

My garden will never make me famous,
I'm a horticultural ignoramus.
                                    Ogden Nash

I once had a sparrow alight upon my shoulder for a moment, while I was hoeing in a village garden, and I felt that I was more distinguished by that circumstance that I should have been by any epaulet I could have worn.
                        Henry David Thoreau

World Health Organisation estimates that stress- and depression-related illness will become our greatest sources of ill-health by 2020. The cost? A staggering £77 billion each year!

Add the fact that stress is a key factor in a range of chronic physical illness including asthma, arthritis, diabetes, strokes and heart disease as well, and we can soon appreciate how important emotional health and wellbeing is to us all.

We can engage with nature at three different levels:

Firstly, we can see nature through a window, in a picture or even on television; this serves as a reminder of what we are

missing. Having flowers and plants indoors is a simple way for us to connect.

Secondly, we can benefit by having nature around us. Living in the country or being near a park or nature reserve adds to our perceived quality of life – we will probably even pay a premium for the privilege of living near such places.

And finally, we can deliberately seek some active participation with nature – in our gardens, trekking, camping or working on our local nature reserve.

Apart from the psychological and stress-busting benefits, gardening is also good physical exercise; an hour's digging is

When I go into the garden with a spade, and dig a bed, I feel such an exhilaration and health that I discover that I have been defrauding myself all this time in letting others do for me what I should have done with my own hands.

Ralph Waldo Emerson

To forget how to dig the earth and to tend the soil is to forget ourselves.

Mohandas Gandhi

almost as effective as an hour's running, and we gardeners know that it is certainly more productive!

Obesity is a massive problem in developed countries now, and will soon overtake smoking as Britain's biggest killer – a mere 10% increase in adult physical activity would save £500 million every year and some 6,000 lives.

It is no surprise that organisations like The Wildlife Trusts and the Royal Horticultural Society are so serious about pressing gardeners to encourage wildlife into their gardens, because we know that thanks to development and intensive agriculture, our gardens are vital refuges for songbirds, insects and even the nation's favourite – the hedgehog. But I would go even further and say that we should have wildlife in our gardens because we can admit that it is good

for us, too. We like to see birds on the feeders and even – dare I say it – the incredible antics of grey squirrels as they try to steal the bird food.

Just add water

The therapeutic and wildlife value of a garden can be further enhanced by adding water, an essential ingredient for both people and wildlife, with the sound of a babbling brook or pond probably the most calming and contemplative sound there is. Water is, of course, vital and deeply elemental, and if you are fortunate to have a pond in your garden you will know what a magnet it is for a wide variety of wildlife. If you do build a pond, don't forget the oxygenating plants, and make sure that at least part of it has gently sloping sides to allow the wildlife to access the water. Fish, although undoubtedly therapeutic, are not really suitable for a pond as they will eat tadpoles and the larvae of insects like dragonflies.

The final ingredient is probably the most overlooked. We are often so busy gardening that we don't allow enough time to enjoy the fruits of our labours. We all need to spend as much quality time in our gardens as we can; watching the birds, listening to the sounds of the different plants and trees swaying in the wind, and of course there are the tastes and smells of the fruits and the flowers – even the unforgettable aroma of the freshly mown grass. We must not be afraid to set aside plenty of time and space in our gardens for meditation and contemplation – after all, the Buddha found enlightenment while sitting under a tree...

I value my garden more for being full of blackbirds than of cherries, and very frankly give them fruit for their songs.

Joseph Addison

CHECKLIST Keep a record of the creatures that visit your garden

	DATE FIRST SEEN	NOTES
MAMMALS		
Fox		
Badger		
Stoat		
Weasel		
Rabbit		
Hare		
Hedgehog		
Mole		
Common shrew		
Pygmy shrew		
Wood mouse		
Yellow-necked mouse		
House mouse		
Brown rat		
Bank vole		
Grey squirrel		
Muntjac		
Common pipistrelle		
Soprano pipistrelle		
Natterer's bat		
Leisler's bat		
Daubenton's bat		
Noctule bat		
Brown long-eared bat		
Serotine		
BIRDS		
Blackbird		
Song thrush		
Mistle thrush		
Redwing		
Fieldfare		
Starling		
House sparrow		
Robin		
Dunnock		
Wren		
Great tit		
Blue tit		
Coal tit		
Long-tailed tit		
Goldcrest		
Nuthatch		
Treecreeper		
Chiffchaff		
Willow warbler		

	DATE FIRST SEEN	NOTES
Blackcap		
Whitethroat		
Bullfinch		
Greenfinch		
Goldfinch		
Chaffinch		
Siskin		
Redpoll		
Pied wagtail		
House martin		
Swallow		
Swift		
Green woodpecker		
Great spotted woodpecker		
Woodpigeon		
Collared dove		
Turtle dove		
Magpie		
Jay		
Carrion crow		
Jackdaw		
Black-headed gull		
Grey heron		
Mallard duck		
Ring-necked parakeet		
Barn owl		
Tawny owl		
Kestrel		
Sparrowhawk		
Buzzard		
Red kite		

REPTILES & AMPHIBIANS

Grass snake		
Viviparous lizard		
Slow-worm		
Common frog		
Common toad		
Smooth newt		

BUTTERFLIES

Large white		
Small white		
Green-veined white		
Brimstone		
Orange-tip		
Red admiral		

CHECKLIST

	DATE FIRST SEEN	NOTES
Small tortoiseshell	_____	_____
Peacock	_____	_____
Comma	_____	_____
Painted lady	_____	_____
Holly blue	_____	_____
Common blue	_____	_____
Small copper	_____	_____
Speckled wood	_____	_____
Meadow brown	_____	_____
Gatekeeper	_____	_____
Ringlet	_____	_____
Large skipper	_____	_____
Small skipper	_____	_____

Identification of garden insects, with a few notable exceptions such as the butterflies already listed, or the stag beetle, takes a little time and experience. Rather than provide an extensive list of potential garden species – which would fill several pages of this book (for example, there are about 2,500 species of moth alone in the UK, very many of which are frequent garden visitors) – we offer a sampler list of common species. By using identification books, such as those listed on page 278, try to find the species on this list first. Having discovered these in your garden, you will have started to gain an idea of the diversity and relationships of insect families, and branch out your knowledge from there.

MOTHS

Hummingbird hawk moth	_____	_____
Elephant hawk moth	_____	_____
Large yellow underwing	_____	_____
Brimstone	_____	_____
Silver Y	_____	_____
Black arches	_____	_____
Angle shades	_____	_____
Common footman	_____	_____
Garden tiger	_____	_____
Cinnabar	_____	_____

DRAGONFLIES

Large red damselfly	_____	_____
Common blue damselfly	_____	_____
Azure damselfly	_____	_____
Blue-tailed damselfly	_____	_____
Southern hawker	_____	_____
Brown hawker	_____	_____
Emperor dragonfly	_____	_____
Four-spotted chaser	_____	_____
Broad-bodied chaser	_____	_____
Common darter	_____	_____

	DATE FIRST SEEN	NOTES

OTHER INSECTS

	DATE FIRST SEEN	NOTES
Buff-tailed bumblebee		
White-tailed bumblebee		
Early bumblebee		
Red-tailed bumblebee		
Common carder bee		
Garden bumblebee		
Mason bee		
Common wasp		
Tree wasp		
Hornet		
Marmalade hoverfly		
Pellucid hoverfly		
Cranefly		
St Mark's fly		
Bee fly		
Stag beetle		
Ground beetle		
Cockchafer		
Click beetle		
Soldier beetle		
7-spot ladybird		
2-spot ladybird		
14-spot ladybird		
Hawthorn shieldbug		
Froghopper		
Water boatman		
Common pond skater		
Field grasshopper		
Oak bush-cricket		
Green lacewing		
Earwig		
Snake millipede		

OTHER INVERTEBRATES

	DATE FIRST SEEN	NOTES
Harvestman		
Wolf spider		
Cellar spider		
Garden spider		
Zebra spider		
Pill woodlouse		
Smooth woodlouse		
Garden snail		
Garlic glass snail		
Brown-lipped snail		
Garden slug		
Leopard slug		
Large black slug		

FURTHER READING

Some excellent introductory books from The Wildlife Trusts:

CHRIS PACKHAM'S BACK GARDEN NATURE RESERVE
Packham, Chris
Comprehensive and practical guide to enable the reader to transform a humble garden into an important refuge for a wealth of wildlife.

BILL ODDIE'S INTRODUCTION TO BIRDWATCHING
Oddie, Bill
Covers everything you need to know about birdwatching, whether it be identifying the birds you see in your back garden and local park, or further afield. Maybe you want to understand bird behaviour, identify that bird you hear but cannot see, which field guide is best for you, it's all in here.

THE WILDLIFE TRUSTS GUIDE TO GARDEN WILDLIFE
Hammond (ed), N
Offers a wealth of information for expert or amateur, young or old, on identifying nearly 125 of the most commonly encountered garden wildlife species in Britain and Northern Europe. Grouped in categories, each species is clearly described with informed concise text.
(Other books in this series of The Wildlife Trusts Guides cover Birds, Butterflies and Moths, Insects, Trees and Wild Flowers.)

THE COMPLETE GARDEN BIRD BOOK: HOW TO IDENTIFY AND ATTRACT BIRDS TO YOUR GARDEN
Golley/Moss/Daly
Being able to recognise the birds in your garden and to understand their behaviour adds an exciting new dimension to garden birdwatching. This book tells you how to ensure that birds find your garden attractive whether it be large or small and how to put a name to 70 garden birds, common to Britain and northern Europe. An authoritative text is complemented with full colour illustrations.

THE GARDEN BIRD YEAR
Beddard, Roy
Describes and explains, season by season, the bird activity in your garden. Offers practical advice on how to manage your garden for birds. Key species described individually. Illustrated throughout with original art work and photographs.

NICK BAKER'S GARDEN BUG BOOK
Baker, Nick
Nick Baker takes a fresh and dynamic look at the fascinating lives of insects, spiders, snails and other invertebrates. His lively approach reveals a spectacular microcosmic world and offers a wealth of practical tips for a closer exploration and appreciation of bugs.

THE FOLLOWING BOOKS WILL HELP YOU PLAN YOUR WILDLIFE GARDENING IN EVEN GREATER DETAIL:

How to Make a Wildlife Garden
Baines, Chris
Elm Tree Books

The seminal book that started the wildlife gardening revolution in the 1980s, and is still the standard text on the subject. Read Chris Baines' own garden reflections on page 39.

**All About Compost –
Recycling Household and Garden Waste**
Pears, P
HDRA/Search Press

The Butterfly Gardener
Rothschild, M & Farrell, C
Michael Joseph

The Complete Guide to Garden Composting
Bardos, P
Taylor Marketing Services Ltd

Composting – The Organic Natural Way
Kitto, D, Thorsons Publishing Group

The Country Diary of Creating a Butterfly Garden
Warren, ESM
Bounty Books

Creating a Wildlife Garden
Gibbons, B & L
Chancellor Press

Field Guide to the Bumblebees of Great Britain & Ireland
Edwards, M & Jenner M
Oscelli

Field Guide to the Dragonflies and Damselflies of Great Britain and Ireland
Brooks S & Lewington, R
British Wildlife Publishing

Field Guide to the Moths of Great Britain and Ireland
Waring, P, Townsend, M & Lewington, R
British Wildlife Publishing

Gardening for Butterflies
Vickery, M
Butterfly Conservation

The Influence of Trees on House Foundations on Clay Soils
Building Research Establishment Digest 298

Making Wildflower Meadows
Lewis, P
Frances Lincoln

The Natural Gardener
Bourne, V
Frances Lincoln

Organic Gardener's Composting
Solomon, S
Van Patten Publishing

Pocket Guide to the Butterflies of Great Britain and Ireland
Lewington, R
British Wildlife Publishing

The Pond Book – A Guide to the Management and Creation of Ponds
Williams, P et al
Ponds Conservation Trust

RHS Practical Guide to Hedges
Dorling Kindersley

The Rodale Book of Composting
Martin, DL & Gershuny, G
Rodale Press

Sticky Wicket: Gardening in Tune with Nature
Lewis, P
Francis Lincoln

A Technical Guide to Creating and Managing Wildflower Landscapes
Lickorish, S, Luscombe, G & Scott, R
Wildflowers Work, Landlife

Tree Root Damage to Buildings
Biddle PG
Willowmead Publishing

Tree Roots and Buildings
Cutler, DF & Richardson, IBK
Longman Scientific and Technical

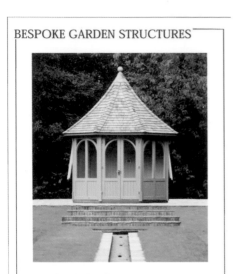

INDEX

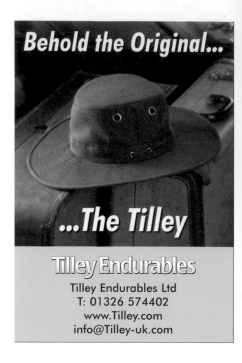

GARDEN NOTES

GARDEN NOTES